SCHOOL LEADERSHIP
TODAY

L. CRAIG WILSON
University of Delaware

ALLYN AND BACON, INC.
Boston · London · Sydney

SCHOOL LEADERSHIP TODAY

Strategies
for the Educator

TO HELEN

for the thirty-three years

Library of Congress Cataloging in Publication Data

Wilson, L. Craig.
  School leadership today.

  Includes index.
  1. School management and organization. 2. Teacher participation in administration. 3. Teacher participation in
curriculum planning. 4. Human ecology.
I. Title.
LB2806.W545   371.2   77-25118
ISBN 0-205-06019-6

Contents

v

SECTION TWO

THE IMPACT OF SURVIVAL BEHAVIOR ON
ROLE AND FUNCTION   59

CONTENTS

CONTENTS

x

Preface

Open access is the key to academic excellence and economic survival. However, pervasive economic problems cloud the issue by placing such high price tags on the educational tools of survival and success so that both the traditionally poor and affluent classes are simultaneously jeopardized.

There are many elaborate rationalizations for balancing the budget by a return to dogmatic management practices. It is said that we have a closed ecological system demanding constraint in resource utilization. Such parallels are drawn as justification for redirecting the aspirations of those whose dreams exceed their power.

Educators, in applying similar logic, argue for access constrictions for the sake of "standards," though here the real snag is encountered. The mind is not a closed system. Educators who assume it necessary, program for adaptation. Although reconstructive problem solutions are not denied, neither are they enthusiastically advocated. Personal inventiveness is feared and inadvertently suppressed. Thus, ideals disappear and with them self-motivation.

Social crisis first triggers the survival behaviors of the most maneuverable, typically the powerful and the wealthy who have personal territories to protect. The second-phase crisis response is the survival behavior of the middle classes, necessarily a group reaction requiring time to solidify. Profoundly revolutionary in concept is the observation that colleges and universities "are moving toward the broad policy of universal access" and that public policy "should make possible universal access to higher education by the year 2000." [1]

The best response calls for a workable middle ground in which the long-term best interests of the masses are not compromised by the short-term panic of the privileged. This middle ground is already in sight, namely, economical conversions of the educational establishment guided by the principle of open access.

Although open access was a good idea before the current economic disruption; it is an even better idea during it. How to make the concept operational in response to urgent social needs is what this book is about. It is a matter of survival. It is also a matter of being proud of how one has handled the crisis after it is over.

1. Carnegie Foundation for the Advancement of Teaching, *More Than Survival: Prospects for Higher Education in a Period of Uncertainty* (San Francisco: Jossey-Bass, 1975).

Acknowledgments

It is my good fortune to have come into contact with many talented advanced students of school administration, primarily through my High Honors Leadership Seminars. We meet for the purpose of brainstorming alternative solutions to current educational problems. Through individual contributions and group critiques, a refinement of individual thinking has resulted, and the outcome of these students' outstanding synthesized efforts will remain for further study by future groups.

Occasionally, it is possible for me to share the products of these efforts with the larger profession by adapting them for inclusion in a book such as this. I gratefully acknowledge:

- Judith Meyer, a state supervisor in Delaware, who has conducted the on-site comparative study of "open education" in England and America.
- Donald Butcofsky, Director of University and Public School Communications Centers, who has explored methods for converting program content for maximum access in open curriculum designs.
- Bob Barker, part-time professor of Business Administration and full-time college planner, who has directed his attention to the human side of planning.
- Barry Ersek, who, though trained in engineering, has accepted a high school principalship, and helped us apply systems theory to educational planning.

ACKNOWLEDGMENTS

I also wish to acknowledge the continuing interest of my former writing partner, Madison Byar of East Tennessee University, in the "tripartite power theory" which we originally published in our *Sociology of Supervision*. Some of the material that I have consolidated and transferred to the current manuscript (chapter 10, "The Power To Change") represents that portion of his original work which seems to have the most enduring relevance.

I am indebted to the University of Delaware for allowing the personal autonomy that serious writing requires, as well as for the sabbatical leave that provided me the time to work finishing touches into this manuscript.

Finally, I am most appreciative for the continuing support of Paul Solaqua, Senior Editor of Allyn and Bacon's Longwood Division. He and his team of critical, and extremely helpful ghost reviewers have provided me with essential national feedback on currently controversial theories without jeopardizing eventual publication through hasty marketing judgments.

SECTION ONE

Survival Symptoms
and Leadership
Responses

1

The Survival Mentality

Survival behavior is most obvious during periods of economic stress, when economic support must drop below a tolerable minimum in the cost efficiency equation. The concept of "minimums" is not foreign to educators, yet survival without quality loss has always been an elusive goal.

Most institutions seek management solutions when their survival is threatened, but the schools have not traditionally entrusted their managers with reconstructive functions. However, unyielding economic pressures have redirected educational leadership—and on an unprecedented mass scale. Unfortunately, this alien leadership style is proving to be more destructive than helpful.

In this book the automatic institutional survival behaviors that produced an "age of managers" are examined. Concurrently, the more perplexing problem of surviving the management syndrome itself with a recognizable concept of quality schooling is explored. The hypothesis is that schools respond poorly to overmanagement. The search is for a suitable style of leadership that teachers will not perceive as oppressive. The hope is that budget stresses will produce new, responsible variations of open access education.

REGRESSIVE REVOLUTION

The tone and technique of leadership in American education has indeed changed. The mission remains vague but still conveys a regressive expectancy that now is the time for austerity, certainly not expansion and probably not even creative adaptation. In an energy conscious world this conservative persuasion has become the political norm yet doubt remains as to whether or not universal access to education will be sacrificed in order to balance the budget. Open educational institutions sustain a society that values individual achievement as opposed to financial inheritance or the rewards of political power. This is a long-term consideration. The silent beneficiaries of past gains in social justice —racial minorities, the poor, and women—tend to be the first casualties of financial regression. Their silence is, however, no reason for complacency.

Where goals are more pragmatic than idealistic, a generation of up-through-the-ranks school administrators has been passed over in favor of promoting a new breed of managers. Few would deny that power has significantly shifted in the administrative hierarchy but to call it a "coup" would not really be accurate or fair. It is not certain how much of the power shift can be attributed to outside forces, simple opportunism, or genuine leadership. Nothing as complex and precipitous has ever happened to schools; there are no precedents. It is survival behavior of the least rational type. A common panic somehow generated a stereotypical response. Only the rigidity of the institutional structure explains the same response of the local school to economic crisis.

NEW FACES IN MANAGEMENT

The new managers are, for the most part, new faces—not people who were trained for new duties or who, for other reasons, would have normally been in line for high positions. Most of the new managers are not well known by the educational establishment; a few are former economists or politicians. There are many examples of this especially at higher levels. When Edward Aguirre was appointed Commissioner of Education by President Ford, he was described by his colleagues as "very strong on management but without a good background in education."[1] President Carter's selection for Secretary of Health, Education, and Welfare was similarly portrayed a short time later. The major political parties had changed but the image of the educational leader remained low-profile and conservative. Within the current system, it appears that the less one knows about the mission, substance, and process of an institution, the easier it is to "manage" it.

A similar example of this is found in private schools. A recent advisory publication for private schools proudly announced it "does *not* venture into curriculum . . . is definitely *not* a newsletter . . . does *not* reference extensive back-up data." It concludes with a statement that the publication *is* "an advisory service for management." This separation of the management function from its subject matter was explained as follows:

> . . . most trustees who have management experience find schools an enigma because they don't fit the pattern of the business

1. *Education USA* 19, no. 41 (September 27, 1976):31.

world. After all, schools are not dealing with profits, products, or other inanimate things. They are concerned entirely with people and the development of children—schools are people intensive.[2]

Thus, the case is made for school management being a special kind of generalized management, having an existence separate from that which is managed. Therefore, the regulation and control of personnel becomes the subject matter of management in this "people intensive" institution.

This type of management transformation first began in industry with the replacement of engineers by business administration specialists. The "bottom line" preoccupation of non-technical managers readily converted a technical business into a "money business." Budgets became more important than product quality, employee predictability more valued than invention, and centralized quality controls more trusted than individual standards.

In some industries problems with product quality have prompted a renewed reliance upon technicians rather than industrial psychologists and business administrators. Nevertheless, the trend continues to run in the opposite direction. Financial panic makes this appear inevitable until it is observed that consumers are purchasing the more durable product and abandoning the cheap imitation. The world-wide ascendancy of the Japanese motorcycle industry and the concurrent demise of the British industry is a case in point. Tradition cannot hold its own against technology. Of course, some classics like the German BMW possess both strengths. The success of Honda, for example, can be attributed to the organizational independence of research and development forces from generalized corporate management.

2. "Ideas and Perspectives," *Independent School Management Advisory Bulletin* (1976).

MANAGEMENT TECHNOLOGY AND
LEGALISTIC THEORY

There is no question that politicians, public officials, business-men, industrialists, and professionals from all fields often trust computer programs more than they do the judgment of individual employees, consumers, and constituents. Two consequences of this practice are "high risk" insurance policies and bank "redlining" of questionable territories for mortgages. Evidence abounds, from the ice cream store owner who computer analyzes every purchase in order to stock the most popular flavors to the oil magnate who decides to drop small neighborhood dealerships. Universities computer analyze test scores, admission applications, and credit-hour costs. Banks control consumer credit through instant feedback on master charge, and police depend upon instant retrievals from crime data banks. When instant retrieval by public opinion pollsters is combined with TV reporting, even the American presidency can be predicted.

There is great power in the *appearance* of being "on top of things." Some will remember the first statistical politician, Robert MacNamara, whose Pentagon projections "justified" the folding wing fighter plane that would later become a disappointment. Even when it is conceded that "command decisions" are an unknown mixture of illusion and substance, no one expects the awe-inspiring new tools that make them seem administratively possible to be abandoned. There seems, however, to be a wide range of limits any one manager can impose—or deliberately refrain from imposing—on himself. The ultimate problem lies less in the technological capability of management, and more in the public attitude that the invasion of privacy is the price of security. The "if it exists, register it" philosophy produces great bureaucracies but solves few problems. Leash laws for dogs, for example, do not keep the parks clean but the vulnerability of individual dog owners makes everyone *feel* better. Thus, the politician who advocates dog control does the public bidding by removing a small freedom. The fact that dog licenses are recorded on computer tape is inconsequential. Eventually, people may learn to protect themselves in a high technology–low trust environment. Presently, however, "executive privilege" is favored over individualism and legally protected personal rights and privileges.

This cultural condition affects schools, as well as other public institutions, with its legalistic concept of administrative accountability. The depersonalization of management results when fear of disruption, crime, vandalism, or the loss of control allows modern technology with its threat to personnel to appear feasible and desirable. Add to this the ever present chance of legally mandated change and the manager begins to look for administrative models that, if carefully followed, will reduce his vulnerability to law suits or the withholding of governmental funds. For example, an eastern state recently requested planning assistance from a federally funded research laboratory when it was ordered by the federal court to desegregate. The management plan that resulted detailed sixteen long-range goals, over one hundred events to fulfill those goals, and more than seven hundred specific actions of an administrative nature. It was seen as a step-by-step timetable for a complete desegregation plan, applicable to eleven school districts. These districts were temporarily merged to facilitate planning by a single "interim board." The point is that *all the traditional forms of community, professional, and governmental planning are necessarily shoved into lower priority slots once such a pattern is established.* If bureaucratic planning is coupled with the technological dependence described earlier, there is no way to avoid setting into motion an agonizing array of survival behaviors on the part of teachers, parents, students, and other involved parties. Local school management, often caught between legal mandates and discontented teachers,

8

is finally forced to accept adversary relations as unavoidable. Apathy is a theoretical option, but it tends to be even more detrimental to the educational process than perpetual conflict.

The vulnerability of the schools to a foreign (business, industrial, military) leadership style is often underestimated. The reason for this is long and successful dependence upon an accountability system that assumes good faith, voluntary initiative, and self-discipline on the part of teachers. The gentle people who have been traditionally attracted to teaching have been slow to realize that their administrators, once colleagues in a common cause, have switched to an adversary system. Having once felt safe because they were trusted, they have now become suspicious, fearful, and angry. They sense a degradation of their role, once assumed to be "professional" in spite of its meager financial rewards. This deflation of morale and self-image are the beginnings of militance and protective secrecy ("low profile" behavior). Distortions inevitably result and the situation becomes worse.

Fear can generate conformity in teaching but not excellence. The primary reason is the helping relationship's heavy dependence upon private inspiration and personal example. The schools have not yet confronted the "power abuse" issues that are surfacing with increasing frequency. Grievances, dismissals, and bitterly negotiated contracts are symptomatic and obvious but they tell only part of the story. The employee who is afraid to file a grievance is a serious problem; the "polite" administrative reprisals which generate such fears are even more serious. Subordinates typically fear management when management fears something else (or itself) so much that ruthless dealings with subordinates become "logical." The most likely setting for power abuse is found where management teams (1) stay on the telephone with themselves constantly (checking procedures, obtaining preliminary approvals, reporting problems, etc.); (2) keep long office hours (for fear that absence or reduced visibility will increase vulnerability to criticism or worse, information lag); and, (3) keep extensive personal files (diaries, appointment calendars, confidential memos, chronological accounts of personnel encounters). Missing in most teacher discussions is the fact that administrators are vulnerable too. When they are burdened with too much pressure, problems break out everywhere. Power abuse may be a symptom but confusion is the usual cause.

COLLAPSE OF THE ERROR CORRECTION SYSTEM

As the legitimate uses of authority become the central issue, a major institution can suddenly appear to grow weak and powerless in all of its operations. Like the familiar quicksand analogy, the harder the captive struggles, the quicker the end comes. Educators have never tried harder or accomplished less. It's a weird isometric exercise in which one part of the institution pits its strength against another in a desperate attempt to regain control.

One is tempted to question whether or not the current forces of management really understand the dynamics of the schooling enterprise. For example, the schools have always been managed through a bureaucratic pyramid in which a large base of relatively powerless teachers contrasts sharply with the small decision-making elite. Incomprehensible to many of the new managers, the organization was *kept loose on purpose,* not because of inefficiency but because the traditional administration knew that a *tremendous error correction factor* would result in the steady stream of small *decisions being made daily and anonymously by individual teachers* behaving in a manner that they considered "professional." Removing this intentional looseness in the name of accountability has had an opposite effect. It is interesting that endless speculations about declining test scores have yet to include possible links with the new error correction mechanism.

Even under the most enlightened management, economic decline brings out the worst in the schools. Access is what schools are all about. Access to knowledge, to opportunity, to privilege, to tools, to interaction, to recognition, to productivity, to power— all have price tags, either widely advertised or simply understood. Remove financial support and something has to give. Someone has to make the painful decision to reduce someone else's success or survival potential.

Most administrators will admit that the management function is part academic, part political. The proportions vary with individual administrators deciding which function to emphasize. Moreover, budget priorities are determined by the chosen emphasis; the tendency is to maintain support for whatever is perceived to be the "primary" goal while reducing the "secondary" goal's support services. Unfortunately, the problem is not solved simply by opting for an "academic" rather than a "political" priority because practical programming requires a fusion of the two. The key value question, "What is primary?" remains. If the choice is "people" over "things," little is resolved because education is a "people business." Different parts of the school program have traditionally dealt with different student needs. When these juvenile groups enter the adult community, and gain power, the result will be a social class. The school budget has been one of the more effective forms of "equalized" wealth distribution. Planned public support offsets the possible selfishness of the more fortunate in recognition of the common interest in community stability and prosperity. The limits of voluntary equalization are not known, but politicians watch carefully for in-group survival to assert itself in competition with the needs of some other groups or the community at large.

A LABOR-INTENSIVE
ESTABLISHMENT

Teachers, too, are a part of any budget-cutting plan. The schools are also a labor-intensive industry, consequently, any serious constriction in funding means that some teachers will be offered terminal contracts. But which ones? Those assigned to low-priority programs? Those who have little power in the community and are thought to be the least likely to seek legal or political redress? The least competent?

Because they are more expedient, more common are such familiar cutback schemes as "last in, first out" (release the newest nontenured teachers before they earn guaranteed employment status). Another tactic is to capitalize on "natural attrition" by not replacing retiring or resigning employees at all or hiring cheaper nontenured beginners as replacements.

Still another possibility is "balanced program deduction" —that is, unchanged priorities but less money for all. This is probably the best choice, provided that financial support for a certain subprogram is not cut below the minimum requirements for survival; also provided that the recession does not create new problems that would come to have priority over the needs of the original program.

Another budget-cutting technique aims at program constriction, deleting personnel almost coincidentally. The excuse is that the program must get "back to the fundamentals." The assumption, however, that fundamentals are always older than frills, is, I think, a decided disservice to such modern fundamentals as the civil rights of minorities, women, and juveniles.

Other fundamentals are, on the other hand, as old as the school system itself, though some are not so secure. The tradition of the self-disciplined, responsible individual, for example, is endangered. The urban individual assumes that dependence on public institutions for safety and security is not as risky as reliance on the individual. The problem is, of course, the changing definition of personal rights, often inadvertently influenced by the schools. This kind of cultural reinterpretation goes on all the time but is magnified by economic decline. The management part of the problem begins with the assumption that administrative accountability must take precedence over professional obligation or personal loyalty. The budget-balancing decisions about teachers must be made by administrators alone; they are not forced to consult the teachers, thus tension begins to build in spite of everyone's good intentions. As social distance increases, survival responses tend toward unnatural calmness in the classroom and conformity. The teacher's anxiety may not be transferred directly to instructional methods but the attitudinal effect of a survival-oriented teacher versus a true believer in personal achievement and social progress is rarely avoided.

All of this begins to happen almost instinctively as soon as school administrators are convinced that a major financial adjustment is inescapable. It is an awkward process, though, one with which few administrators have experience, and one that is destined to end in failure as long as the defined task is to cut back rather than to rebuild.

The recent history of the schools shows that the establishment has no reverse gear. Survival behavior is used mainly for increased maneuverability in financial matters, no one has yet invented a workable conversion formula for the overly stabilized institution. It is difficult for most educators to admit that a conversion is needed because every gain the schools ever made has been instantly fixed into law; intricate financial aid distribution plans, teacher certification regulations, and backup policies and regulations formulated by state, local, and municipal boards of education. The educational machine, under the pressure of profound economic decline, is malfunctioning at all levels in such a way as to jeopardize the traditional values that at one time were thought unassailable.

For example, innovative programming has ceased due to legislative fund withdrawals accompanied by the fear of any risk venture at all in a period of decline. There is little faith in the ability to invent alternative schooling models which could be both cheaper and better. Another value distortion is revealed in the curtailment or abolition of "compensatory education" programs for the culturally deprived—those who are most hurt by a recession. It is somewhat like raising the price of food stamps because the need for them increases. And, of course, anything considered "new" has had to go, not because it was failing but because it was unprotected by either administrative conviction or institutional identification. The most conservative kind of invention is sought, because its purpose is to protect a survival value. Already, the escalating costs of higher education have divided student bodies into the children of the wealthy and the scholarship-supported representatives of the poor. The middle class is disappearing—indeed, it is sometimes observed that history may be forced to label the current generation "the last of the middle class" in recognition of communal high-rise rental housing replacing the American dream of a single family dwelling, mass transit replacing cars, and formal education being terminated by cost rather than achievement potential. Thus, it seems that the institution that lacks a turnaround tradition is nevertheless most vulnerable to changes in funding levels.

THE ROOTS OF HIGH COST AND MEDIOCRE PERFORMANCE

It appears that the key to reform lies in doing the "right thing for the wrong reason." What has been "right" all along has been

(1) to redesign for efficiency based upon a criterion other than the costly "teacher–student ratio" and the "self-contained" *building,* and in the process (2) to adopt an alternative institutional model that is considerably more "open" (and coincidentally cheaper). Such changes are profound. Consequently, only a crisis of the current proportions could make high-level heresy feasible for even the most courageous administrator. Now, seemingly opposite systems of logic combine to produce the "impossible alternative": high-quality schooling at low cost. For management it is a "king-maker" opportunity.

Movement toward open curriculum models while schools are under financial pressure requires disciplined leadership. As vast as the public school network is, it still does not compare with the size of the proliferating nonsystems that serve all age groups other than the captive years of six to eighteen. The forms range from GED (general education development) tests taken by individuals to qualify for high school diplomas to international correspondence schools. There are adult evening schools, television and newspaper credit courses, "free universities," special-interest classes, educational computers with individually retrievable self-teaching programs, the military occupational specialty courses, storefront schools in urban areas, and hippy-type "survival schools"—all of which defy the "credentials culture."

Openness is, thus, accurately equated in our culture with an optimization of access. Multiple access routes to educational resources do not lead to a reduction in standards; indeed, personal performance becomes more important as the familiar "quality controls" of formal instruction give way to alternatives such as self-instruction, peer teaching, apprenticeships, and performance testing.

"Differentiation" is the key word in open programming— differentiation of types of content (stable, contested, exploratory); forms of interaction (cooperative, competitive, individualistic); dimensions of desired competence (skill, knowledge, value); kinds of evaluation (closure, performance, awareness of alternatives); goal emphases (process mastery, project definition, problem-solving missions); resource controls (direct learner access, access by petition, access by prescription); and time commitments (full-time, multiple purposes; full-time, single dominant purpose; part-time, secondary purpose only)—for every major component of design in the educational environment.

The "image" of a survival curriculum is critical. The desired image is the combination of a supermarket and a recipe book. The individual "cook" can make choices from the resource base and the alternative dishes that can be prepared. The cook never intends to try every available recipe, nor is it assumed to be desirable to test every ingredient on the shelf. A personally satisfying combination is the goal and no one pattern is thought to be "better."

Small modules are easier to put in the shopping basket and make far more interesting combinations. The novice cook should be able to try a Chinese meal without signing up for a lengthy course in oriental cooking. Yet, the modules should be planned in such a way that the full course will remain an option, given a specified selection and arrangement of modules.

The schools persist, especially under accountability pressures, to do too much "teaching" in relation to the amount of "learning" that can be documented. The practice is both costly and ineffectual. Just the opposite should be true, that is, there should be much more learning than teaching. Teaching should stimulate learning and thereafter avoid competing with it. There are many conversion points for curriculum rebuilding, the over-teaching phenomenon is just one. Another is the imbalance between "performance" and "structure." For example, the entire English class is able to diagram a sentence but no one is capable of writing an article. Similarly, art students easily drift into electing courses in the history of art rather than develop their own skills. In general, this tendency tells us where the "overteaching" is occurring—in the oldest, most securely established disciplines: the "basics." The language arts curriculum, including the full range of programs from elementary reading to high school English, would probably be dramatically improved if cut in half, thereby making room for the badly needed performance studies (modern journalism, for example).

PANIC IN THE MIDDLE CLASS

The generation of practical school improvements is an endless exercise of the imagination. The most fascinating new development is the serious involvement of the college bound. Heretofore, this privileged group was willing to consider "curriculum conversions" only for the disadvantaged or the handicapped. The motive was charity, not sound educational theory; the remedy was good for someone else, but not good enough for self-application. The child born into a white collar family comes to school with predispositions guaranteeing both success and boredom in the structural phases of the language arts. Yet, he wades through a dozen years of exposure to the obvious and the trivial without complaint. And, in the end, he shows up at a PTA meeting to demand the same "high standards" for the next generation.

But, no longer. The middle class now feels as threatened as the groups they once considered beneath them in good fortune and talent. The new survival requirement for all is personal competence in one or more recognized areas of cultural need, literally defined as some kind of occupational competence. The "college prep–liberal arts" status has become as irrelevant as a soldier's "good conduct ribbon." No longer will there be a need for such status-reinforcing concepts as "honorable failures" (a

"D" in French, for example, rather than a "B" in the less presti-
gious Industrial Arts). The practical need has become *exemplary
performance*.

When this idea is restated as advocacy of "no-failure
schools," the indoctrinated middle class responds instinctively
with a charge that "standards" are being lowered. Not so. It
simply means that the middle class is going to have to perform
too, not as a class but as individuals. The "culture-neutral economy" has already arrived (there are no middle-class parents rich
enough to guarantee the prosperity of their children), and the
"culture-neutral school" has become a middle-class survival
necessity. Almost half a century ago, a depression-motivated professor, George Counts, posed the question, "Dare the schools
build a new social order?" The answer then was "Try if you
wish but don't expect to succeed." The intervening years have
produced a competency-structured culture. If the schools once
again decide to participate—and they really have no choice due
to the crisis motivation of the middle class—Professor Counts'
dream might come true.

2

Conditioners of Survival Strategy

It has become increasingly obvious that the best chance for educational quality on an economic mass scale lies not in prescriptive fundamentalism, but in a reaffirmation of open access structures for personalized learning. In the previous chapter, this kind of openness was characterized as manageable though not entirely compatible with orthodox educational traditions and certainly not readily understood by managers who equate job success with the regulatory control of the teaching–learning process.

In this chapter, we will examine complexities in the educational setting that often confuse and interrupt planned remediation.

MEMORIES OF FAILURE: THE RECENT PAST

The schools are still being affected by the quick succession of school reforms that occurred during the 1960s. The combination of these reforms has necessitated a transformation in managerial leadership.

Some of these reforms were:

1. *Differentiated Teacher Roles.* This reform originated as a legitimate effort to raise the specialization levels of teachers by assigning some of their tasks to paraprofessionals. When the same idea was applied to school administration, the "business management" function rapidly gained distinction, and the planning function was quickly captured as an executive privilege. Thus, "administrative teaming" assimilated curriculum design and supervision. When the differentiation trend ended, teacher roles reverted to their familiar undifferentiated "grade level" and "teaching field" designations, leaving management as the only successful separatist group.

2. *Social Remediation.* Solving the problems of prejudice and deprivation are recurring primary goals. It has been said that many of these programs have failed their experimental tests; however, only the cynical will trivialize large-scale humanitarian efforts. The schools did not succeed in remaking the world, although they did try to face up to their inadvertent contribution to social injustice. It appears that the schools are ineffectual change agents when they are given assignments that the larger culture cannot handle successfully.

3. *Interdisciplinary Programs.* This reform may be considered survival behavior for the liberal arts because it sought primarily to reestablish the relevance of the basic disciplines while the number of applied fields of knowledge was rapidly multiplying. Although the old categories of knowledge remain constrictive, and irrelevant, they still exist. But, they are becoming obsolete as "career education" follows "vocational education" and remains separate and almost autonomous.

4. *Flexibility.* In its extreme form, it became permissiveness; "too much free time," the critics said, when computer-generated "flexible, modular" schedules were able to make high schools look and act somewhat like colleges. The personaliza-

tion of learning for some was the greatest advantage. This individualization, however, was both good and bad. A new form of oppression emerged unexpectedly as the good intentions of "individualized teaching" undercut traditional student anonymity which protected individuals trying to survive in impersonal institutional settings. In the end, this reform backfired with "high density" (no free time) schedules returning to replace the short-lived flexibility.

5. *The Behavior Modifiers.* Some educators believe that the remaking of others is both feasible and desirable. Given the possible abuses of freedom by those advocating permissiveness and the concurrent development of new control strategies (from behavioral psychology), it was inevitable that the relative power of the regulators would increase. It is a great problem to contend with especially when reinforced by the philosophical compatibility of the "new managers."

6. *Deschooling.* Not even Ivan Illich, considered by some to be a neocommunist, really believed that he could unravel the school bureaucracy by documenting how the most well-intentioned institution can become harmful at some unknown point. What he did accomplish was to provide a temporary antidote for the behavior regulators who did not have answers to the provocative question, "Wouldn't we be better off to dismantle the schools?" His long-term contribution was to introduce the healthy proposition of "alternatives" *to* schools, and *within* school programs. The positive developments of the future will undoubtedly come from this idea. To whatever extent people are willing to turn their private lives over to bureaucratic management they need to invent "escape routes" for dissenters. Such a safety valve begins with the idea of alternatives.

7. *The Libertarians and the Lawyers.* The "rights" movements are powerful, proper, and desperately needed. They have called attention to oppression where it was so common it came to be invisible. They have given a voice to the powerless, thereby helping to define issues of both cultural and educational significance. They have also, however, created a back-

log of administrative hostility, and some rigid and confusing precedents for legalistic decision making in an otherwise peaceful professional setting. Unionism, an important dimension of the problem, is here to stay. It is the only vehicle outside the courts with enough muscle to guarantee the teacher a hearing in the halls of management. Liberty and justice for students and teachers were once the "gifts" to individuals in the educational establishment. Now they are being defined legalistically, one "right" at a time, for groups rather than favored individuals. The process is as necessary as it is painful. And, it has only begun.

8. *Back-to-the-Basics.* The schools never abandoned the basics; they sincerely tried to up-date some of the definitions of "fundamentals" but quickly returned to the security of the three Rs when money ran short and criticism high. The test makers claim that literacy itself is in jeopardy and that the schools are to blame. They are probably wrong but the authoritative allegation is as damaging as truth. Different groups benefit in different ways from the confusion. Most harmful is the implication that some kind of high-cost frivolity has drifted into schooling to the point of crowding out more important things. Attitudes toward self-development, the challenge of work, and the rewards of service probably *have* eroded but the schools cannot be blamed for creating the problem. Unfortunately, "back to the basics" has become the catchword for the irrelevancy of the entire educational effort and needs to be exposed as such.

THE POWER TO CHANGE: EMERGENT PATTERNS

Recession responses, including those just mentioned which remain from an earlier time, have already set into motion trends that no knowledgeable planner will ignore. Some of these trends are positive; others are counterproductive; and the value of the remainder seems either obscure or neutral. All those of major significance have a power component reflecting the necessarily political implications of any institutional conversion considered potentially permanent. Access is still the common denominator of all forms of educational power. Being pervasive, it reaches the powerless as well as the influential, and through new national governmental policy on all subordinate (e.g., state) educational operations has an impact on everyone. The United States does not yet have a federal system of education, but one would not know this by the speed with which fifty state school systems respond to a new beat of the drum in Washington. This is, therefore, where the illustrative list of new educational realities begins.

I. EMERGING EDUCATIONAL POLICY: FEDERAL AND STATE

A. A major shift in federal policy toward education, only in part recession-related, stresses *"practical" institutional reform* rather than psychological research of the type that started with the "Cooperative Research Program" of the late 1950s and was politically rejected in the 1975 budget of the National Institute for Education.

B. A near reversal in educational policy plays down the remediation of the alleged "needs" documented by the National Assessment Program in favor of sanctioning *"alternative education" models* invented by local districts. The former policy was prescriptive and deficiency oriented; the latter is flexible and survival oriented.

C. A shift, particularly on the federal level, from "categorical aid" (earmarked project funds) to *general fund transfers* (revenue sharing) with legal compliance *"riders"* supports the civil rights of minorities, women, and more recently, juveniles. Legal intervention as a change strategy is now recognized by most educator–preparation programs.

D. Having experienced a decade of disillusionment with project-induced change, a transfer of initiative to *"class action"* test cases in the courts, and the building of *"forced change" implementation* strategies into administrative guidelines, many colleges of education commit themselves to prescriptive teaching (behavior modification) but have hardly begun to recognize legalistic change. An even better choice would support alternative or open models because of their survival potential but this option remains low-key and ineffectually advocated.

II. REDISTRIBUTION OF PROFESSIONAL POWER

A. The realignment of professional influence has *reduced the control of colleges of education* in favor of external program accreditation and "performance" definitions of teacher competence.

B. Early signs of union–management confrontations modify the above trend in the achievement of a *working definition of "seniority"* (tenure) to offset abuses in competency assessment. Most educators have little interest in accountability but much concern for job stabilization as state tenure laws are challenged by school boards in order to gain more maneuverability in inflation adjustment.

C. The seemingly irreparable *separation of "management" from "career teaching"* and the *continued centralization* of power on the *district level* is being countered by teacher *union militance.*

III. ECONOMIC SURVIVAL BEHAVIOR

A. Student enrollment and financial support are declining for two powerful reasons—the end of the baby boom, and the deepening recession. The labor-intensive school system faces the painful alternative of *staff reduction* as well as a roll back of services and programs. Most schools and colleges, both private and public, are in the same boat regardless of their geographic location. Nonlocal forces have clearly overridden previously dominant regional subcultures.

B. "Last in, first out" has been, as previously noted, the rule of thumb in staff *reduction;* and the "young, cheap, and untenured" teacher, a target for *recruitment.* Competency challenges for tenured employees have backfired to upseat more administrators than teachers, yet the redistribution of teacher age groups continues, and its effect on curriculum and students is still unknown.

C. Teachers are "digging in" rather than risking job loss through mobility of any kind. Even study in residence for higher degrees is considered risky because school districts cannot guarantee reemployment. "Keep your job and study with us" is the lure of the flourishing mail-order companies offering graduate degrees. Personalized programs are being advertised; job security is what is being sold.

D. Higher and more varied credentials are sought by educators for personal advancement, and for enough flexibility to survive reassignment on the job (even though increased college tuition is making this step almost impossible for some, and admission constrictions continue to block others). Colleges which separate their degree programs from certificate up-grading ("extension" work) are not doing all that is needed to promote the survival of their students; degrees still count when the competition gets rough.

E. Survival options are being reduced when the teacher's need is maneuverability. Program reconstruction and staff redeployment are the only sensible means of maintaining quality while cutting costs; however, the processes of invention remain suppressed. This is, of course, *the great immediate need.*

F. Meanwhile, informal education is flourishing but often with only reluctant professional and official sanction.

Education has already been "deschooled" but school people have not yet admitted that a permanent adoption and support of *informal adaptations* might be a part of their responsibility. The recent resurrection of community education is one of the more powerful movements using its survival value to override establishment cynicism.

G. The recognition that *the planning, management, and operation of informal educational programs is as much a legitimate concern to colleges of education as the training of a second grade reading teacher* is long overdue. The traditional schooling functions may have decreased with lowered enrollments on the elementary and secondary levels but the educator faces a greater challenge. *Education is not diminishing; it is just changing form.*

ROLE-ORIENTED SURVIVAL SYMPTOMS

Pervasive problems in education demoralize the total profession while they are pushed aside in favor of the more narrow, pragmatic concerns that generate survival symptoms of the following variety. Management survival behaviors are:

1. Movement toward an "officer corps" mentality—psychological affiliation with the "administrative team," separate and above teachers and teaching.

2. Primary personal specialization in the technologies of planning and regulation. Interest in the attainment of legal and financial power; relatively little interest in maintaining personal competence in traditional academic or educational fields.

3. The substitution of public relations "image building" for professional involvement in planning; more reliance upon

secrecy in decision making (executive privilege) than in the alternative of self-correcting "open management."

4. Primary interest in political and legal concerns; supporting "standards" that the powerful and the prominent prefer.

5. Conservative in matters of financial priority, personal value, and institutional stability. Tendency to oppose extensions of personal "rights."

Teacher survival behaviors are:

1. Retreat into a labor union mentality; primary concern for job security.

2. Ambivalence when confronted by polarized career choices, namely:
   a. administrative
   b. an academic role as a career teacher
   c. militant group (association or union) leadership.

3. Tendency to side with management in hard-line discipline policies but to simultaneously hold on to as much personal autonomy in the classroom as possible.

4. Diminished sense of power in curriculum development, tendency to plan creatively only within prescribed teaching roles, leaving the broader innovative design possibilities entirely to management discretion.

Student survival behaviors are:

1. Low enthusiasm for scholarship; a semi-serious approach to personal studies for reasons of economic survival.

2. Job anxiety becomes stronger than zeal for social reform.

3. Passive acceptance of budget cutting alterations (reductions) in school offerings.

4. Development of a separatist notion of personal happiness in the form of true indifference to what others think of them.

5. General uncertainty that the free enterprise system and the democratic model of government can solve pervasive "quality

27

of life" problems; tendency to distrust larger political solutions, developing, instead, strategies for personal survival.

SUPERMANAGEMENT VERSUS DEMANAGEMENT

The personalization of survival behaviors by teachers and students poses special problems for management, especially since they are left with a feeling that no one else is really interested in directing the institution. This, in turn, breeds overmanagement.

Administrative overcontrol has not gone unnoticed. The Los Angeles School Board plans to establish new precedents for management control by establishing its own "independent watch dog unit to check up on the administration and to do long-range planning." [1] The sponsor of the proposal (which was unanimously accepted by the school board) said he wanted the unit "to analyze performance progress on board and superintendent goals, check to see whether policies were being carried out, and to do long-range planning for the board." Top administrators, he said, were "too busy with daily tasks to perform those functions." He also said that "the administration had assumed power which belonged to the board." To me, this is obviously one more giant step in the wrong direction. More planners and managers will only continue the deactivation of the traditional system of quality control.

Perhaps the schools can no longer contain a loose confederation of self-policing professionals; if not, a case can be made for the provision of an alternative kind of quality control. The

1. *Education USA* 19, no. 6 (October 11, 1976).

present mixture of the old and new forms of control negates the effectiveness of either one. This is, of course, what precipitates the question: "supermanagement" or "demanagement?"

Paradoxically, rather than remaining at opposite poles, attempts at "demanagement" often serve the interests of "supermanagement." For example, the 1976 National Meeting of State School Boards defined the problem as "restoring public confidence in education . . . by restoring the influence of the public on education." Yet, the proposal for doing this was to create "an independent staff for state boards . . . using federal funds on a matching basis to support such staffs." [2] Thus, because state departments of education are thought to be unresponsive, a second "shadow department" would be created. Double the forces of management in order to demanage!

Another dimension of the problem is the idea that self-limiting executive power is a sign of weakness or incompetence. The end result is not unlike the fearful driver whose white-knuckled grip on the steering wheel produces not stability but high risk.

Educators' control problems are not unique. Actually, some of the best examples of rebounding overregulation come from other areas. For example, Britain's harsh gun control laws have not only failed to halt the violence in Northern Ireland, but a Cambridge University study of the overall effectiveness of English gun control now concludes:

> No matter how one approaches the figures, one is forced to the rather startling conclusion that the use of firearms in crime was very much less when there were no controls of any sort . . . Half a century of strict controls on pistols has ended, perversely, with a far greater use of this type of weapon in crime than ever before.[3]

2. *Education USA* 19, no. 7 (October 18, 1976):49.
3. *Guns and Ammo* 20, no. 11 (November, 1976):33.

In the sixties, overreacting school administrators accidentally produced similar results in their campaigns against deviant
hairstyles, drug use, and public demonstrations by dissenting students. Similarly, the Catholic church's unrelenting policies on
birth control and divorce have brought this ancient institution
to a crisis of declining membership.

The school's growing "crisis of confidence" in its own leadership is not less serious. The overmanagement urge seems to
know no bounds. Examples can be found in all institutions and
in any culture, perhaps explaining the persistence of the "balance of powers" logic. Demanagement, like open education, remains suspect because controls are still considered a need.
However, a few visionaries are beginning to realize that the call
for demanagement is, in reality, a call for *shared* management,
for cooperative decision making. This would be an unrealistic
longshot if it were not for the school's long history of successful
self-regulation, a way of getting the job done that has been sus-
pended but not forgotten.

3

Adjusting to Forced Change

In-service education, an obvious tool for survival, is in fact a fraudulent "change agent" because it does too little, too late. It operates on the assumption that "adult behavior modification" is desirable and possible, and that this kind of "involvement" is beneficial.

The conventional procedure calls for less than two weeks a year—typically only half that—to be devoted to total staff program planning and evaluation. Spread out over the 180-day school year, the result is a couple of days to open the school year and an equal number to close it. The remaining days are interspersed. Thus, administrative orientation, ceremonial morale building, and discussion, often without decision, become the only feasible agenda items. This tradition is totally out of tune with the current rate of change. It is a procedure clearly incapable of modifying the basic direction, structure, and process of school management, and it is precisely these larger dimensions of programming that are at stake during economic disruption.

Schools *can* be changed quickly, notwithstanding the late Paul Mort's "fifty-year lag" studies, but only through *forced change,* as opposed to the more gradual process of democratic persuasion and consensus building. If that idea is not acceptable

—it is not acceptable to most educators who entered teaching when it was a "unified profession"—it may be time for everyone to honestly examine the assumptions underlying "class action" law suits, supreme court rulings on discriminatory structures for schooling (demographic definitions of prejudice), national legislation dealing with the sex-neutralization of all laws, prohibitions of privacy invasion on the national level, and the endless number of administrative guidelines tied to nonlocal funding which require legal compliance for continued support.

Less forceful but still in use are the categorical aid programs which identify target groups and offer rewards for movement in a specified direction. General fund transfers from a higher level of government to the level below (revenue sharing), supporting "approved plans" of institutional development can also be powerful. Discretionary monies (creativity inducements) are potent change facilitators but they are always among the first cutbacks during a recession. (This is particularly unfortunate because it is quite possible to "invent" quality-sustaining adjustments.)

Forced change has thus become the norm while it is still being rejected or ignored in the literature of leadership and management theory. A revolutionary period has begun and the tendency is to value power over process and ends over means. If these values are taken to the extreme, democracy itself can be destroyed. Only if this change is exposed, understood, and contained within a larger democratic concept is it possible for the values associated with individual choice and public consent to survive. "Conversion strategy" begins at this point.

CONVERSION STRATEGY CHARACTERISTICS

When conversion strategy is defined as "forced change," the understood relationship is between the change agent and the impersonal institution. Institutions are more than manifestations of their temporary custodians. They are also a combination of past practices, rituals to which people have been conditioned, rule structures that continue to exist although they may have become useless, and a network of powerless roles that were never intended to include the responsibility of institutional improvement. Attempts to change such a pattern result in defensive, job-saving responses from the powerless.

In education, this category includes almost all teachers. It is a natural response but, nevertheless, catastrophic for converting the schools into a streamlined and efficient kind of institution. Yet, teachers cannot be held "accountable" for reforming the schools; that is management's responsibility. Almost any kind of economy-oriented reform will hurt some teachers. At the same time, though, it should strengthen others. Likewise, administrative roles, subjected to an authentic upgrading process, will change too. If casualties occur, they should be the by-products— minor side effects—of institutional rearrangements. Only in this spirit can one comfortably advocate forced change in a democratic culture.

Conversion strategies have distinctive characteristics, some of which refute the conventional wisdom of education's planning and evaluation processes. They include the following:

1. Conversions are not "experimental"—they are the change agent's best judgment concerning the substitution of a promising new practice for an obviously faltering current practice. The strategies do not start cautiously on a small scale, relying upon diffusion processes to spread success; rather, they end with the same scope and degree of involvement with which they started. There are no secondary, follow-up steps.

2. Time lines for change are short—rarely more than a single school year. The schools literally "start over" every fall. Multi-year change projections typically break down by retraining and indoctrination requirements. Conversions pre-

vent problem development, making second-year project participation a matter for employee contracts, not a matter of
personal persuasion.

3. Conversions limit participation in the redesign process. Large
groups inevitably tend toward political consensus; conversions require just the opposite—the invention of radical alternatives. The process is sometimes called an "executive
appraisal" in recognition of the design work being done by
the current management team. Consultants may be used in
the brainstorming process but those in authority accept full
accountability from the beginning.

4. Conversion strategies require a moratorium on testing. The
need is not for clever solutions to nonexistent problems but
for practical, surefire remedies for inefficiencies. There is no
concern whatever for documenting ("pretest," "post-test"
style) the small dimensions of change; consequently, the
danger of statistical assessments becoming change inducers is
avoided. Conversions properly begin with executive position
papers and end with sociological–historical progress reports.
At no time does the volume of paperwork exceed the importance of implemented ideas.

5. Transformation tasks are delineated, including deactivation
of the "rebound mechanisms" which would, in time, override
new practices with resistance and limited support while out-
wardly continuing to advocate project success. The transformation model is thus comprehensive and autonomous; the
design is fail-safe.

6. Conversion projects, as implied earlier, are designed for self-
perpetuation. It would take a certain level of cynicism, however, to "people-proof" the models completely. This could
only guarantee failure as constant change conditions make the
new model another cultural artifact. A good example of this
kind of error is the "windowless school" ("climate-controlled
year-round,") which failed to anticipate the inflation–energy
crisis. The best conversion projects lean toward self-per-
petuation but accept human intervention and thoughtful

redirection in light of new insights or needs. They are thus dependent upon people though vulnerability to prejudicial or accidental destruction is kept under control in the early high-risk stages.

CONVERSION MODEL SOURCES

It has been noted that in using conversion strategies several key assumptions are made, namely that:

1. Excessive cost can be eliminated without influencing quality; indeed, schools may often be improved in the process.
2. Movement toward openness is the proper direction for change when resources become scarce. The reason for this is that increased maneuverability for survival promotes inventiveness and thrift.
3. Conversion plans are practical, engineering-type specifications for customizing specific school operations. Always present in such models are the following: (a) a specific focus for the proposed conversion; (b) a clustering of both primary and secondary variables to obtain a "critical mass" of employee commitment (thereby making administrative regulation unnecessary); (c) a carefully programmed series of administrative initiatives; and (d) a highly visible, short timetable for all employees affected by the particular conversion to accomplish their mission.

Conversion plans can be limited or comprehensive depending upon the checklist used by the planner. The author's checklist focuses on access, specifically on its seven partially controllable dimensions:

1. Invention (the right to discover and create).

2. Choice (personal decision making).

3. Production (the right to be a worker; the right to have dignity without work).

4. Security (the stabilizing of crisis points—illness, retirement, death, unemployment, etc., and sufficient environmental protection to sustain the quality of life over generations).

5. Safety (freedom from the fear of unprovoked violence, and more important, freedom from overprotection by a paternalistic government; guaranteed individual initiative, privacy, and divergent life styles).

6. Conservation (protecting the public's survival interests against resource exploitation for short-term profit; detecting neglected improvement for reasons of power or political popularity).

7. Justice (support for the emerging awareness of injustice).

Figure 3.1 is intended to relate these seven planning and monitoring points to the phenomenon of access. Planning models must be defined by each individual. Note, for example, the emergence of "sex neutral laws" and the civil rights of juveniles under the "justice" heading. Also included is the "right of privacy" movement against electronic "bugging" devices for criminal investigation and control by computers in the commercial world.

In each of the seven categories it is important to check the relationship of the private and public sectors. Economic recession can induce public institutions to transfer certain responsibilities back to the individual, thereby cutting costs. Conversely, as individuals "lose control" for economic reasons, they look to public sources for help. Many of these practices affect the schools directly; others set precedents which are soon followed for no better reason than they appear to be working elsewhere. Figure 3.1 provides an overview of relevant factors in institutional behavior, inviting educators to question, monitor, and respond to the larger struggle for access.

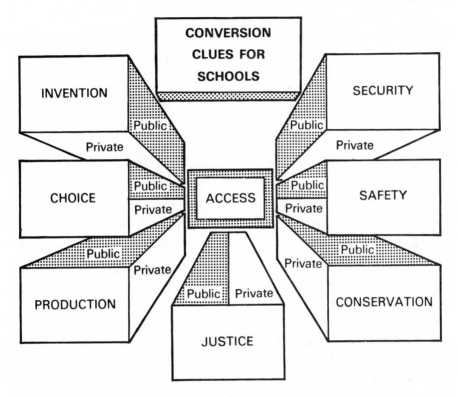

Figure 3.1. *Planning and Monitoring Points for the Evolution of Access*

SURVIVAL KITS

In pursuing the issue of access, reform proposals can be visualized as four basic survival kits for (1) students, (2) democratic processes, (3) public institutions, and (4) the open culture.

Survival Kit 1 for students must assume the desirability of extending and diffusing personal power. Since the schools have no way to extend the kind of power that results from wealth or property, the only programmable option is technology. This option presumes both increased *access to tools*—those which one might think of as the "technology of the common man"—and, a high level of *personal competence in the use of these tools*. A justification of careers in technology may be preferred by many but this need not be the schools' controlling assumption. Access and competence are essential; future jobs, less predictable and beyond the jurisdiction of the schools, should not be the primary concern.

Survival Kit 2 for the participation process equates "progress" with the *broadening of public knowledge*. It is assumed that the public communications network is partly the responsibility of the schools. With "truth" being contested and political, and a culture relying upon its institutions (including schools) to make decisions for people rather than with them, a major dislocation of power is occurring. Institutions are taking more prerogatives but using them less wisely. The schools are the last bastion of local autonomy and have the power to aid in a *rebirth of the concept of community*. Recessions sharply reduce family mobility, thereby increasing the importance of local communications networks. The schools are even stronger than local governments in regulating public policy for both adult and juvenile groups. The schools can and should reactivate their traditions of community leadership, especially in the urban and suburban areas. In the rural areas where the idea of community has always been strong, the guideline should be to "think small"—small schools, small school districts. Legalistic forced change (court-ordered desegregation, for example) thrives on oversized political, educational, and governmental jurisdictions. More diversity will result in better schools and stronger communities.

Survival Kit 3 for institutional self-regulation calls for further development of the planning function. The schools have come to possess the technology of community development almost by accident. Population monitoring is necessary for enrollment forecasting, and for property-based school support. If the local data banks were used together with the state data system, the result would be the most comprehensive computer-based monitoring system available to any institution.

Of course, the unrestricted accessing of data banks maintained for other reasons—law enforcement, banking, credit, insurance, welfare, retirement, etc.—allows the social security number to be an instrument for the invasion of personal privacy and a code for the development of a deeper understanding of community behavior. The former may be unjust but is not yet considered illegal. The power-motivated administrators seem unable to eliminate the overabundance of paperwork. Institutional development should begin with the establishment of regulatory guidelines for its technology. Such things as timetables for the destruction of individual and family records, access guarantees, information dissemination restrictions, etc. should be instituted. Community monitoring is much more promising without posing such a serious threat to individual liberty. It might be interesting to have environmental quality computer simulations in which current trends in land use, housing types, pollution levels, transportation patterns, employment prospects, etc. could be used in presenting issues concerning new school locations, curricular provisions for emerging careers, educational interests related to age distribution, social service requirements related to neighborhood economics, etc. The idea is not to use confidential community data to make decisions for people (thereby making institutions stronger and individuals weaker through lack of knowledge) but to communicate the new information to the public in such a way as to promote interest and discussion concerning alternative programming possibilities.

Survival Kit 4 confronts the schools' need to invent a better structure for the changing definitions of social justice. Justice cannot be defined explicitly by the courts or anyone else. Attempts have been made, over and over again, with such concepts as "racial balance," "parity for blacks," "proportionate power," having been invented, tried, and then abandoned in favor of new ways of perceiving a difficult problem. Older remedies for injustice are, of course, still around, useful for some purposes and some people because the relationship between school policy and the several liberation movements—race, sex, and age—is still uncertain. Territorial and statistical definitions of prejudice are currently in vogue but the real problems are programmatic and attitudinal. The needed structure for justice will provide for program and attitude changes as the concept of justice itself matures. Justice may finally be recognized as a cluster of issues related to "access"; meanwhile, survival adjustments in the curriculum call for increased access for everyone without specific regard for any one group. When access patterns become more open, everyone will benefit.

The four "survival kits"—access to *tools,* to an *extended communications* network, to a more efficient *institutional planning* function, and to a modernized *structure for social justice*—add up to the political component of school administration. Administrators are, thus, the sources of access regulation—the intervention points for social change through education. The uninitiated may often wonder how the schools ever became the testing ground for cultural transformation. The reason is simple; no other institution is in possession of an equal power base for handling change.

PARADIGM FOR PLANNING

Since conversion strategies are, first of all, administrative action models, and more specifically, models that seek economy through a transfer of authority back to the people, a paradigm can be a useful planning aid.

The model, just discussed in survival kit form, is pictured in Figure 3.2 and shows the interrelationship of the three main components of the planner's task: (1) conversion assumptions,

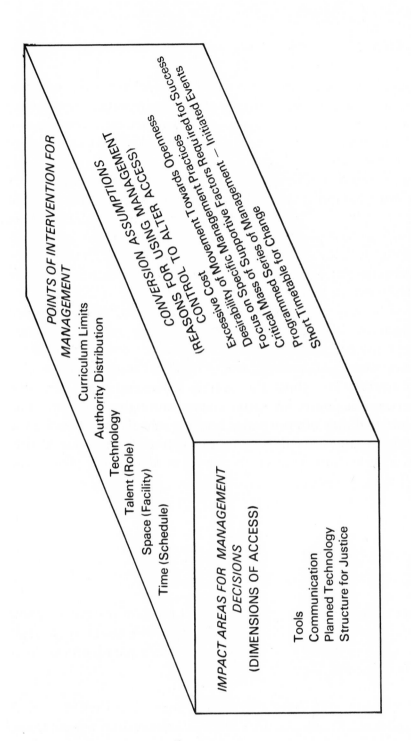

Figure 3.2. *Paradigm for Conversion Strategy Planning*

POINTS OF INTERVENTION FOR MANAGEMENT

Curriculum Limits
Authority Distribution
Technology
Talent (Role)
Space (Facility)
Time (Schedule)

CONVERSION ASSUMPTIONS MANAGEMENT
(REASONS FOR USING ACCESS)
CONTROL TO ALTER OPENNESS

Excessive Cost Towards Success
Movement of Management Factors — Initiated Events
Desirability of Specific Practices Required for Success
Focus on Supportive of Management
Critical Mass Series of Change
Programmed for Change
Short Timetable

IMPACT AREAS FOR MANAGEMENT DECISIONS
(DIMENSIONS OF ACCESS)

Tools
Communication
Planned Technology
Structure for Justice

41

(2) management controls, and (3) the dimensions of access. There will be many conversion "plans," some large, others less ambitious. They can all have powerful results if a "cancellation effect" is avoided through careful attention to philosophical compatibility. Such is the intent of Figure 3.2.

In conclusion, the educational institution is a great bureaucracy with a built-in resistance to any kind of change. Laws, regulations, and financial formulas are so much more enduring than superintendents, principals, and school boards that comprehensive planning is the only realistic antidote for the possibly resulting extremes of apathy or tyranny. Since participation in decision making is limited by both tradition and impracticality both directions and strategies are necessarily selected by the few for the many. This is forced change. It is a counterculture idea in many respects but nevertheless an accurate assessment of how things are actually accomplished. Whether the result is democratic or otherwise depends much upon leadership orientation and the intelligent use of communications resources. There is still much to be learned about the application of democratic values to the decision processes in large institutions.

4

Creative Conversion
Possibilities

It is said that designers are "limited only by their imagination."
This is, of course, untrue. If certain results are desired, some
kinds of inventions are necessarily contraindicative. Reconstruc-
tions that establish priorities and cut seemingly less important
goals may sound logical—provided one does not try to investi-
gate why certain goals of obvious worth are abandoned. The
schools have accidentally produced some very creative "hatchet
men," whose reform recommendations leave no doubt about
their partisan assumptions. Within these constraints—even because of them—a few promising conversion points can now be
identified.

LEAVING THE PATERNALISTIC
ENVIRONMENT

The prolonged physical, moral, and educational overprotection
of youth is expensive. In an earlier cultural period it was considered necessary, regardless of cost. Today, the practice has be-

come outmoded by modern youth's resistance to all forms of authoritative guidance. The price is high, not only financially, for retaining institutional control of behavior after general support for it has been lost.

The most visible symptom of the problem erupts periodically in high schools in the form of school riots. School principals have waited too long to admit that only the most peaceful environment can withstand the mass movement of one thousand people six or seven times a day through narrow corridors where physical contact is unavoidable. The master schedule that mandates adult surveillance both in class and between classes will surely be challenged as an invasion of privacy as the juvenile liberation movement gains momentum. Meanwhile, educators do not want to lose sight of the fact that paternalism has gone too far. There is a large number of schools that can't keep students in school with enough regularity to benefit from the attendance-based state support system. There is now good reason to base school support on student eligibility rather than on daily attendance. To falsify school attendance records for the purpose of retaining a sufficient number of teachers to handle peak enrollments, or to force reluctant learners to stay in school for reasons other than their personal benefit is beyond justification.

The solution is so obvious it can be easily overlooked. It is not the British "open classroom" that is needed but the American *open campus* quarter system—junior college style. In this setting, authority within the classroom is maintained but the conduct of scheduled student–teacher affairs is strictly personal. Traffic management is simply removed from the master schedule, thereby completely short-circuiting the crowd control problem.

The discipline problem disappears as self-regulation becomes a practical criterion for the privilege of attendance. The teacher's responsibility becomes a balance of scheduled group encounters and personalized, self-scheduled counseling or problem-solving relations with individuals or small groups. No longer is it necessary for all teachers to be full-time employees, nor for all teachers to have identical workloads. Alternative teaching career patterns can emerge from the disciplines being taught or teacher preferences. Administrators have tried for too long to be advocates of student freedom while denying the freedom of the teacher. But no school has ever been able to transmit more freedom than it is willing to allow its adult employees.

Is "deschooling" an irrelevant futuristic theory or the current reality? The latter seems to be the case, the only unfortunate fact is the school administrator's reluctance to admit that there is value in informal education. They have the choice to either continue to resist the inevitable, or find ways of cataloging, programming, and giving credit for alternative expressions of personal competence. Positive trends include performance testing for either career certification or academic credit qualification and voucher-type experiments, which approve the learner's objectives, provide support, and allow the learner to decide where to attend school and the conditions of time and attendance. When schools adopt the deschooled options, the evidence will be larger catalogs, more liberal credit patterns, and much more variety in individual programs. And, in the process, costs can decrease as quality is improved.

MAKING PEACE WITH THE LAW

Programmatic desegregation is one of the most important needs of our time. It is hard to tell whether it is folk wisdom or simple prejudice that produces public resistance to the destruction of the community school. People want justice, but something tells them that it should be possible without court control over their most accessible public institution—the school—which may be so close to home that they can see it from their front porch.

In a previous chapter it was noted that "the self-contained school building" is the heart of the problem. If every school program has to occur under a single roof, then each school must be "comprehensive," necessarily the most expensive model. This leaves the courts no choice but to seek in-school statistical evidence of nonprejudicial programming. Racial balance becomes the logical target, not only in the school at large but in the various subprograms that may tilt the overall balance through grouping, tracking, or even personal choice. The overlooked alternative is to access all the educational resources of the school district, retaining, in the process, the "neighborhood school" for the traditional functions it performs best.

The weakness of the "comprehensive" school has been its minimal capacity for specialization. By attempting everything, it could not have exemplary programming. The higher the grade level, the greater the distortion. On the other hand, it is fairly easy to achieve a critical level of resources and faculty commitment in the school that has a specialized function. A "school for the performing arts," for example, cannot be compared with a one-teacher drama department in a typical high school. The same can be said for any other specialty whether it be artistic, humanistic, or scientific. Schools are much more efficient when they incorporate programs that promote high standards of personal performance.

Schools that are being accidentally destroyed by well-meaning courts should move the school system toward the next highest level of specialization—the inter-neighborhood or inter-district academy—then, make these new performance centers available through a combination of exploratory rotation and personal choice without regard to race or neighborhood origin. The schools need specialization and by nondiscriminatory sharing of the new resources the issue of lingering prejudice can be resolved.

The local school can be maintained—indeed, it *should* be kept. The only difference would be that a portion of the student body would always be on special assignments outside the neighborhood. Academic specialization and cross-neighborhood integration are probably most effective on the high school level. Whether or not a child's *education* (as opposed to a child's *school*) is desegregated has to be judged by the changing patterns of interaction over the entire twelve years of compulsory schooling. If special career path monitoring and assessment plans are needed, then educators should proceed to develop them. Meanwhile, judges and educators need to begin thinking about nondiscriminatory school programs, not desegregated schools. The former is the substance of justice, the latter may not even be its shell.

The other major movements for educational justice can also be supported programmatically rather than structurally. Reference is made to the combined liberation movements for minorities, women, and juveniles. These are areas of school improvement that often cost nothing. Cost neutralization occurs because some historical forms of institutional prejudice have required the costly duplication of services in order to keep certain groups separate. On the other hand, the installment of previously omitted programs will cause cost increases. However, a reduced number of duplications tends to balance the required additions, making major change possible for only minimal cost. Teacher attitudes are often a particularly troublesome dimension of prejudice. Some propose behavior-modification in-service education, but a more promising approach may be to revise teacher recruitment and assignment patterns. A change in administrative practice is relatively easy; a change in people almost impossible.

Closely related is the idea of access which may be built into the structures of guidance, discipline, scheduling, monitoring, and management. There is no better treatment for the problem of prejudice than an analysis of access because it can be depersonalized and changed with only minimal resistance. This does not completely reach the classroom interaction part of the curriculum but it does invite a reconsideration of attitude through the removal of official constraints. And, "making peace with the law" ultimately assumes that people of good will, free of institutional imposition, will, in fact, progress toward the equalization of rights and privileges.

MAKING THE TOOLS OF
ECONOMIC SURVIVAL
MORE ACCESSIBLE

Career education is widely advocated in American schools. A part of these programs, almost invariably, is some kind of work experience. Yet, there is an interesting paradox—the schools rarely see themselves as the employers of their own trainees. It's not that the expertise is lacking. Berea College of Kentucky is a good example, with students earning their total college expenses by participating in far-flung, but still college-based, work–study programs. College enterprises include a farm, hotel, gift shop, and furniture factory, and work is available in commercial crafts as well as in a variety of more conventional office-type or instructional aide assignments. Appalachian poverty motivated the original program design but sound education sustains it.

The recession, of course, has produced similar conditions almost everywhere but especially in industrial cities. The opportunity exists to take career education seriously enough to designate a number of salaried school positions for the rotation of trainees. Minimal compensation, coupled with the teaming of trainees to cover otherwise full-time assignments, could simultaneously expand school services and reduce school operating expenses. A work-based, engineering-type model for precollege education would have great appeal for some, possibly much greater than the liberal arts advocate would dare consider. Yet, those who would not choose to participate could be exempted. Alternative education, in this case, should mean many personal alternatives within the overall program. One appealing elective might be to help run the educational establishment itself.

On the topic of economic survival for individuals, the schools have yet to fully capitalize on the "access to tools" idea that gave birth to *The Whole Earth Catalog* and related counter-culture literature. Of course, direct-access, personalized education was counterculture only originally. School librarians haven't yet caught on but college bookstore operators are much less naive about what modern youth find appealing enough to buy without the school requiring it. Concepts and theories are "tools" by this definition, along with the conventionally accepted commercial products and mechanical inventions.

The school problem is two-fold: (1) everything has traditionally been rationed to students ("scope and sequence" curriculum guides block spontaneous individual access, make all access teacher-dependent, and usually offer only a superficial coverage of the presumed "fundamentals"); and (2) the schools' "tool collection" is typically modest to meager in scope and is managed in such a way as to block the transition from tool introduction, to individual tool ownership, lease, rental, or free public access for the purpose of developing high personal skill. Since the schools are so underbudgeted and underequipped at present, no money can be saved here. The long-term picture may be just the opposite, however, as vastly increased tool access is converted into salable production skills.

REMOVING MANIPULATION
FROM THE CURRICULUM

Traditionally, teaching is defined as an authoritative act. Science, when applied to education, does not challenge this assumption but procedurally refines the related and sequential acts of diagnosis, prescription, and evaluation. Unchallenged, this assumption preempts most of the learner's rights to his or her own purpose and to the preferred means of achievement. Economic recession seems to fortify this questionable practice.

However, "doing your own thing" is no longer a counter-culture idea; it is, rather, the main response to a rapidly changing world. The idea is that while the big problems seem to defy everyone's efforts, a distinctive personal life-style is still an attainable objective.

"Behavior modification" and "accountability"—very much supported during the recession years—are still around but at long last reasonably well contained. Some of the special education projects and testing programs (achievement monitors) that were generated are token demonstrations of the "clinical model" (still considered to be the last word in some teacher education circles).

The courts, in responding to recent class action law suits, have attempted to stop "target group" programming. In less sophisticated years, the same practice was simply known as "earmarked legislation," but the "prescriptive mode" brought it to the level of mild warfare in which the learner becomes a "target," his disabilities having been previously documented, if not scientifically, at least statistically. The important thing now is that the "patients" have made it quite clear that they do not wish to "take the cure"—at least not this cure.

Students want survival, but what they want to see survive is the right of educational self-determination. This means, for the curriculum programmer, not more prescriptions but more varied alternatives for making the school's resources accessible. Tracks won't do because they are the traditional perpetuators of social class. They are, of course, alternatives of sorts but they are too few, too insular, and they commit the learner for too long a time —usually from the ninth grade onward.

The economics of personal choice are ambiguous. Theoretically, with each learner becoming to some degree his or her own teacher, more can be learned and with fewer teachers. Yet, technological and general resource backup systems are more crucial when the goal is to personalize education. This, in turn, calls for a variety of nonteaching types—clinicians, technicians, librarians, managers, etc.—within the education environment along with a new breed of teachers. Thus, what is diminished in one category is increased in another. The total budget rarely goes down, at least for this conversion. It is an essential conversion, however. It links the schools with the restless survival-oriented students who will have much to do with any future economic adjustments requiring community support.

No one really knows how to program for multiple life-styles. When it has been attempted, the common error has been to revert to the dangerous assumptions of target grouping. The alternative is similar to the practice of supermarkets; sell the raw materials and let the customers plan their own meals. Some subjects would still be taught prescriptively, authoritatively, and without apology. It is just a question of which ones and to what extent.

REDUCING COMMUNITY ALIENATION

"Think small" may well be the best advice for relating schools to the alienated community concerned about its economic future. Many educators gave up the commitment to local autonomy years ago. Consolidation had been vigorously advocated by reports that claimed that no high school with less than one hundred students graduating could be truly "comprehensive." Simultaneously, the "nonlocal" political and financial community had gained so much strength that many local school boards complained of powerlessness. In those days, "metro" was the key word. Bigger was better; duplication was wrong and so was inequity; equalization and coordinated planning were desirable. Management technology had only just begun so no one gave serious thought to the possibility of any bureaucracy becoming "too efficient."

But, the fast change rate was linked with technology, politics became cynical and manipulative, the levels of authority above did show a decided tendency to "solve" problems for the levels below, and no one seemed able to confirm that schools had improved. Disillusionment was strongest in the big cities where loss of control had degenerated into street crime and marginal employment. When the recession came, it naturally hit the hardest those who were already staggering under a burden too big to carry alone.

Afterwards, a positive survival behavior made an unexpected appearance with the revival of the community school in the urban setting. Advocating such new ideas as "voucher plans" and old concepts like "local autonomy," the new movement even turned to "self-policing" for neighborhood safety and "self-teaching" (schools of the "street theater," "storefront" type).

A community's frustration is difficult to distinguish from the calmer determination to regain or retain control. Two examples are the Charleston, West Virginia (Kanawha County) textbook censorship case and the Boston busing problem. In both instances, the issues were superficially publicized. At the core of each problem was the citizens' struggle to reassert their rights and to reclaim some of the authority delegated to governmental and educational bureaucracies.

The community participation process has not yet completely renewed itself. Citizens rise to meet common enemies but become complacent again between crises. The need is for permanent institutions, principally the schools, to stabilize planning, to practically monitor and report on community successes and failures, and to begin making available its increasingly potent community development tools and personnel for a broader definition of the mission of schooling. There is probably some irony in the community school movement coming first to rebirth in the cities, then to the suburbs and back to rural locations. The goals of making schools "small" and "manageable" as well as "diverse" and "individual" are especially promising for the country's future. Educators are fortunate to be at the focal point of such a mission.

STABILIZING PERSONNEL POLICIES

No real progress can be made for school improvement if teachers feel insecure. The assumptions of the accountability movement had produced mild intimidation even before school enrollments began to decline, automatically reducing state support and the number of available teaching positions. Tenure is a mild check on capricious administrative action but this too is now threatened in several state legislatures. The reason is that declining revenue conflicts with personnel policies that make inadequate provisions for needed staff reduction.

The alternative is to update the tenure laws with a new concept of seniority that would give strong job support for about two-thirds of the teaching staff. Also essential would be self-terminating contracts that could be renewed if funding permitted but could also be allowed to expire if necessary. Such roles could be flexible, including part-time service, adjunct retainers, teachers in training, or migrant teachers. "Differentiated staffing," considered an experimental failure, probably did not go far enough since the schools rarely employed more than a few teacher aides and educational secretaries. The current situation would permit creative faculty diversification which could become a blessing in disguise.

In-service education was already failing before union contracts set its limits in both financial terms and clock hours and thereby signed its death warrant. Yet, good schools do not stay good without keeping their personnel up-to-date. If in-service education is out, then some kind of arrangement for teacher involvement in group planning becomes a must. But nonauthoritative planning backlogs recommendations on the desks of the few administrators trying to make too many specialized decisions for impatient half-involved teachers. A revival of the supervisory function in a more decentralized form would be beneficial. It would be technically feasible and professionally sound; teachers, who are the talent base of the academic disciplines, could broaden supervisory potential beyond the "generalist" role.

There could be a problem elsewhere, however. Supervisory personnel like to think of themselves as teacher helpers but their employers see them as company oriented. Thus, a contest of power might precede the only thing that would allow teachers to seriously assume the curriculum updating responsibility—the relocation of the entire supervisory function to consolidate curriculum planning with teaching on the one hand, and acceptance of a leaner management function on the other. Leadership would be proper on both sides—quite a switch from the current thought which reserves the leadership function for administrators only.

Thus, two needs could merge to become one major school improvement conversion—namely, the "new seniority" and teacher-level curriculum leadership. The bonus will be that the needed flexibility for personnel policy reconstruction will also prevent unwanted political intervention.

REINVESTING SOCIAL CONTROL ROLES

Nothing so vividly reveals the social control commitment that schools have drifted into as the role of "assistant principal for discipline." The role is on the level of the "second in command," raising the expectancy of disobedience and disorder to such proportions that one would think if it did not occur by student initiative someone in power would almost have to provoke it. High power will either be exercised or begin to atrophy. The fact is that few disciplinary principals are in danger of running out of work.

Student survival requirements and the heavy hand of school authority are on the verge of breaking the entire machinery of school government. A positive, deliberate shift in the concept of management could still leave the institution intact, but the changes would have to be made fairly soon, beginning with a simplification of the rule structure of the school. The school is an automatic decision-making machine, uniformly imposing requirements, defining options, monitoring production, recycling failures, and suppressing dissent. If the power of the process is doubted, one has only to examine a school that has recently experienced a total administrative change. A year later, many students will still not know that they have a new principal; even more disheartening is the fact that many teachers will know his name but will not have yet perceived any other implications for themselves. If the school secretary is efficient, the school will run smoothly, as if on autopilot; if the secretary leaves, the school may be in trouble.

The juvenile rights movement has already started to unravel the many student regulations that schools have invented. A number of constraints have been added through the years that have never been taken off the books. The master schedule contains even more constraints, as do the invisible policies of selection and placement. Schedules can easily be returned to a subcomputer level through faculty reorganization for decentralization. If this resulted in increased responsibility for the teacher the guidance staff would be free to abandon the regulatory role almost completely—and, the assistant principal could be reassigned to curriculum development. The disciplinary problem will be solved through interpersonal relations between teachers and students.

A reconstructed guidance service could be especially creative in adopting a community concept of interagency service. For example, staff organization has yet to reflect the most important educational aspect of "the drug culture"—the large number of students now coming to school on behavior-modifying prescription drugs provided within the law by family physicians or mental health services. The typical school nurse is as helpless as the teacher since her authority is limited. Similarly, the criminal justice system has long needed liaison supervision beyond the well-meaning but limited services of "youth aide officers" assigned to schools by the police. Educational transfer services, particularly of the "deschooled" variety which can be fit in around work, have outgrown the traditional college or employment referrals. The deteriorating economy raises the importance of vocational counseling and "performance tests" for job qualification or technical training. The point is that a restructured guidance service could swap the faltering disciplinary function for a powerful interagency relationship to which several public budgets could contribute. Youth services could be improved substantially, and, most likely, with no cost increase at all. The school cannot handle the whole job of youth management and should stop trying. The great "discipline problem" contains only one message: the schools have been trying to do the wrong thing. The intention has been commendable but the current assessment is that the outcome has been unsatisfactory. The age of self-determination for youth is at hand and the schools should help make it work.

In summary, program conversions are necessarily controversial. There is no significant change in a school setting that does not violate somebody's security. We have not yet found a way to democratically generate voluntary role changes on a large scale. The possibility may be that teachers have a backlog of ideas for school reform that no one has bothered to solicit. However, there is an even greater possibility that the suppressed ideas are role bound—that is, confined to the teacher's contract duties.

The ultimate conclusion is that conversions such as those illustrated in this chapter have dimensions well beyond the standard teacher contract. They are, therefore, administrative in nature, even requiring administrative initiative for a preliminary hearing. It is a great responsibility so often avoided by practitioners that one can safely assume that they, too, are role bound. As long as this condition prevails it is unrealistic to expect schools to reform themselves.

The Impact of
Survival Behavior
on Role and Function

5

Primary Role
Adaptations

Professional roles in large bureaucratic organizations are designed for minimal change. Unfortunately, a culture in crisis can suddenly begin pressuring for transformations that individual employees do not consider possible or proper. The person in the position, whether teacher or administrator, feels trapped and lacking in adaptability.

The new expectancies are typically nonspecific. There are serious doubts about employee competence but no definite, appropriate remedies. Contract agreements derived from institutionalized, past requirements are just the opposite—highly specific, linked with financial and legal guarantees of employee security, and daily reinforced by informal interpersonal relationships. When threatened employees are forced to choose, they almost always drift in the direction of the most specific alternative.

By opting for no change and rejecting nonspecific external criticism, the bureaucratic captives unavoidably offend their critics. These employees trivialize the legitimate anxieties of parents and taxpayers at a time when they are in no mood for being ignored; they, too, want survival.

This chapter focuses on management and teacher survival and on the behaviors that are produced from too much external pressure and too little employee adaptability. The intent is to introduce the general concept of role disruption, which subsequent chapters will treat in more detail.

MANAGEMENT SURVIVAL

When the management of any bureaucratic establishment is threatened, the security of all the employees is immediately jeopardized. There is no time lag. Rumors of unrest at the top spread fast because of the certainty that equilibrium can only be restored by doing something that will necessarily affect some vulnerable employee, lower echelon of authority, or selected organizational component. The quickest, easiest way to reassert the privileges of power is to blame others. That is the most expedient way to strengthen internal obligation patterns and to suppress vocal dissent, but, the reason—fear—is as wrong as the truth-evading motive. And, in the schooling enterprise, there are almost always devastating results in the classrooms as caution replaces spontaneity. No good school can remain that way once the faculty's high values are displaced by silent conformity and the teacher's primary motivation shifts from student welfare to self-defense. The same can be said of the defensive administrator who, for personal reasons, withdraws essential support from his teachers. He may momentarily feel more secure but this kind of euphoria is shortlived. The trust relationship is much easier to break than to rebuild and no administrator can enjoy long tenure without it.

This unfortunate sequence of events is important to understand because economic disruption tends to trigger much more insecurity "at the top" than most teachers realize; consequently, survival behavior in the administration is quickly interpreted as tyranny. This, in turn, sets in motion political forces of significant magnitude that keep the chief school officer's job in a constant state of rotation. With management possessing considerably more power than the average career teacher, and having considerably less time to exercise it, the hypothetical tyranny becomes an unavoidable reality. Change by executive contract becomes the resulting school board practice—"The job is yours if. . . ." Democratic participation by teachers is thus laid aside before it can even be tried.

Decision-Making Emphasis

Few administrators want to become a part of the cycle just illustrated because a slip in timing makes it too hazardous for even the most adventuresome. Yet the contracts of administrators in some of the country's most prominent cities continue to document the existence of a "gypsy" management that easily moves from one short-term executive appointment to another, according to the whims of troubled school boards. Four types of candidates are on the circuit: (1) "change advocates" who do not envision themselves beyond the proposal stage before moving again but whose charismatic dialogue charms audiences everywhere, (2) "change agents" who basically market preselected problem solutions (desegregation plans, for example), and (3) "change arrestors" whose principal function is to curb the fast changing establishment. Those are the exploiters, however; the contributors stay long enough to correct some of their own mistakes as well as make subtle shifts in institutional priorities and processes for long-term stability.

The problems that produce opportunism in management are built into the patterned policies and automatic decision-making arrangements that are typical of most bureaucracies. Policies tend to be cumulative rather than successive, each new addition is written indelibly to perpetually compete with past or future policies.

The following options reveal the possible changes in decision-making emphases.

1. Options that *mandate* (legislative, judicial, and administrative attempts to force change on a reluctant establishment)
2. Options that *induce* (incentive plans which invite but do not force)
3. Options that *authorize* (permissive legislation that legalizes but neither forces or invites)
4. Options that *transfer, withdraw,* or *ignore* (redefinitions of jurisdiction and mission)
5. Options that *protect* (through restrictions on tools, the accessibility of information, rights of participation, or the power of decision)

Clearly, options 1 and 5 are the greatest temptations in a troubled time. Examples of "mandates" are court-ordered desegregation plans, fair employment riders on appropriation bills, school-board-ordered drug-abuse classes, and accountability testing. The "protective" options, in general, have tended to cause alienation. In the seventies, the juvenile civil rights movement merged with the liberation movement for racial minorities and women to bridge the gaps caused by protective segregation. Then, the economic crisis slowed the trend with economic restraints. The tug of war in education continues but a real war rages in the larger culture, which seems to be on the verge of deciding that individuals should be less vulnerable to their institutions.

Nevertheless, the individual's protection against arbitrary search and seizure has no meaning in airport terminals. Presidents seem to feel the need for over one thousand secret service agents for their own protection, electronic security monitors remain a booming business, and no big business seems able to run without the automatic decision capability of the computer. The dominant cultural feeling favors a new individualism as the remedy for a besieged middle class. However, evidence in institutional behavior shows an opposite trend: when people are economically threatened they opt for more security and instinctively equate it with an increase in authoritative control. A different kind of security, one which comes from liberty rather than obedience, is important at this point.

Evolution of the Leader–Follower Options

At any given moment, what appears to be an autonomous action of management is often a second-phase adaptation to a changed attitude of its followers. Three factors in constant interplay are:

1. Institutional authority (leadership)
2. Voluntary subordination (followership)
3. Self-regulation (a conscious reduction in subordination)

To illustrate, government in the mid-sixties was typified by a pursuit of power that was eventually to erupt as the Watergate scandal in the early seventies. Manipulation was assumed to be legitimate leader behavior. The followership, however, must have been less enchanted than the contenders for power because a noticeable degree of voluntary subordination was quietly but swiftly withdrawn. President Nixon was later to hypothesize the existence of a "silent majority," that he thought to be his following. He could not have been more wrong. The average citizen was attempting to reclaim private privilege in direct proportion to a faltering faith in public authority figures in general.

This is a fearful sensation for a leader once the truth begins to sink in, and a typical response is to coerce the disaffected to reestablish loyalty. Just the opposite is, of course, what happens

—resistance to the attempted coercion and a greater shift in political allegiance to the self-reliant individual. The survival options listed below illustrate positive and negative responses to change. The list of possibilities demonstrates that subordination can be invited but not commanded. The leader's survival options are:

1. public defense of his actions
2. elitist retrenchment, or
3. institutional reconstruction

The follower's survival options are:

1. revolution
2. subversion
3. apathy (political disengagement)
4. selective loyalty
5. high morale, high trust in public officials

Options in self-regulation are:

1. retreat
2. sustaining defense
3. developmental expansion

After sufficient time lapsed, the mid-seventies policy showed signs of favoring, for the leader, elitist retrenchment, and for the follower, a blend of political disengagement and selective loyalty. This ruled out the more fearful dimensions of political dissent, but it also projected little likelihood for an exciting reformation of the private–public relationship. The public leader who worries about survival should probably attend to his personal authenticity. The fast-changing economy, at least in part, necessitates a return of public confidence, and this can never be commanded, only invited and earned.

Demanagement

Research documentation will eventually confirm the high-pressure predispositions of school managers to:

1. Reduce staff participation in budgeting, spending, and accounting, reserving for management exclusive rights to allocate scarce resources.

2. Decrease the frequency of faculty meetings with serious planning content, relying instead on a small group of trusted subordinates to help make and carry out basic policies.

3. Be much more sensitive to expectancies from above (in the chain of command) than to colleague or subordinate needs and wishes.

4. Inhibit dissent to the point of equating employee "loyalty" with agreement with management; ultimately, channeling "merit" resources into rewards for the "most cooperative."

5. "Run the organization" with mid-career lieutenants and opportunistic beginners, minimizing seniority rights and privileges in all matters related to decision making.

6. Subtly resist both program expansion and innovation as a matter of policy (for inflation control).

7. Increase employee evaluation, stressing performance *within* specific roles. ("Behavioral objectives" are ideally suited to this purpose.)

8. Divert staff energy into self-evaluations that define and promote group harmony as a psychological rather than an institutional phenomenon (encounter groups, sensitivity training, value clarification).

9. Extend management control to include everything not specifically delegated to the classroom instructor—instructional technology check-out systems, certification of individuals for status changes (graduation, placement, etc.), security management based on limited access assumptions, master scheduling, rule structure oversight, etc.

67

10. Directly control all matters of public relations, institutional evaluation and interpretation.

The net result of supermanagement is the intellectual disengagement of large numbers of professional employees. As individual roles are perceived to be "eroding," morale soon follows suit. Role constriction and low morale combine eventually to reduce voluntary accountability, the real "glue" that has always held the educational establishment together. From this point no management team is good enough, or big enough, to accomplish more than low quality institutional maintenance. Quality and economy were the original motives of supermanagement; in the end, quality is sacrificed and costs increase. The alternative is demanagement.

Richard Corneulle's *Demanaging America: The Final Revolution* is a landmark in the tradition of Ivan Illich's "deschooling" of education. Interestingly, the American intellectuals have conceded that too much of a virtue can become a vice but none of the futurists foresaw the need to unravel the officer corps. It is necessary to go all the way back to Spengler's pessimistic *Decline of the West* to pick up the prediction of a self-destruct phase in institutional development. However, the assumption that the free world will inevitably decline is unnecessary in facing the need for demanagement. Indeed, voluntary demanagement may be the remedy that contradicts inevitability in all such theories.

The idea of demanagement is straightforward. Two Americas are visualized, one increasingly managed and failing; the other informal and largely successful. For example, population stabilization, the answer to Malthusian economics, is not occurring as a result of governmental distress signals or even family planning clinics; it is the aggregate effect of millions of women making an equal number of private decisions after having been given access to the chemical technology of birth control. The "big picture" was not planned first and then imposed; it evolved from paintings by individual artists, each creatively contributing to a larger collage.

Corneulle's "taximeter" analogy is particularly revealing.[1] He notes that the New York City taxi system transports millions with a remarkable efficiency resulting from only one management constraint—"keep the meter running." If the educational management was to have undertaken a similar project, they would most likely have developed a computer model similar to a high school schedule—a finite number of pickup points and destinations, a predictable number of passengers and routes, a controllable cost accounting system to identify efficient drivers for merit rewards and inefficient competitors for replacement. No doubt, such a system would have standardized driver dress codes and in-service workshops to "professionalize" the driver–passenger relationship. Initially, many "improvements" would be cited by management, but in the end, it would not be able to document its claims in two critical areas: passengers and profits.

There appears to be a point in managerial evolution beyond which administrators must proceed or fail. The world's "planned economies" are working, in their way, as Castro's example attests. However, so are the taximeter subsystems of a free economy. Co-existence is possible to the extent that voluntary or imposed management constraints prevent the destruction of democratic communities and their built-in accountability systems.

The public, as previously noted, is uniquely vulnerable to management domination. Even so, the school system still has a number of autonomous enclaves at work. The oldest, the elementary school's self-contained classroom, has withstood such powerful invasions as team teaching, nongrading, accountability assessments, merit pay, exotic computer schedules, personalized systems of instruction, departmentalization, a variety of teacher-

1. Richard Corneulle, *Demanaging America: The Final Revolution* (New York: Random House, 1974).

proof curriculum packets, and technological self-teaching with built-in performance standards. Yet it remains almost universal and with surprisingly few scars to show for its endless encounters. The permanence of the autonomous teaching station seems virtually guaranteed.

Perhaps this is the clue to demanagement as a positive school improvement initiative—the legitimation of the autonomous structures throughout education and the concurrent withdrawal of possible threats. If done in good faith, the almost immediate result should be the return of diversification and invention as primary survival behaviors. The bonus might even be cost reduction as thousands of self-governing professionals begin to balance the budgets. Management's presumption that waste, inefficiency, ignorance, and corruption are always to be found on the level below has proven to be false. When this assumption is effectively reversed, the demanagement trend will have begun. The schools will benefit and the surviving management will deserve its new security because it will no longer be a countercultural force.

TEACHER SURVIVAL

When the schools are under economic pressure, teacher survival has two dimensions: stabilization of the teaching role, and adjustments in the thinking and practice of the individual teacher. Attitudinal factors always come first; role changes follow much later to confirm the altered perceptions of the majority.

Teacher as Manager

When the demanagement idea first surfaced some observers expected it to become an impetus for teacher militance. But this was not so. Surprisingly, teachers perceived that: (1) they would be able to manage themselves within their delegated territories (e.g., classrooms and academic disciplines), and (2) they would personally benefit from administrative control. In the latter instance, they still perceived management's functions to be the maintenance of an orderly environment, a stable backup system for resource procurement, problem solving, and personal counseling. Equally important, they saw administrators as guardians of a "civil service" type system from which their job security derived—an especially important factor because of the disturbed economy.

Perhaps because of the fact that all school administrators are teachers first, a stable management may have represented both a comfortable present and a secure future for the ambitious teacher. Even so, there seems to be an inexplicable amount of naivete concerning the "freedom" that a teaching contract grants. How can so many feel free in the face of such obvious constraints? Any administrator knows that the effect of "high density scheduling" will be the reduction of teacher options as well as a constraint on student mobility. It often becomes a remedy for parental complaints about students having "too much free time" and teachers being "permissive." Freedom for the teacher can be increased or constricted by the schedule maker whose actions are usually a deliberate form of behavior modification.

The so-called "flexible modular schedule" tends to give teachers powers and privileges that are lacking in a conventional five or seven period day. If given a choice, I think few would elect to return to previous practices. Once given freedom, people want to keep it, but they rarely report abrasive situations before the change is made. Eventually, these same teachers realize that the "flexibility" in certain schedules may not be permanent, but the rigidities do not become apparent until they switch reference points to, for example, a quarter-system junior college schedule with an open campus plan. Criticism rarely comes until an external criterion assuming the desirability of more freedom is used for purposes of evaluation.

Conflict among Colleagues

It is not uncommon to find teachers who believe that some of their fellow teachers have "too much freedom." The special education teacher is often a target because, in special education, student–teacher ratios are small, scheduling is a matter of teacher judgment, mobility is permissive, and academic standards are subject to unilateral teacher adjustment. It should be remembered that there are a few other "good jobs" that have been long in existence, notably agriculture, coaching, on-the-job career supervision, and driver education. The industrial and studio arts also rank high in teacher autonomy and unobstructed mobility in comparison to the typical formality in English classes.

The nonconventional, flexibly scheduled teacher roles tend to be harshly criticized by many teachers who perceive that their own work load is increased in direct proportion to the freedom of their "more fortunate" colleagues. "Give those music, art, physical education, reading, and special education teachers regular classes and the whole school will be better off!" There are two other reasons for their wanting the specialists in regular classrooms: (1) individual children are often "pulled out" of regular classrooms for special help, leaving the home-base teacher frustrated by broken continuity and no perceptible decrease in class load, and (2) specialists sometimes imply that errors in regular group instruction may have been the cause of individual learning disabilities; hence, they are perceived as usurping the supervisor, perhaps even reporting alleged teacher deficiencies to the principal. With job reductions a common practice, such behaviors are considered job threatening, presumptive, and unprofessional. At this point another external force comes into play to aggravate an already unfortunate situation. This is the "back to the fundamentals" movement which administrators translate into more teacher–student contact hours (longer days, more teaching periods), causing load increases, especially for the regular teacher.

Generally, for the wrong reasons, internal pressures are antispecialist. If it is new or different, the chances of a highly unpopular role surviving recessionary cutbacks are slim. External funding for projects such as those dealing with "learning disabilities" helps but cannot or should not be thought of as perpetual. The system should be self-adjusting so as to be able to take over all essential services, not to merely ebb and flow at the whims of federal politics. And, professional conflict, which promotes the expendability of all new things, must be checked. It is in the interests of all teachers to: (1) stop trying to distinguish between fundamentals and frills, and (2) move all teacher roles away from the prescriptive, centrally managed scheduling patterns. Regular teachers should work toward having personal schedules similar to those that specialists have, rather than trying to destroy specialization.

The Production of Producers

If people want schools to get back to the "real fundamentals," then they should be prepared to talk about *productive performance.* Grammar is *not* what is "fundamental" in English; effective communication is. Consequently, it would be reasonable to put half of the English teachers on a schedule similar to that of a special education "crisis teacher." The assignment would be to institute a "communications performance laboratory" utilizing the format of television, radio, and newspaper production. The key word would be "production"—in script writing, broadcasting, and news reporting.

In this revised form, the teaching format would comfortably blend with "career education." Career education is almost, by definition, practice in the general competencies from which *not the purpose of (word) ed.*

(should it be?)

practical job specifications are derived. Incidentally, the career education movement is not working well, not because the idea was fruitless but because the groundwork for the project had not been properly prepared. And, there is no chance of repairing the mistakes until people *go forward* toward *new fundamentals.* The idea of going *back* to the fundamentals assumes a timelessness and universality in certain skills that is simply not true. A past generation's academic and career behaviors may become obsolete because of time and technology.

Demanagement Means Deschooling

The "deschooling" ideas of Ivan Illich are not only philosophically profound, they are a fairly accurate description of what had already become fact before he could find a label for it. However, teachers, administrators, and librarians have been reluctant to endorse anything that they identified with the counterculture. They virtually ignored the growth of independent education— survival literature, which can be found in private bookstores around every major university campus in the country. The *Whole Earth Catalog* is the most famous, but it is not alone. Bibliographies of hundreds of high quality, useful references can easily be compiled from those shelves. Yet, surveys of high school libraries reveal glaring omissions. To acquisition librarians, this is "hippy stuff," replete with offensive vulgarities. To teachers, the enthusiastic endorsement of individualized learning may be an implied criticism of their function. The fact is that such a widespread interest in this kind of education is creating a learning-intensive culture, which can only be an advantage for the schools. The attitude is pervasive and powerful. The option exists for the schools to intentionally catalog and advertise some informal means of achieving its goals, as well as to invent credited curricular parallels to some of the more popular or needed alternatives that the community has invented for its own survival.

Teachers must remind themselves that schooling is just a subset of learning. At best, schooling is an important component but it should never aspire to the claim that it is synonomous with education. Once this is acknowledged, teachers can abandon their defensiveness and begin to help students become self-reliant "managers" of their own lives. "Demanagement" and "deschooling" thus become the same thing, administrators specializing in one, teachers in the other. With formal and informal education working together and supporting each other, the whole "curriculum" can increase in scope while declining in cost—a survival feature that would be welcome in any community.

[handwritten margin note: Teachers aren't taught to teach this way yet]

Protection of Private Life

One area in which the school can begin to "demanage" should be the private lives of the students. The budding movement to define the "civil rights of juveniles" will eventually clarify the school's boundaries in personal matters, but in the meantime, some serious attention should be given to the motivations and impact of the school's initiative to manage students' personal lives, justified as "values clarification."

Is it the school's intent to reintroduce traditional values to a generation that some adults perceive as "experiencing everything and valuing nothing?" Or, is it the opposite—the reflection of a culture having so much interest in personal valuing that it is bringing about a "values reformation?" Are the "behavioral sciences" (notably psychology) and the "humanities" (principally philosophy) uniting to invent a new body of curriculum content? Another alternative, a political one, would be the goal of student body passification via a modified form of group therapy.

Traditionally, the schools have been able to teach about anything—even controversial subjects—as long as participation in the study of "contested truth" is acknowledged as such and made elective. Deliberate attempts to modify values or behavior have sometimes resulted in classroom disasters and accidental reprieves because of ineffectiveness. Either way, the school's attempts can only be considered highly presumptive, to say the least, and perhaps as seriously illegal as the invasion of privacy of the home. These psychotherapeutic methods invite quackery when used as a political tool to force values that the adult community may still be debating at the end of the century.

Change through Autonomy

For teacher talent to become more self-directing in creativity and accountability, semiautonomous teaching-learning stations must be created. There is no way to "get more out of teachers" without reversing the management trend of reducing the scope and importance of the teacher as a responsible professional. Removing some of the restrictions that were produced through the accountability movement is the only way to break the dependent passivity that is robbing teaching of its vitality.

As hinted earlier, an unknown number of teachers have found new security in their limited job descriptions and the dependence upon centralized management to handle any problem of serious import. If this group resists more responsibility, the recommended, autonomous teaching stations may have to be selectively assigned to those who function best with maximum freedom. Role differentiation in teaching has failed to date but may succeed under a modern survival plan using new bases for sorting out legitimate role differences.

Such a plan can, and in many cases should, be part of a *larger staff reduction and redeployment plan.* This is not a popular idea but there is no other way to find support for school operations by an average community trying to financially survive. Illustrative guidelines for such a plan would include:

76

1. a 30–50 percent reduction in staff

2. concurrent "deschooling" and "demanagement," meaning: (a) creation of selected autonomous teaching stations, (b) maximum utilization of informal education resources, (c) descheduling teachers up to 50 percent of the time for self-redeployment to different types of teaching, counseling, and planning, (d) withdrawal of selected management constraints which inhibit teacher initiative

3. recognition of several major career patterns, such as: (1) "high specialization, long-tenured service," (2) "renewable annual appointments—specific contract services" (no tenure), (3) "temporary management service" (3–5 year terminal appointments reverting to conventional teacher tenure), (4) "adjunct faculty retainers" (on-call, special-purpose assignments)

4. development of a model for collective bargaining which supports *a financially adjustable teaching establishment* (one which does not: (a) break city budgets with uniform nonnegotiable demands, (b) hold out for everyone on tenure, or (c) use the "sacrificial lamb approach" by cutting such perpetually vulnerable fields as the arts

In summary, teacher survival and administrator survival are interdependent. If either one tries to survive at the expense of the other the chances are that both will fail. Role adaptation *appears* to be the central issue; however, it is not. Redesigning the institutional framework for increased role flexibility is. The old container simply cannot hold the new wine.

now is the time
no more old school
I run schoolhouse

6

Survival of the Developmental Staff

Many half-visible roles fill the void between the classroom teacher and the school executive. These accommodate the superintendent's backup staff for planning, supervising, and researching. Although essential for the survival of the school system, these assignments are the most vulnerable in the entire fabric of schooling. If they can survive long enough to rescue the school system from its present economic crisis, they may someday be institutionalized.

SURVIVAL OF THE PLANNER

Educational planners are unseen, unknown, academic "ghosts" who move unpretentiously through the halls of the powerful. They are not politicians, and they cannot influence social policy without the supervision and consent of the visible holders of power. Occasionally, they are transformed into politicians, but the results are usually disastrous because:

the genuine man of words can never wholeheartedly and for long suppress his critical faculty; he is inevitably cast in the role of the heretic. Thus, unless the creative man of words . . . (aligns) himself with practical men of action, or unless he dies at the right moment, he is likely to end up either as a shunned recluse or in exile or facing a firing squad.[1]

Americans have grown accustomed to the planner's presence in politics, but planners are even more essential to the large school bureaucracy where it is not always possible to "vote out" practices no longer supported by the public. Yet, the educational planner is a newcomer who occupies the most insecure and least understood leadership role.

The political superintendent may be eloquent but the public expects action. Thus, the superintendent's energies are devoted to action and too often this person has little time to be theoretical or reflective. But superintendents cannot afford too many mistakes in judgment. They need help in keeping their behavior and utterances in line with the public expectancy. For this kind of help superintendents can rarely turn to subordinate lieutenants whose backgrounds and deficiencies closely resemble their own. Political superintendents know this, so they look to the planner, a person they may not really understand and may be afraid to trust, but who seems to offer the missing ingredient for their political success.

Superintendents see in the planner possible extensions of themselves into areas in which they know they lack preparation. By "listening" to planners, they can be credited with a certain erudition that in reality they lack. Because they know this, their first concern is with the statements they will make publicly—speeches, written policy statements, proposed problem solutions, and legislation. They need a person who understands them well enough to "put words in their mouths," capturing strongly held

1. Eric Hoffer, *The True Believer* (New York: New American Library, Mentor Books, 1951), p. 154.

values, habitual speech patterns, and previous political commitments—above all, adding visionary projections and the philosophical consistency of a sound long-range development program. Modern superintendents, beset by public demands, stand little or no chance of achieving favorable reputations in any other way.

When superintendents sense their obligation to the planner conflict arises. Superintendents generally do not like to owe this much to anyone; consequently, their reaction is similar to that of a man who has negotiated a big loan at the bank: he appreciates the help but shies away from the banker because the banker is a constant reminder of the debt. This creates a touchy situation for the planner, as social distance increases in direct proportion to the amount of the contribution made. The irony is: the better the planner, the more strained the situation. Because of the increased tension, the planner becomes less capable of creative work. In the end, however, it is the superintendent who will lose. The planner will most likely move on in search of an environment that rewards rather than penalizes creativity, an openness to ideas, and a unique problem-solving approach.

In service to a school system, planners often pay a great price. They necessarily withdraw from public attention because of its threat to the boss. They write, but always for someone else. They see their ideas and plans materialize under the apparent leadership of others. In this they may gain a measure of secret satisfaction, but in the process, their personal rewards become increasingly deferred and indirect. The institution has no built-in system of rewards and recognition for planners, thus planners must create their own. The "king-maker" role is an uncomfortable one for planners and will remain so until the planning function is securely institutionalized and protected as an integral part of the educational structure.

Planners have few restrictions in their planning, especially if they are hidden spokesmen for senior political administrators. They are asked to "dabble" in a great variety of fields, and to maintain a respectable degree of consistency between and among them. This is the only assurance politically oriented administrators have of a comprehensive program covering all facets of their operations. The public image of the total institution will depend upon the planners' successes in producing synergistic plans, internally consistent yet acceptable outside the institution.

Long-range school progress requires that a basic concept unite otherwise separate ideas. Such a concept must remain in an evolutionary or fluid state, identifiable but changing. It must be disassociated from specific individuals in order to remain viable and continue to stimulate thought and creative effort. Individual "solutions" fostered by typical administrators frequently evolve from a need for expediency or from an established personal bias or limited knowledge. Consequently, they may become inconsistent with the admitted or verbalized basic concept. In time, the separation between verbalized aims and operational theory becomes complete since the action bears no resemblance to the spoken theory. "Theory" is then discounted as interesting but rather worthless and quite separate from the practical, which refers to the "action" taken. Theory and practice are thus established as two separate things.

Theory denial is often the beginning of the end for serious planners unless they, very quickly, learn to pay principal attention to operational values and ignore the publicly acknowledged but nonfunctional beliefs. Consistency between theory and actual practice does not seem to be necessary to any basically dualistic society. Operational theory, philosophy, and values do tend toward consistency but they are virtually secret, internally held, and individually preserved as such. None of those inside the culture are disturbed by the familiar dualism. Acceptance of this contradiction breeds the permissiveness and outward friendliness that makes the system work. But, nothing ever completely submerges the conflict between what is verbalized and what is actually done.

The "faith" of the whole system is in the leadership, not in the potential of the masses. To the neutral student or other intelligent outside observer, there are inconsistencies everywhere. Leaders openly say one thing and appear to do another. Frequently, they speak of democracy, advocate plans for better technology and extensive employment of experts, then decide to continue the old method and "make experts" out of loyal supporters. By manipulating the in-group and placating the masses with "proper" ceremony, they keep the public aspect clean and consistent with popular beliefs, but major decisions are still reached on the basis of in-group policies.

Thus, planner's ethics limit them. If they apply scientific analysis to the "real" operational theory—which ought to be a sure way to cause change—they violate an institutional taboo, that of seeking to control the in-group. If, on the other hand, the planners limit their theorizing to that which is merely ceremonial, they are totally ineffective. Faced with this difficult choice, they may too frequently pick the former and cause their own personal insecurity. It may come to be assumed that if the planners really belonged to the group, they would understand it and not seek to undermine it by analyzing what everyone already understands and accepts.

Yet, while planners work for the in-group, their real power is derived from what they hold in common with the larger society. This factor explains why planners are good ghost writers. It does not explain, however, the public's continued support of position-oriented leaders, known by their constituency to operate on an entirely different basis. Regarding this paradox, it is important to remember that all of the institutional rewards and punishments (except the ceremonial ones) stem not from the larger, obvious ethic but from a hidden, inner ethic. The public is caught in the same web as the planner—that of multiple values, each operational, each specifically suited to divergent purposes, and each openly used by people in high positions just as though they were internally consistent and entirely logical.

Planners, or truly plan-oriented leaders, continue to voice their assumptions about change. They usually include beliefs such as the following:

1. Change comes at different speeds, from slow to rapid; the speed of change does not determine the merit of the change.

2. Understanding the ease with which human beings adapt themselves to change is the key to planning better schools.

3. People fear change because they fear for their own security; if change, or proposed change, promises increased security, it will become acceptable.

4. The ultimate security of people is in their control of change rather than in the absence of change.

5. Observations by alert individuals from outside the system may yield better ideas of what can be done than the observations of those within it.

6. People are unequal in both needs and capacities; social and educational improvements will come from applied uniqueness.

7. There are useful and creative people in all levels of any culture; real progress comes only from the free exercise of creative powers wherever they exist.

8. True educational leadership lies both in the recognition of the deep-seated problems of the school and in identifying and applying the cultural means needed to solve them.

9. What people believe is what they know; most people will accept new beliefs if and when they better serve their needs.

10. Consensus may often be "pooled ignorance." It is not necessarily a sound basis for decision and it is especially inappropriate as a device for planning innovations. Consensus is best reserved for the final evaluation of total plans or the end results of change.

11. Public institutions have an obligation to take the initiative in reforming themselves. They should not only respond to public dissatisfaction. Institutional improvement should stem from study and action, not just from reaction.

12. Institutional change—especially in public schools—calls for positive administrative action in removing the obstacles to change and in freeing creative individuals to devise and implement improvements.

13. Educational change can and should be anticipated and designed comprehensively, implemented on a broad front, and evaluated in terms of its total impact as a means of achieving recognized goals.
14. Research and experimentation in the social and political sciences, including education, are equally as important as in the natural and physical sciences. Research can provide new and useful knowledge, a key to institutional reform.
15. A deliberate, modern preparation of public school leadership is increasingly necessary; the rapid infusion of new technological specialists into responsible positions is a primary requisite to progress.
16. Schools as democratic institutions are capable of meeting unprecedented demands for institutional change, but they can do so only through the great, sustained efforts and dedication of avant-garde educational planners.

The educational planner's assumptions about change and his or her role in it are necessarily process centered. This is because the planner seeks to establish a system and institutionalize only the most basic principles, never specific methods, which to a planner are always temporary.

The process ordinarily begins when a person of position comes to the planner for help in converting a general idea into a plan. Generally, such a person, perhaps a superintendent or other top administrator, actually seeks only a new method. This person seldom envisions the invention of a self-renewing social system, in which any specific method is secondary to the system or the principles involved. Actually, leaders who seek the help of planners are more likely to look for solutions to immediate problems instead of the creation of more appropriate, modern structural arrangements. The sure definition of the problem and the implementation of a process to solve it are generally too involved and complicated for easy solution or assimilation into the old structure, which may itself be a contributing cause of the problem. The danger that lies in the making of any plan is the possibility that it will last beyond the period of its prime usefulness and become an institutional anachronism.

To counter this tendency, the planners' methods must always be considered temporary, changing, and subject to every new thought and technological (methodological) principle available, but not necessarily subject to any very rapid change in philosophical or logical principle.

It is important to distinguish between operations pointing toward the establishment of "permanent" methods and those that seek to keep principles in the forefront. These two processes lead directly into distinct types of administration; one results in an enslavement to method, and the other produces diverse means of applying a principle. When principles are institutionalized and adhered to, there is little trouble as time passes on. Definitions of true principles are powerful and enduring, but "great definitions" in the form of methods are quickly outmoded and thereafter serve as restraints (such as the forty-five minute period and the Carnegie unit in high school).

School planners are constantly pressured to abandon this position. Many school officials prefer a definitive method set up as an institutional process. They tend to shy away from theoretical and undefined principles that fail to tell them exactly what to do. Many school officials use the term "I'll buy that" or "I can't buy that." They frequently seek something to buy or reject. Ideas that require development or reorganization are not popular because they are too slow to mature, require a long time to properly evaluate, and seem questionable because they have not been proved.

Planners' strategies vary; their crucial techniques derive from the uniqueness of their mission and the ever-shifting climate in which they work. The first task is to gain enough personal acceptance to be permitted to function as a planner. They know from the outset that it is impossible for them to acquire the kind of following an accepted superintendent may have spent an entire career cultivating. They must be selective. They obviously need the stable and assured friendship of a few key people at the very heart of the institutional power structure; this is a primary essential. Outside of this small group of supporters, planners must depend on the quality of their work to win friends and supporters. They need as much support as they can muster, but they can only acquire a close circle of friends from selling themselves as opposed to the more indirect route of selling their ideas. Selling themselves may be a great temptation, but it is dangerous because: (1) their actions may be interpreted as an ambition to move into direct political leadership, and (2) they may sacrifice so much time in group association that they may never get around to the primary task of planning. Therefore, one of the most important human relations techniques involves deciding which opportunities to take. Planners must operate in terms of their goals and should seek support from those who would be most helpful.

Having made this first decision—that their job is to work with the public only *through* the office of the superintendent— planners are then free to open other avenues of communication and seek direct, outside support of their specialized work. They must identify themselves with other planners outside of their own institution and beyond the subculture in which they operate. These other planners may be found in colleges, universities, private foundations, or in a variety of other places. The important thing is not where they are from, but that they represent a larger community of ideas and knowledge upon which planners must draw. They may draw upon their nonlocal communities for many things, including moral support for their minority opinions. They can also use these communities to cross-check their more questionable ideas (especially those too controversial to be debated locally), and look toward them as a primary source of new ideas. Most planners have these kinds of contacts before they accept a field assignment. The great problem is to maintain these ties in spite of the unfortunate gap that currently exists between scholars and practitioners. If these ties become too tenuous, planners have only one choice—to leave their local assignments and return to the world of ideas in another capacity. If they make the decision to cut themselves off from the nonlocal community, it will only be a matter of time before the local culture weakens their convictions, compromises their plans, and reduces them to the status of a local element, too familiar with the culture to see the need for planning ahead.

Assuming that planners can successfully maintain membership in the local power structure and also maintain contact with outside sources of ideas and constructive criticism, they are ready to go to work in earnest. They usually have only the authority of persuasion at their command, a limited staff, if any, and no recognized structure or organization. Yet, they are almost immediately bombarded with the "wild ideas" secretly held by individuals within the institution, who, before the planner's arrival, had no neutral person with whom they could share ideas or complain to. As there is often just a shade of difference between a complaint and a creative idea; so once again planners find themselves treading on thin ice. Their employers will wonder about the stream of solitary visitors beating a path to the planners' doors. These administrators may wonder why the visitors do not come to them; they may confuse their own authority with the planners' power. The visitors themselves will wonder how much of what they tell planners will reach their bosses.

Planners cannot assume neutrality because they one day might be in the process of writing a policy or preparing a plan that expresses a definite view on the question at hand. Their only alternative is, therefore, to be completely honest and to continue encouraging people with ideas to come to them. They must learn to hold ideas that might jeopardize the individual who dared to advance them in complete confidence. And when ideas are safe for limited sharing, but not mature enough for administrative decision, they must provide an opportunity and a sheltered environment for small groups to develop them further. One of the planners' chief services is the creation of a buffer zone between fragile new ideas and the likely premature rejection of them by those in authority. In time, most authorities come to appreciate this service because it produces two striking results: (1) the ideas that do reach them for decision are better, more comprehensive, and complete, and (2) staff morale immediately becomes higher due to the increased emphasis on sharing ideas, individual participation, and creativity.

Beyond these fairly distinctive techniques, the planners' methods are not unlike those of any other scientific worker. They identify promising ideas, help people separate assumptions about the society from known facts about it, aid in the establishment of nonpersonal purposes, assist in the creation of plans to carry them out, and finally serve as participants in the evaluation. These processes help to develop planners into the kind of people they become; their roles shape their personalities. Thus, the planning process can become an identity in a local culture where people are inseparable from their ideas.

Planners are not superhuman. They have the same basic desires, needs, and motivations as other people. However, the realities of their unusual calling tend to magnify some characteristics and minimize others.

Some of the demands of the school planning environment and some of the personality adaptations which it necessitates are:

Environmental Realities	Reactions of the Planner
relatively long periods of time alone	without feeling lonely
constant evaluation by others as a person as well as on work	without feeling personally threatened
"deferred rewards" and indirect recognition	without feeling slighted, ignored, or used
the target of misplaced blame, without control, recourse, or rebuttal	without becoming defensive or vindictive

no authority beyond persuasion, yet results expected in organizing and coordinating the activities of others

without being overcome by a feeling of futility

few confidants, but responsible for understanding the motivations of many

without distorting judgment

theoretical consistency in a setting of conflicting ethics

without becoming argumentative or eclectic

being on record with less maneuverability than associates

without feeling trapped or betrayed

no guarantee of tenure, yet the necessity to plan beyond the foreseeable future

without feeling expendable and thereby tempted to "spoon feed" ideas to others for self-protection

dramatic changes of pace in responsibility—pressures and deadlines followed by relative inactivity and no routine to fall back on

without feeling guilty when judged by the "clock punching" habits of others

expectancy of "minor miracles" in the form of a steady stream of creative contributions

without pushing beyond normal endurance or becoming resentful of those who make unreasonable demands

dependence on a large non-local community with poor communication lines

without feeling abandoned

consistently high quality, difficult scientific or theoretical work crammed into a political timetable

without becoming neurotic, a perfectionist or a pseudo-scientist

uncertain social status in the institution—close to, but not part of, the highest echelon of leadership, and apart from all lower echelons

without feeling that one has no status at all

Other "realities" and "reactions" could be listed, but these should suffice to illustrate the point that only very few people should aspire to the role of educational planner. The inner directed person is best because an added margin of self-assurance is needed to sustain production in association with people who are largely otherdirected. But their self-assurance must not cross the thin line that separates it from insensitivity. The planners must be acutely aware of the people with whom they work. They have to be evaluative, but their evaluation must be directed toward ideas rather than people. Planners must make some judgments, but their appraisal should never include a rejection of others because their perceptions are different. Planners must therefore be unusually tolerant in human relations.

Although preferably slow to anger, planners should nevertheless be capable of "righteous indignation." The planners' dedication to principles and purposes should cause them to reject the "anything goes" definition of tolerance. If they really care about others, then what people do and think is a matter of importance. Planners are especially interested in the people still to be influenced by the institution.

Unless future politicians become superhuman the number of planners affiliated with all great institutions will increase. Therefore, it is important that the principles of planning become institutionalized.

THE SURVIVAL INSTINCT IN SUPERVISION

The supervisory role predates that of the planner and in a number of important curricular areas is its direct predecessor. Consequently, many of the previously expressed concepts concerning planners apply equally to supervisors. The trend, however, is not toward a joining of the two roles, but toward divergence and further specialization.

Survival for supervisors could be defined as a problem of technique updating but that would obscure a much more serious philosophical issue. Supervision has traditionally reflected the democratic commitment to unlimited educational opportunity. For many, the use of schools to liberate the underprivileged has been an "educational religion." However, hidden beneath the zeal for "high standards" has been an undeniable trace of elitism. There is much evidence of this, including ability grouping, career tracking, and the entire field of "admissions." Given outside political encouragement, supervision has shown an alarming potential for restricting as much access for some as it extends to others.

Intentional corruption of the dream of universal opportunity through education has, nevertheless, been slight. The transgressions that have been committed began as good intentions, but supervisors became overzealous with such goals as "weeding out incompetent teachers." But, accidental tyranny still seems to be deliberate oppression to the victim. The good intentions must somehow be monitored and kept within safe bounds, but monitoring itself sometimes produces oppression. Thus, the problem often remains unsolved by external supervision.

The supervisor's capability for self-regulation has been questionable. Otherwise, how does one explain the necessity for citizen groups to use the courts to correct such abuses as those resulting from IQ testing, special education stereotyping, and admission plans based on prejudicial definitions of talent—all of which can be linked with supervision in one way or another?

The underlying philosophical problem revolves around private versus collective security; self-regulation versus institutional standards; professional trust versus political allegiance. Unfortunately, many supervisors are so deeply involved with the establishment's procedures that they are usually too doubtful about the possibility of the self-regulating professional community. It is hard for many to believe that the teacher of high-integrity should be considered an accountable professional; somehow, the rule structure of the establishment seems more stable and certain.

The "open-culture instinct" has to eventually overcome the destructive suspicion of subordinates. Teachers should not have to prove their worth, justify their creative impulses, or take more than their share of blame for their students' learning difficulties. Teachers have to be assumed both innocent and competent; only then can a suitable relationship develop between teachers and supervisors.

There is some reason to believe that the militant scientism that has steered supervision toward the opposite direction may have run its course. However, "adult behavior modification" must be perceived as expansive and dangerous before some administrators will stop trying to balance budgets by diminishing the important of the teacher.

The supervisor who is overtrained in the psychology of B. F. Skinner may not be able to make the transition back to the democratization of schooling. A humanistic movement simply does not stem from Skinnerian assumptions. There are competing schools of thought in psychology (Carl Rogers for example) but the competition seems weak when compared to politically reinforced Skinnerian doctrine. Because the existing anti-Skinnerian movements have not become sufficient antidotes for authoritarianism, other disciplines must fill the void.

Supervisors with survival interests have a serious value choice to make. If they elect "power" instead of "persuasion" their tenure and effectiveness will most likely coincide with that of their own immediate supervisors. The alternative requires allegiance to teachers and to the quality of the ideas they create. An efficient school system can be run either way, in spite of the widespread misrepresentation of open education as a source of permissiveness. True freedom is possible only within a structured context, so a supervisor's survival decision cannot be based upon structural concerns; it is really a matter of the supervisor's primary allegiance.

If the choice of a commitment to the teachers' cause would seem to stem from an insubordinate attitude, it is probably because the schools have accepted an inevitable adversary relationship between management and teaching. Supervision, of course, links the two and should serve both. The survival decision should therefore be one that would keep communication lines open, work for maximum voluntary harmony, and build the needed curriculum designs to support the personalization of learning. Thus defined, the supervisory role could contribute significantly to the survival of both the institution and, most importantly, its clientele.

SURVIVAL OF THE RESEARCHER

As a logical step in the development of their professional calling, researchers have identified their field with:

1. the extensive use of verified, widely used and well known tests and measurements
2. precise definitions of hypotheses related to the measurements selected, and
3. noninterference with the variables tested during the course of the investigation.

At first glance, these characteristics appear defensible—even commendable. They are loaded, however, with pitfalls that the practicing educator inevitably encounters. These include the following:

1. Testing, especially in designs calling for pretests as a bench mark for change, tends to:
   a. come too early for a comprehensive understanding of the experimental and developmental purposes.
   b. foster defensiveness and introspection on the part of staff members when the need is greatest for externalized, visionary projections of goals and the highest possible level of consensus.
   c. be irrelevant, or even contradictory, to many important development purposes—objectives that are beyond existing measurement technology, or are either too personal or too general for practical assessment.
2. Hypotheses, suitable for classical research, tend to:
   a. shift the rewards inherent in a school improvement project to favor participants with imitative interests as opposed to exploratory, creative, or philosophical tendencies and competencies.
   b. focus the leadership commitment on something that is more specific than visionary—usually a project that is considerably less than comprehensive, multivariable analysis, which is the greatest current need in school improvement design.
   c. commit the leader to a rigid timetable for program change that makes the leader unadaptable and most vulnerable to criticism, misplaced blame, and job insecurity.
   d. force on the leader a burden of data processing, analysis, and reporting that takes the leader out of the position of group leader at a time when it is least affordable to lose contact with those supervised.
3. The idea of "pure" research, with its uncontaminated variables, tends to:
   a. encourage, and in some cases demand, the withdrawal of leadership, particularly from those factors in which measurable effects are predicted.

    b. cultivate suspicion that experimental groups have special supervisory sanction; conversely, that control groups represent practices that have fallen from administrative favor.

    c. align the project sponsor with little understood consultants, and with data processing technology generally perceived by the "in group" to be evaluative, somewhat mysterious, and potentially critical of present practices and accomplishments.

Faced with these concerns, administrators react in several rather predictable ways. Their common response is to verbally encourage others to undertake studies or experiments, but studiously avoid their own personal involvement. Another reaction is to assume the role of research publicizer, diffuser, applier, and interpreter, but again, to dodge the direct commitment to become a producer of research. Still another response is to authorize externally conducted and directed studies and surveys that use local school subjects, but demand no other form of participation, especially excluding the responsibility to implement recommended changes. Finally, there is an option to reject research altogether, or to redefine the term to make the entire process more compatible with the administrator's own perceived reality, even though classicists would not consider this research.

This final alternative seems to be gaining the most momentum. Its proponents engage in activities that are usually defined as "development projects" or "demonstrations" rather than research. Basically, participants in such activities:

1. defend large scale program change in terms of administrative judgment rather than research documentation

2. rely on pragmatic results for quality controls, rather than tests and measurements which are merely quantitative

3. emphasize new applications, rather than discovery, as the basic process of institutional advancement

96

4. show a willingness to change or extend the program's goals in light of new insights gained during the process of experimentation, not only after the final results are in and reported

5. communicate and diffuse "findings" through conceptual models for program planning, rather than specific situational results

"Research" and "development" have thus become a dichotomy of rather distinct camps of school improvement practice. Even the major sources of funding for projects have been roughly identified along the same lines. So sharply has the line been drawn that it is not uncommon to find a public school system applying separately and concurrently for both "research" funds and "demonstration" support—to underwrite a single school improvement project.

A leader's first allegiance must always be to "development and demonstration"; a luxury, if it can be fitted in, is research. The problem is that a combination of the two approaches is not currently recognized. To both camps a combination would be perceived as something less than either; hence, the administrators are caught in a dilemma even when they attempt to solve the problem through compromise.

Yet compromise seems to be the only possible solution. Encouraging evidence shows:

1. an increasing interest on the part of researchers to conduct their studies in school systems where important things are happening; where people have already started altering significant variables and development style and are in need of an evaluation of the results they are getting

2. the researchers' realization that school improvement is a science of institutional development, not just another case for social force analysis (sociology), individual responses (psychology), or teaching methods (pedagogy)

3. a growing backlog of theoretical constructs (stemming largely from demonstrations rather than research) that are in need

of further development into major theories of social change in which education is the controlling dynamic (as opposed to classical "determinism")

4. a general acceptance of the idea that the pace of twentieth century change calls for more relativistic definitions of knowledge and the processes of its acquisition (as opposed to classical research anchored in behavioral psychology)

5. an increased use of computers to bring research timetables more in line with supervisory decision-making deadlines; also, to reduce data processing for schools that are not staffed and budgeted to make extensive commitments

Research has become one of the more significant new administrative specialties. It has often been linked with supervision, which is currently changing to include institutional planning as one of its dominant functions.

With this much reshaping of the entire administrative structure of the schools, authority becomes uncertain, diffused, and in the case of the newest functions, nonexistent. Who has the authority to plan and initiate a research project, to direct one, to report and interpret one? Does the type of study make a difference? If it involves fact finding preceded by program change, are different people involved? Is research something that exists apart from a program? Or, is authority for research one and the same with authority for the program? Is research something different depending upon the authority level sponsoring it? Or, are there vertical authority lines that link all echelons of power and control? Is the superintendent the only one with enough power to authorize a study of significant dimensions?

Clearly, there are different and contradictory answers to questions such as these. The only constant in the whole picture is the unattached nature of the research function and the ambivalent attitudes of administrators toward it. It is, for this reason, a high-risk function, especially for its chief advocate (the principal investigator), but also for its institutional sponsor, the usual "subject" of the research, as well as for the investigator's employer.

The typical pattern that research follows, since it does not have a stable foothold in the institution, is sporadic. Although research once flourished in many school systems, it quietly declined when the individual sponsors moved on to other jobs or projects.

Whether or not this pattern will continue indefinitely is questionable. Up to this point, research in public education has been the contribution of a gypsy-like band of individuals who progress professionally through scheduled projects (usually completed within one to three years) rather than permanent positions within a single school system.

Effective research is powerful, just as clear thinking in critical situations has always been a source of human influence. In the case of the gypsy researchers it is either a borrowed or usurped power. It makes no difference whether the researcher operates under the title of supervisor, consultant or administrator, it is only a matter of time before the sponsoring institution insists on one of two things: (1) making the researcher an integral part of the official power structure (thus commanding allegiance to all of its constituted rules, formal and informal), or (2) controlling the researcher's every move until his or her total energy is committed to safe, approved activities.

It is true that some institutions, like colleges and universities, are more hospitable to the research function than are most public schools. State departments of education usually have a person or division in charge of research, but they do not perform the kind of research that helps develop better school plans. State research is usually limited to the routine collection of statistics that are recorded but left uninterpreted, thereby useless as guides for program development.

Yet, even in the university system contradictory ground rules control the types of projects that are undertaken. For example, developmental research is not well-accepted. A university-based researcher must too often make the choice of performing "basic" research on static situations (for example, the public school's backlog of "safe," permanently unsolved problems) or having his or her academic respectability questioned for becoming involved in change-oriented projects that liberal public school leadership is willing to support. The choice is unfair: respectable research on insignificant problems or high-risk, disapproved research on the pressing, semipolitical kinds of problems that accompany institutional development and reconstruction.

Obviously, the problem of stabilizing the research function and identifying it with leadership so as to make it an effective planning tool is a conceptual one. First, it has to be decided that stabilization is desirable. Next, there is the matter of clarifying the functions of research and several closely allied services. Individual roles are likewise involved, and these will also be difficult to ascertain and organize. All three—concepts, functions, and roles—converge from time to time in a single place to demonstrate the power of an efficiently organized research and development service. The perpetuation of such a service, however, has few precedents. The use of research as a developmental tool in an open access setting is close to being successfully demonstrated. If research remains antithetical to openness at a time when survival strategies are moving in that direction, then research must be classified, and thereby condemned, as a counterculture force.

TEAM SURVIVAL

Planning, supervision, and research have all become early victims of economic cutbacks partly because of their historic separation.

Each has a different history, yet there appears to be overwhelming evidence for supporting them as parts of a single developmental process. Planning can be thought of as a protective function, supervision as interpretative, and research as evaluative. Arrange them together—and the power to redesign the schooling enterprise emerges.

This composite system of competence is, of course, more than a matter of matching up credentials that are distinctive yet compatible. The teaming for major reconstructive development would have to assume:

1. the reconstructive mission itself (and, this is partly a matter of personal philosophy—especially regarding demanagement and deschooling assumptions)
2. the necessity for an overall decision-making system permitting everyone to participate in each major phase of development (one way, perhaps, would be to rotate chairships so that the initiative could shift to the one with primary responsibility for a particular assignment)
3. a healthy degree of operational autonomy for each of the three functions within the larger model (including the right to challenge the developing master plan, but not to the extent of unilaterally destroying it)

The initiation of a developmental team after staff resources have already been reduced by forced budget cuts will probably be the most formidable task. There would be no way for this to be accomplished unless the policy-making board can trust the chief school officer more than it fears the political opposition to increasing staff. The decision has political as well as professional logic behind it, however, when it is conceded that there is no foreseeable end to the need for redesigning the schools for increased efficiency—and there is no possible way for overloaded teachers or staffless school executives to get the job done.

The necessary remedy is to temporarily increase investments so that plans can be made for an even greater, and permanent, cost reduction. Cost reductions will necessarily come from new revenue or the redeployment of funds currently earmarked for instruction. Teachers, and most especially their self-protective unions, will surely object until they realize that, one way or another, costs will have to be reduced. However, the most palatable argument for making such an unpleasant decision under a master plan is that a new basis for employee security can be invented in the process; furthermore, that the new tenure can be accompanied by new importance for the teacher.

The goal of simultaneously upgrading and stabilizing teaching cannot be accomplished without the widespread support of teachers. And, direct participation is the only route to this destination. Thus, *the survival plan for the developmental staff must include the sharing of planning, supervision, and research with teachers.* Only a diffused, widely shared, and nonrestrictive plan can produce autonomous, "invisible hands" partnerships. Without these partnerships, a weakened form of teaching may survive, but the development team will not have a chance.

7

Curriculum Stabilization

Curriculum stabilization can only be achieved through the maximization of choice, or alternatively, increased managerial control. In previous chapters a strong preference for individual choice has been expressed. At this point, it has hopefully become logical to identify survival with open access programming and to highlight the dominant survival factors in open programs.

The school bureaucracy appears to have been a paradoxical combination of stability and mediocrity. The survival of individuals in schools that are also attempting to survive is possible under a wide variety of curricular designs. But survival should not depend upon the endurance of the system, but upon the quality that can be sustained. Thus, excellence and survival become the same.

The higher mental processes generally correspond with higher human motivations and operate best in the absence of manipulation and external constraint; thus, the drive for educational excellence leads inevitably to the advocacy of open access curriculum models. Regrettably, openness is often associated with libertarianism, waste, and excessive cost.

The fashionable thing to advocate when money is short is conservation. Everyone would agree with this necessity; however, it takes disciplined thought to aim for the type of conservation that results from self-governance. It is strange that this logic must be forced. The American experience clearly identifies the virtue of thrift, even self-imposed frugality, with independence and self-reliance. Indeed, there is much evidence to prove that public greed and financial recklessness correlate directly with the transfer of responsibility from individuals to public institutions. Such concerns become specifically meaningful in the following analysis, which deals with curriculum-related survival factors.

SURVIVAL FACTORS

There are six factors that affect curriculum stabilization: content differentiation, sanction of the superdisciplines, multiple entry and exit points, separation of the social control function from learning, teachers as curriculum contributors, and distinctive resource collections. An analysis of each survival factor is presented in this section.

Content Differentiation

The obsolescence of most current school programs is due to a factor that is so obvious it has become invisible. It is that about half the academic content in every discipline has moved from the category of *stable knowledge* (fact, truth, popular consensus) into one of two much newer categories—*contested truth* (public forums, value revisions, new scientific information) or *exploratory hypothesis* (research, inspiration, creativity). The schools did not initiate these changes, nor is it fair to say that they resisted them. The legitimate charge is that schedules, teacher assignments, and testing procedures were originally established on the assumption that the school's most important task was to transmit factual information, and that the lesser task was to teach about the culture that generated these facts.

Many examples demonstrate that most of the newer categories of knowledge have not even been included within the better programs. A technology-based "total communications" approach to language development is not yet available to students, in spite of the constant bombardment of electronic, instantaneous worldwide entertainment and news coverage. Reading is still important because a critical component of communications will always be in book form. Theoretically, many students have a chance, not only to read, but also to access records, tapes, films, and computer libraries—modern extensions of the book. Few schools, however, let students use these devices to express themselves. Indeed, the schools are still trying to find enough room in the schedule for writing, speaking, and listening, in order to compete successfully with the older emphases of literary history, language structure, and reading. Even in the scientific areas, the college bound student has extreme difficulty in accessing the impressive modern technologies that the "tracking" system has accidentally relegated to vocational schools, technical centers, and commercial departments.

It would be proper for each discipline to be permitted to define its own "basic," "contested," and "exploratory" content, appropriately distributing technological studies across the three categories. Similarly, since the three types of content elicit their own unique methods—lecture, seminar, personal research—students can access their chosen disciplines through processes with which they are most comfortable. These options should be reconsidered so that the needed opportunity may be provided to quickly update all disciplines with a new "soft" content, which is more oriented to search than certainty but which is no less respectable because of its relevance.

Sanction of the Superdisciplines

Examine the transcripts of a number of undergraduate college students and the new subjects become readily apparent. Elective clusters in the social sciences, for example, include "Urban Affairs," "Black Studies," "Women's Awareness," "The Criminal Justice System," "Population Control," "Consumer Law," "The Multinational Corporation," "Religions of the World," etc. Additionally there will be transitional labels such as "Cultural Anthropology," "Political Science," "Community Education," "Human Geography," and finally, the even more traditional categories of history, geography, economics, and sociology. Turn to the sciences and the old and new categories also appear —"Marine Studies," "Computer Sciences," and "Energy Alternatives" are at one end of the spectrum and biology, chemistry, and physics are at the other.

One way to analyze the emerging patterns is to sort out at least three orders of content:

1. Social Problems Applications
2. Multidisciplinary Studies, and
3. Root Disciplines

Clearly, this poses another "forcing structure" in which the Root Disciplines are neglected in order to focus upon the other two subject areas. A related problem especially for the public schools is teacher certification in the basics and a tendency for school districts to give teachers specific assignments related strictly to the traditional content designations on their licenses rather than to the emerging crossdisciplinary applications of knowledge. Elective systems permit some updating through teacher initiative but the reinforcing combination of basic specialization licenses, school board contracts, and orthodox patterns of school organization, is too much to be overcome by even the most extraordinary teacher.

Organizational remedies currently being defined on the local school level will eventually outweigh the creativity currently being generated by Colleges of Education or State Education Agencies. Most, for pragmatic survival reasons, represent unique political–academic inventions that will permit the super-disciplines to remain in a healthy state of evolution. These remedial models almost always represent a delicate balance between the organizational model, which mentions no academic commitments whatever ("schools within schools," "self-contained classrooms," etc.), and those that overemphasize the academic assignment and thereby freeze its normal evaluation (the "English Department," "Science Program," etc.). The superdisciplines ideally prevent schools from reverting to either exclusively political patterns or out-of-date commitments to the basic disciplines.

Multiple Entry and Exit Points

Turnpike planners have no way of knowing how many travelers will always take the long trip so they arrange for frequent entry and exit points. The driver does not have to get on or off just because the option exists but having once entered the turnpike is obligated to proceed at least to the next exit. If U turns are not permitted every decision is important even though only a limited commitment is intended.

Schools are like this too. Originally the design had no interchanges; once committed one completed the long journey or "failed." The modern school calendar, as well as the school day, clearly indicates that the inflexible pattern has been broken. The first breakthrough was the short-term course, still the most popular feature of the open access curriculum. It is important because randomly placing three-, six-, and nine-week courses effectively challenges unnecessary content sequences and eventually blocks tracking. Another, almost hidden, advantage might be called "Project Restart." The chance to start over without penalty may be the most important advantage because it can happen over and over again, not just in childhood. Exploration without penalty is most strongly supported when the permanent record accepts no failing entries—just a "mission accomplished"

SECTION TWO   The Impact of Survival Behavior on Role and Function

statement or an "incomplete." No one will know, anyway, when "incomplete" means "permanently withdrawn" or simply "temporarily sidetracked." And, even if the grading system is used for motivation or control, this standard will still hold because credit is withheld pending project completion.

Equating the academic task with a "mission" indirectly sanctions the project approach to teaching. This, in turn, encourages the engineering emphasis in everything—the applying and performing sides of the discipline that can ultimately form a tangible product. Schools have traditionally taught fundamentals first, then illustrated the mastery of these fundamentals using the "classics" (citing the successes of others), and finally, if time permitted, invited learners to try to create their own classic. However, even when time did not run out for the final phase, motivation did. The "classics" are overwhelming and the "basics" take a long time and are boring. The way to get students past the hurdles of a traditional program has always been to schedule their schooling "upside down and backwards"—that is, projects and advanced material first. Then, show the examples of success by others, and lastly, develop personal skills (fundamentals) as the project reveals a need for them. This does not preclude skill introduction on a formal basis but it does tend to shorten the initial time investment and cause excitement for learners when they have a chance to be creative. Multiple entry and exit points are dependent upon content that is differentiated both in terms of stability and a recognition of the super-disciplines. Figure 7.1 summarizes the relationships that provide the needed flexibility for truly unique "people paths" sanctioned by the school.

Separation of the Social Control Function from Learning

Nothing so thoroughly contaminates good teaching as the confusion of disciplinary functions with the liberation of the learner.

108

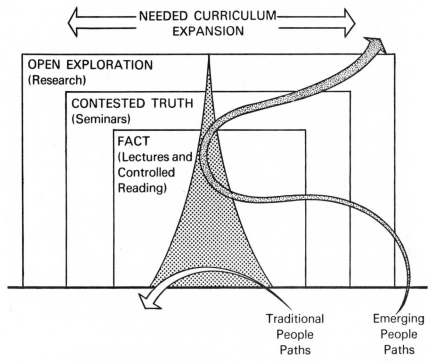

Critical Features:
1. Multiple rather than single entry points
2. Increased scope of content
3. Abandonment of extended sequences and related tracking
4. Learning styles related to both the nature of the disciplines and the methods of inquiry
5. Differentiated teacher roles

Figure 7.1. *The Open Access Curriculum. From L. Craig Wilson,* The Open Access Curriculum *(Boston: Allyn and Bacon, 1971), p. 19.*

This is not to argue that learning can proceed from disorder, but it does mean that strategies for pupil discipline are often the antithesis of the best teaching strategies. To force the student to behave in socially responsible ways is an interesting thought to begin with; to say that a change in behavior is evidence that learning has occurred is a common though frightening idea. Behavior modification *may* be the purpose of some legitimate teaching, but probably a very small amount, and in any event, is safe only if fully advertised and made a student elective (like going to weight-control meetings or seminars to stop smoking). The school provides access to tools and permits learners to examine them. But the result is that certain tools are sometimes judged by learners to be inappropriate or simply not interesting. No behavior has been modified and no tragedy has occurred. Others may examine the same tools and develop an interest in them. Proficiency may follow practice, just as practice follows familiarization. But, again, the goal of changing student behavior is unnecessary in the teaching–learning act. The implied manipulation of the learner builds a negative relationship at the outset, later on becoming an authority confrontation if the learner does not begin to change in the preselected ways.

In many ways, teachers are efficient "stock room managers," at other times, they are "tool salesmen" and "demonstrators." They may become "learning counselors" as their customers select certain tools for personal mastery, and later they may appropriately become "performance evaluators" as students need to know how much proficiency they have developed. Throughout the learning process, the guidance relationship is healthier than any other relationship that begins with a behavior modification assumption. As previously acknowledged, there is a place for behavior change; there is also an institutional need for a sensible degree of order. But, learner-assistance is something different from either and should not be permitted to follow the precedents of directive psychotherapy.

Teachers as Curriculum Contributors

It would not make sense to advocate openness for students and deny it to teachers; indeed, it may be dangerous to do so. The teaching role traditionally demands too little thinking, planning and creating and too much routine behavior management, repet-

110

itive information transmission, and ritualistic advisement. Economic problems have not helped either. Incoming teachers are better qualified due to tough-minded recruiting from a labor surplus. But currently employed teachers worry about continued layoffs and protect themselves by toned-down dissent and artificial interest in pleasing management. Supervision, meanwhile, easily drifts away from the advocacy of openness to the more comfortable role of resource management and personnel evaluation. One of the great intellectual paradoxes of modern education is the tendency for many to see "open access supervision" as a contradiction of terms. The result is a death blow to both the evolution of access and supervision.

To date, the differentiated teacher role has largely failed, along with teacher teaming. The reason is that the differentiation has been made along the wrong lines and has produced a clustering of specialties that are more similar than interdependent. Similarity breeds competition rather than reliance upon the teammate's higher level of competence in a specialty. To complicate an already difficult situation, the issue of whether or not to delegate authority to teams never really achieved resolution either.

An "all or nothing" ideal, with every teacher being either a free agent or a production line captive, is a self-limiting remedy. The changing academic disciplines create part of the problem with movement toward multidisciplinary (nonspecialized) programs. The consolidated arts programs seem to be doing well; a kind of determined self-specialization has provided reasons for respecting the other teacher's right to be different too. Disciplines with heavy technological resource bases, including the arts along with the sciences, find distinctive tools a good excuse for distinctive roles. This appears to be the strongest reason to argue the case for increased teacher autonomy.

But, even within such favored groups one can easily find people with dependent life-styles who honestly feel most comfortable and competent with a production commitment as contrasted to a planning or a decision-making obligation. The problem would probably be solved by simply asking teachers what they want their primary contract commitment to be—producing (instructing, counseling), planning (projects and program development), or deciding (regulating, administering)—and then setting up professional teams with suitable representation from each functional specialty (as distinguished from the academic area within which the functional role would be performed). Different types of authority would thus gain the recognition that could ultimately be reflected in differentiated schedules and compensation. Under such an arrangement it would not be inconceivable for some teachers to be paid higher salaries than their administrators. It would all depend upon three factors: (1) functional role preference, (2) academic role, and (3) preparation and experience required for the two selected roles. Merit pay is not recommended because it tends to politicize rather than professionalize the educational environment.

The necessary logic substantiating the need for a new teacher role stems from the original question: at a time of economic distress is the soundest leadership strategy one that centralizes and constricts decision making, or one that diffuses and shares the concerns of management with teachers? Open access theorists feel that the latter option is best for the future as well as for the immediate crisis. Unfortunately, current management trends still equate democratic practice with nonstress conditions and authoritarian regulation with troubled times. In the final analysis, however, participatory professionalism for teachers is the only avenue to open access schooling.

Distinctive Resource Collections

A good survival school committed to open access tends to appear somewhat like a supermarket. Its resource collection is more comprehensive than that of the average school and the physical grouping of the different types of resources reveals what there is to be accessed. The common resource components are:

1. The tool-intensive learnings: shops, studies, laboratories, data processing centers, field-test locations
2. The information-intensive learnings: libraries, academic reading rooms, electronic access terminals, lecture halls, film and TV viewing rooms
3. The interaction-intensive learnings: seminar rooms, theaters, social centers, planning rooms
4. The skill-intensive learnings: gymnasiums, practice fields, performance centers, skill monitoring and analysis centers
5. The reflection-intensive learnings: private offices and studies, retreats, nonscheduled, nonprogrammed spaces, access routes to the extra-school environment

The resource base comes from the long tradition of building curriculum designs on the single overriding assumption that learning is a teacher-intensive act. High quality survival schools continue to make use of the school's adult personnel but also make it both legitimate and easy for students to access many resources directly. An updated version of the library card will most likely become the general access authorization applicable to each of the outlined resource categories. When this happens, the open access curriculum will have become an irreversible trend.

STABILIZATION THROUGH SIMPLICITY

Most people finally come to believe there is virtue in simplicity. It doesn't matter whether one is buying a new car, evaluating a classical painting, figuring out the best way to landscape a lawn, planning a political campaign, or running a school, somehow, the option that is simplest—while still functional—turns out to be the most durable, easiest to maintain, most versatile, and the most beautiful, too. Ornamentation, while it initially attracts, sometimes lives on to become repulsive. Complexity, likewise, captures the imagination, but produces disenchantment as frailty becomes the price of glitter. Sometimes, of course, complexity is not deliberate, reflecting, instead, only confusion and lack of imagination. In schools, as in so many other applications, the ultimate test of the product is its ability to accomplish its intended purpose within reasonable limits of energy and economics.

Existing Simplicities

The schools have a remarkable durability and the primary reason for this is that several of their controlling characteristics are simple. Some people contend that the school's strength is a result of its independence; in other words, the institution is so independent of its employees as to routinely survive brilliance, creativity, mediocrity, tyranny, or gross incompetence in the very highest positions. Ambivalence is the educator's usual response to this claim. Who wants their employing institution to collapse because of leadership error? On the other hand, who likes to believe that educational leadership is only an illusion of constructive public service?

Regardless, the simplicities that make the school durable remain, and eventually, the school improvement theorist must decide which should be kept intact with little or no alteration and which should be abandoned as useless or dangerous. For now, they can be enumerated as follows:

Frequent Restart Opportunities. The schools literally "start over" every September—with new schedules, new teacher contracts, new students, new obligation patterns, new budgets, and often new principals, supervisors, or superintendents. This guarantees that nothing will get too bad; unfortunately, it is also a guarantee that nothing too good is likely to evolve either. The problem is that the 180-day teacher contract includes a time allotment of less than a week for institutional development—and this is only a maintenance-level investment. The prevention of program erosion is the major accomplishment; product improvement is a virtual impossibility. Yet, there is something very refreshing in "starting over with a clean slate" at fairly frequent intervals. Restart opportunities are not only beneficial to teachers but to students as well.

Indeed, one can make a very good case for increasing restart opportunities for students, via short-term courses, quarter-system calendars, and other similar arrangements. There is no question that survival rates go up under shorter "contracts" with learners. Thus, both students and teachers have their personal security enhanced by the seasonal nature of their work. The peace of mind that results should not be minimized; it is, without doubt, a positive reinforcer of more open approaches to learning.

The Self-contained Classroom; the Autonomous Teacher. This second characteristic is an outgrowth of a long tradition of teacher role definition. The elementary school's "self-contained classroom" is the conceptual equivalent of the autonomous teacher in high schools. Both have the same advantage—limited but absolute authority. The territory within which authority can be exercised is small, but the fact that this authority is secure makes it that much more valuable. A controllable island of personal initiative and privilege within a large bureaucratic establishment is an almost incredible (but happy) accident of history. Without it, the teaching vocation would be much less desirable, and less effective as well. The reason for its effectiveness is the built-in error correction potential on the level closest to the

115

children. Management sometimes alters the educational environment negatively. Teachers hear both the voice of management and the complaints of the learner. The result is often a softening of the official position for humanitarian reasons—and, when this happens, the school once again bends with adversity rather than breaking.

Managers of all sorts, especially those outside the schools, look on this practice as an insubordinate response by employees. Managers feel employees should learn the meaning of "loyalty," defined operationally as total, uncomplaining, and instant obedience. Others challenge the solo performance of teachers on grounds not of disobedience, but of general nonspecialization and resultant superficiality. They advocate all sorts of remedies, ranging from team teaching to external evaluation and supervision. And, permanent inroads have been made. The modern teacher is clearly less autonomous than his predecessors and even the traditionally protected college professorship has become much less autonomous as the politicizing of the campus has increased under the guise of "governance." Nevertheless, the basic simplicity perseveres. The many positive reasons for this are probably not the ones that explain its survival. The reason might be the ease with which specific individual contracts accommodate transients and concurrently give administration a feeling of always being "in control" at the time of contract negotiation. Whatever control is lost thereafter is perceived as a sociological phenomenon, not an error of management. Hence, both the administrative practice and teacher accommodation continue, each with its own set of reasons. The fact that they are different does not reduce the strength of the trend; indeed, just the opposite is true, and a very stable school practice is the result.

Decision Making versus Operation. The school's third, simple characteristic is an almost universal distinction between administration and teaching. The separation of teaching is carefully circumscribed in the teacher autonomy noted previously.

Administration claims all else—budget control, scheduling, personnel employment and subsequent supervision, school plant utilization, public information, etc. There is some overlapping but not much. Administrators do but rarely share the teaching function. Teachers sometimes get involved in minor administrative decisions through such arrangements as department chairmanships, team leader assignments, and special project coordination. However, these tend to be subject to automatic expiration annually, requiring administrative action for reinstatement.

All of the talk about democratic decision making and teaching role differentiation has clearly not produced more than a small change in actual practice. It is apparent that the possession of power is identified with the administrative role and that it is shared only reluctantly. When power-sharing is brought about by organized teacher group bargaining, a big mistake occurs—the modified teacher role is defined as though all teachers should be involved equally. This is no more workable than uniformly denying participation rights.

A type of seniority plan, coupled with the invention of a few new "instructional management" roles, might start a trend toward a higher level of professionalization. Meanwhile, the prevailing practice gives the power to one group and the operations assignment to another—and, the balance of power tends to keep it that way. It has many shortcomings but instability is not one of them.

Self-contained Buildings with Interbuilding Student Migration. Whether an accident of history or accumulated professional wisdom, the fact that most school programs are totally contained in one building is significant to the principal's role. The principal becomes almost sole proprietor—a parental figure —because of the tradition of placing almost all of the essential services everywhere throughout the school district in equal proportions for comparable grade levels and student numbers.

117

Every school has a cafeteria, for example, even though no commercial food chain could survive the cost of a comprehensive kitchen at each restaurant. The same assumption pervades the allocation of all resources from teachers to texts. It is not at all uncommon to hear principals refer to *my* school, *my* building, *my* teachers, *my* kids. It is also often hypothesized that no program can rise above its principal. If the principal is "poor" the teachers cannot offset his or her influence enough to make the school "excellent" or even "good." This is the negative side; the other is that the consolidation of authority is another antidote to bureaucratization.

Principals are not autonomous but the breadth of resources under their control is impressive. The checks and balances arrangement involves, of course, district-wide budgets, a line authority relationship to their superintendents, and a supervisory link with curriculum guides and related teaching and evaluation resources. The point is that the almost universal principalship is basically simple, easy to install, and capable of survival under affluence and adversity alike. The arrangement is not the best, but is very likely to last forever. The reason is that it keeps things small enough to remain under human control. Moreover, it may be significant that the people doing the controlling are the ones closest in residence and kinship to the students being educated. The times being what they are it might be a good guess that a deconsolidation trend of major importance may emerge, coupled with new strength for the self-contained school. It might work this time with "electronic travel" (TV, records, radio, etc.) providing a fair antidote to distant consolidations made operative only by busing.

The Universal Credential. Ivan Illich has had the last word on the negative power of the teaching credential. The argument is that the unbroken link between college training, teacher certification, and teacher role (legal contract) definitions provides a rigidity that bends the entire institution to ultimately serve itself more than its clients.

The point here is not to agree with or to contest this position. Rather, it is to note the enduring simplicity of an arrangement that attracts teaching people almost anywhere, and, through licensing, lets them seek employment wherever they choose to live. The migratory citizen has liked this idea because it has opened access to the teaching professional without too much regional or economic prejudice. Illich contends that the credentialing system blocks self-instruction as well as prevents legitimate involvement in teaching by the talented (but unlicensed) in other vocations. This may be true, but at present, it is difficult to predict the direction of the certification trend. The counterforces at work are obviously an apparent surplus of qualified teachers, and a general population in a mood to remove as many impediments to personal choice as possible.

It is almost too obvious for comment, but the "licensing connection" has one especially bad feature—it accidentally and indirectly contributes to uniform curriculum designs at a time when the larger drive is for open access. Perhaps the incompatibility is only temporary; it all depends on adjusting the credentialing system to permit more diversity in the utilization of teaching talent.

Trends that Complicate

Beginning with an institutional design of overwhelming stability —attributable, in large measure, to the five "simplicities" just discussed—time has produced several unplanned complicating factors. They include:

Teacher Unionization and Collective Bargaining. This event has irreparably shattered the illusion of a "unified profession." Much could be said about the resultant attitudes, but the real story lies in the introduction of legal processes and machinery into the previously almost private domain of the professional educator. Legalistic thinking is not just a personal matter, an alternate form of logic. It is, more precisely, an adversary-based relationship which requires formal processing for issue resolution. There is some reason to believe that the adversary assumption may not even be the best approach to justice in the courts. Even more evidence exists to question its suitability for a co-operative profession in which the progression into management always begins with a career in teaching. It is not easy, to say the least, for people to see their own past in teaching as a set of values and commitments that must be abandoned in order to pursue a career in administration. Teachers and administrators are almost equally naive in legal proceedings—but they are learning, fast.

What is significant is the apparent permanence of the intervention of the legal community into an almost family-run establishment. The schools have been basically simple and very trusting in matters of personal and intergroup relations. This will never be true again. The only thing that can be done is to alter the decision-making apparatus for compatibility with the more complex legal world beyond the school.

Change Initiatives Beyond the Community.   Education was designed for local consumption and this was originally interpreted to include an equal proportion of local control. No more. The combination of migratory citizens and nonlocal wealth was enough to initially activate political forces on the state and national levels. The first modest efforts have since accelerated through legislation and class-action court cases to become a major avenue of change in every community in the country. The original political design for administering the schools did not rule out federal participation but neither did it anticipate this authority becoming more influential than the state. Desegregation suits and nondiscriminatory employment guidelines are recent examples of national mandates overriding state and local practices and traditions. The concern here is that the enduring "simplicities" are now being so seriously challenged by external legal and political forces that they are becoming confused. A resimplification of decision making may need to be considered but has not yet been proposed. Without some kind of legal antidote, external intervention can be assumed to be a major factor in the permanent design of every community's school system.

The Separation of Teachers from Curriculum Control. This has been mentioned in earlier chapters but is too important to ignore in a list of trends that have disrupted the otherwise simple design of the public school. When schools are small and simple, everybody does everything. Specialization comes with increased size and it is this process that has increasingly pushed teachers into becoming instructional technicians, and simultaneously shifted to supervisors the sequencing and arranging of content. Support from the commercial world for the "curriculum" effort has extended simple scope and sequence outlines into elaborate "programs" covering multiple grade levels and most of the academic disciplines.

At the peak of this movement one often heard references to an "eroding principalship," reflecting the inability of that role to ward off or accommodate the far-reaching initiatives of district-level supervisors, each marketing their chosen "curriculum package." Autonomy without control of purpose is the ultimate frustration that this condition fosters; in other words, the local school becomes an institution without the power to control its direction, but no less responsible to the local community for the quality of the overall offering.

The Nationalization of Evaluation. The first big wave of the accountability movement is past, but the low profile "National Assessment Program" lives on. Such is the way of all technology, and the testing technology of the schools is no exception. The movement is big, imposing, and aggressive—but patient. When people complain, the tests are still given but fewer public reports are made. Teachers, of course, know that the near hostile attitudes toward the accountability movement and the assumptions of nonlocal testing are identical. They, therefore, continue to adjust their professional activities under surveillance, almost always in a conservative direction. Not much complaining is heard except when administrators feel that their total school system has been unfairly compared with another. Most administrators are not strong supporters of either accountability or nonlocal testing, but they tacitly allow both. The result is two layers of expectancy reaching the teacher—one, the familiar local aspiration pattern; the other, nonlocal. To call the situation complicated is the least that can be said.

The Professionalization of Planning.   Good plans simplify; that is the theory. In education unfortunately, the theory has been just the opposite. The reason is the orientation of the people who have been attracted to the planning function. The first planners were, of course, the incumbent administrators; the resultant planning, political. The second wave of planners were still "educators first" but with added specialization. They had, as a job prerequisite, experienced at least limited political success in school administration before moving full-time into the planner's world where it is often necessary to advocate positions that could never command a majority vote. They had some understanding of the importance of consensus in successful management as well as the need for logic and consistency in any deliberate reform movement. They were products of the academic community but with an engineer's orientation. They understood both the desirable and the possible and often succeeded in combining the two. To this point, the planning function was perceived as a developmental service that extended the school executive's usefulness by sharpening goals and streamlining strategies. The problem came, not in this, but the next phase.

Almost overnight the lure of project money, the availability of computers, and the unlikely interest of research psychologists combined, as noted previously. The earmarked project funds required evaluation proposals, and review boards were dominated by psychological measurement specialists; consequently, the way to be successful was to hire a planner with a similar orientation, putting into the plan the necessary computer capability to remain abreast of the school's increased testing and evaluation commitment. Suddenly, it was not "development" but "research" that was being drafted. The pattern was, furthermore, "basic research"; the authors were inexperienced observers, not practitioners.

As simplicity vanished under the mystique of measurement, the executives who made it all possible were to become alienated. They had no choice but to rely on political processes rather than on the distorted planning function for their own survival. Showcase research projects lingered for a while but soon disappeared as project renewals were not sought. The schools are now trying to regain a sensible level of simplicity in planning and management. Temporarily, the plan includes a moratorium on special projects of the type that obscure facts with statistics. The next step should be a restoration of nonearmarked project monies and the return of the practical planner.

Avoiding Complexity

If a simple educational plan can lead to open programming, then it makes sense to avoid complexity that serves no useful purpose. Some of the practices that could be replaced by new or modified ways of accomplishing essential ends more simply follow.

Schoolwide Computer-based Schedules that Attempt Individual Student Programming. Personal programming is a desirable goal and computers are useful scheduling tools; however, the matching of teachers, students and resources can best be handled in groups of less than 250, preferably less than 125—not 1000 or more as is the "master schedule" practice.

Overly Large Teacher Groups that Report to Few Authorized Decision Makers.   When decision making bottlenecks in a school, flexibility, responsiveness, and openness quickly collapse. Most schools, in spite of national movements working on school reorganization for more than a decade and a half, still ask seventy-five or more teachers to report directly to their principal on any matter requiring authoritative judgment. The system remains committed to a maximum of seven immediate subordinates for all levels of management. Most commercial and industrial enterprises do the same. One possible reason for this practice might be the illusion (perhaps true) of freedom that comes from a low-profile, almost anonymous, teacher role.

Bureaucratic Processes for Curriculum Change.   This is another controllable characteristic of the schools that survives for reasons other than its visible and publicly acclaimed purpose. Its typical form is an elaborate review process for any and all program change initiatives originating in sources lacking official authority (especially including teachers). Stopping teacher-originated change is as easy as raising an official eyebrow. A complicated political process stands between personal inspirations and official responses.

Overapplications of Limited Use Technologies.   The schools are group oriented. It is easier for administrators when a rather expensive technology can be justified on a large scale. This leads to errors of overapplication. A good example is computer-assisted instruction. Most of the large scale experiments have subsided to a reasonable level but originally the thought was to bring every student to the terminal. The same thing happens to the soft technologies that take the form of instructional systems —an example being Individually Prescribed Instruction (IPI). In this experiment, total groups were committed to precise sequences of content and skill development. Only after the controlled phase ended did some schools start doing what they wanted to try initially—that is, to use the materials selectively and randomly to meet individual needs. Tightly managed instructional systems can serve specific purposes very well but fail on a grand scale. The lesson for the schools is to strive for appropriate applications of all promising educational technologies.

Overtesting the "Need to Know." Little needs to be said about this factor. It is common knowledge that there are no decision models being used in school administration into which systematically collected data are entered. Demographic data banks, yes; decision making and policy models, no. Instructional models are proliferating due to the advent of exotic terminals and a growing body of software (Project PLATO style); however, the overall movement remains experimental.

A vast amount of information is being collected and routinely processed by school computers. The information ranges from school attendance (mainly as a basis for school revenue distribution) to student achievement. Several fairly comprehensive plans have evolved from the accountability movement, but in general, the number of collection mechanisms has far exceeded the number of retrieval systems. There is far too much fact finding in relation to fact using. This clear dissipation of energy on pointless activity is hard to justify. Additionally, the intervention effect has reached a serious level. Cutting back the testing and statistical collection process would simply require redefining the criteria for its use. Its use should depend on the need to know and the capability to use the knowledge wisely. The theoretical capacity of a computer should have nothing to do with this decision.

LONG-RANGE SIMPLIFYING AND STABILIZING POSSIBILITIES

Many simplifying possibilities have already been advocated or implied. The more practical options include the following:

1. *The miniaturization of management.* Applications could include everything from reconsideration, pending consolidation, to teacher role differentiation. It should begin with the concept that bigger is not necessarily better. A remedy for overcontrol is needed.

2. *Modularization.* The most significant result is breaking up the thirty-six week school year, as well as all academic sequences with questionable reasons for resisting direct access learning.

3. *Enlarging and reinforcing autonomous territories.* The breakthrough is the creation of consolidated academic disciplines. On levels where this is less appropriate, authority delegations to stable teacher groups engaged in curriculum planning serve a similar purpose. In either case, the search is for a basis of sharing authority with teachers that will not be interpreted as a threat to the administration.

4. *Specialization that avoids the specificity of certification regulations.* The goal should be to define teacher duties in terms of functions, not roles. Thus enlarged, everything within a general employment agreement could be a matter of either teacher option or teacher–administrator negotiation. The highly rigid civil service pattern would thus be broken.

5. *Technology clustering.* Technological centers, medical clinic style, can be used to justify both comprehensive services to teaching and the continuing employment of technicians to keep the service on a professional level. Current educational models are discouragingly fragmented.

6. *Redesigned security systems for school resources.* Open access programs are secured in different ways from traditional systems for the dispensing of all services through teacher monitors. The commercial supermarket model is both open and secure; perhaps adaptation is possible.

7. *Breaking the time barrier.* It is as simple as diminishing all time-related requirements to the point where professional options begin to reappear. An effective level has been reached when high schools begin to look as if they are on split sessions. The junior college precedent is much more appropriate for the flexible future than the current practice in high schools.

8. *Capitalizing on career development.* The liberal arts argument that knowledge is its own reward has less organizing potential for schools than the idea of universal career interest. Openness in curriculum designs, not narrowness, should be the result of switching from an abstract orientation to one that reflects the educational planner's concern for practical applications of knowledge. Certainly, this would appear to be the mood of the generation for which such plans would be made. The pitfall to be avoided is, of course, preoccupation with scientific and technical careers at the expense of the arts and the humanities. For the open education advocate, opportunity lies in the major reform potential of any goal that is comprehensive enough to reach into every corner of the curriculum and to require proof of relevance.

9. *Identification of administrative goals and practices with a worthy social cause.* Nothing simplifies faster than an idea comprehensive enough to make administrative concerns appear as trivial as they are. Unfortunately, educational change cannot be brought about by school people alone. It must somehow spring from the concerns of the larger culture, perhaps triggered by educators but rarely, if ever, created by them.

Between great causes, management turns in on itself and proceeds to complicate and obscure practically everything previously considered fundamental. Managers no longer think and talk about the needs of their youthful clients or values of the culture. Instead, their dialogue centers on the problems of power, privilege, structure, and finance. Economic disturbances foster this kind of confusion in curriculum planning, and make it easy for the discouraged educator to concede that the advocacy of open education is futile. If this situation continues, the next generation of leadership will look for its answers in new places and justify the restraint of the human spirit rather than promote its dreams.

8

Instructional Stability: The Search for New Meanings

The instructional program is often defined as the "heart" of the school. This is where the teacher feels the most comfortable and the most involved, possibly because there is virtually no ambiguity in role, authority, or responsibility. The administratively scheduled student encounter is an automatic reaffirmation of the school's intent, the teacher's centrality, and the student's subservience. It appears stable, and in many instances it is. However, bureaucracies are often tranquilized at precisely such points. The "comfort index" may be a valid criterion for a sense of well being between missions; however, it is much less valid during a crisis situation.

CONTROLLING ASSUMPTIONS

The only stability that has merit in an educational setting is like that of an airplane. It can only be understood in motion, the safest performance always being "high and fast." Some inflation adjustments in schools may be compared to giving a jet pilot instructions to economize by flying "low and slow"—a much more hazardous proposition than, say, trading the jet for a helicopter. The school's risks in changing quality but not design can best be perceived by reviewing the hidden assumptions that are implied in practice by the "instructional program." They include the following (slightly magnified for clarity):

1. Instruction is an authoritative act that begins and ends with teacher judgment.
2. Student success is measured by approved classroom behavior.
3. "Progression" is the adding of one more "block" to an invisible larger "building" of knowledge of which the teacher is not an architect.
4. Relationships between and among building blocks are presumed to be best if nonduplicating, noncompetitive, and logically sequential.

   "Disciplines of knowledge" (academic building blocks) are known to evolve and sometimes regroup; however, college professors worry about such things and when something important happens the texts are rewritten. Keeping instruction relevant means keeping current copyright dates on adopted materials.
6. Teaching is what schools are all about; everything else is justifiable only as a support system for what happens in the classroom. If the goal is better schools, the only way to get them is to have better teachers.

WORMS IN THE ACADEMIC APPLE

Judgmental errors related to the stabilization of instruction derive from one large mistake, itself surrounded by combinations of small programmatic problems. The big error is "overteaching," and this implies scheduled group encounters with students in excess of their tolerance for passivity.

The current overemphasis on accountability leads administrators toward high-density scheduling and teachers toward a largely subconscious increase in prescriptive teachings. When the whole package is assembled, the student has less free time, a decided reduction in discretionary movement (a "pass" is needed to go anywhere), more lectures to sit through, and more tests to take. Conversely, there are fewer projects, few questions about what he would like to be doing, and little opportunity to work with other students.

The seriousness of this well-meaning return to the basics comes from the fact that the invisible line separating intensive teaching from overteaching is crossed. As the scales tip, the student's attitude becomes resistive and the teacher's attitude changes from zeal to personal resentment.

"Overteaching" is an ever present danger because the power to turn it on and off belongs to the principal rather than the teacher. All it takes to activate it schoolwide is a memo conveying a resurgence of lay dissatisfaction with the school's results; a high-density schedule; and a new student performance test that implies the possibility of teacher blame for student failure. This happens so quickly for one reason—the teacher's role definition is too small and too uniform. Hence, almost any type of leadership initiative is suppressed. Two illustrations will be presented representing the current mode, one dealing with a comprehensive instructional resource center for teachers, the other with a values clarification workshop. Both are about as good as such things can become; however, they are both destined, perhaps in different ways, to be neutralized by teachers because the agitation that is created does not deliver the promised increase in power.

The remedy for improving instruction, therefore, will be to redesign the teaching role and to reinforce teacher authority. Hopefully, this remedy will counteract the current instructional problems summarized here:

1. A "bigger than life" image of "instruction" that, through time, crowds out less formally controlled learning, particularly student inspired and regulated self-development. Thus, practice remains frozen in its most costly component—teacher transmitted information—and makes no use at all of less expensive "deschooled" alternatives.

2. A neutralization of both teachers and administrators in the neglected regrouping of territories of knowledge for purposes of updating content, facilitating teacher specialization, and coordinating a professionally interdependent staff. The important area of curriculum design should be a crucial upward extension of teaching (as opposed to a new province of management). Powerful "helping hands" economies are dependent upon the designation of semi-autonomous small-group teaching stations.

3. An unwarranted management dependence on accountability systems that focus production-line style on the upgrading of individual teachers. Adult lifestyles are, first of all, most difficult to change even with the intensive use of behavior modification incentives. The procedure is expensive, ineffectual, and unlikely to escape the reputation of being an intolerably presumptive act of management.

FOCUS ON TEACHING
TECHNIQUE: AN EXAMPLE OF
CURRENT PRACTICE

Once educators announce their willingness to believe that teaching is an applied behavioral science, psychologists immediately volunteer technological assistance. The following outline of instructional development services is an actual example edited only slightly to disguise the school system that created it.

Instructional Development Services

Instructional Development Consultants

In support of the district's instructional program, the Instructional Resources Center provides a variety of services to teachers. Support for improvement and innovation in instruction is provided through the services of instructional development consultants, professionals with both theoretical and practical backgrounds in learning, communications, and instructional technology. The consultants are available on call to assist faculty in developing and improving instruction.

Instructional Development

To achieve maximum benefit from these efforts, instructional development consultants advocate the use of a systems approach to designing, implementing, and evaluating the total process of teaching and learning. This approach, known as instructional development, is based upon research in human learning, and combines both human and material resources for more effective and efficient instruction. The approach focuses upon the learning outcomes expected from teaching as defined by specific learning objectives.

Based on both formal and informal evaluations, recommendations for the improvement of instruction are made. These recommendations may include the need for designing new instructional materials, considering a different instructional method, or simply writing larger on the chalkboard. All consultations, recommendations, and evaluations are held in confidence between the teacher and the instructional development consultant.

Services Available

The following services are available to any interested teachers through the instructional development program by calling the IRC director.

I. COURSE ANALYSIS, DEVELOPMENT, AND EVALUATION

Course evaluation instruments are available or can be custom designed. These instruments are used to measure students' affective reactions to the course and instructor. The types of instruments available are:

A. Course Evaluation Instruments—affective measurements

B. Class Profile—to determine demographic characteristics

C. Mini-Course Evaluation—custom designed, short course evaluation

D. Class Observation Forms—feedback provided on class observations

E. Cognitive Testing—to determine student performance

F. Literature Searches—to locate innovative methods used in a discipline

II. INSTRUCTIONAL MEDIA SELECTION, PRODUCTION, AND UTILIZATION

A. Coordination of the design and production of overhead transparencies, slides, graphics, television, film, multimedia presentations, and slide/tape programs

B. Selection of instructional media and their uses in order to achieve optimal impact upon the learner

C. Consultation on design of new facilities such as audio-tutorial labs, projection systems, and instructional space utilization

D. Selection of commercially available audiovisual materials

III. COMPUTER APPLICATIONS IN EDUCATION

A. Consultation on appropriate uses of computers, such as computer-assisted instruction or testing, computer knowledge or literacy, computer-managed instruction, computer-based problem solving, and computerized simulation and gaming

B. Selection of available programs, data bases, or other materials

C. Selection of hardware and software systems

D. Coordination of the development of new computer-based educational materials

E. Implementation of computer-based systems, including the design of facilities, scheduling, proctoring, and coordinating with other modes of instruction

IV. OTHER INSTRUCTIONAL DEVELOPMENT ACTIVITIES

A. Workshops, seminars, and colloquia on instructional development and instructional media use

B. Assistance on research projects in teaching effectiveness

C. Assistance in the writing of proposals to state, private, and federal sources for grants to improve instruction

FOCUS ON INTERPERSONAL INFLUENCE: ANOTHER VIEW OF PRACTICE

Reference has been made to the "values clarification" trend in the public school classroom. Its parallel when used with teachers has been interpreted as a "process of interpersonal influence." Again, the source is psychology; the presumption is that controllability and quality are the same.

The following example is a training program outline drawn from the agenda of an educational laboratory, edited only slightly to maintain its anonymity.

An Instructional System to Develop the Skills of Teachers and Administrators in Interpersonal Influence

Learn basic concepts about the process of interpersonal influence. Identify your own style of influencing others and how you are influenced. Gain basic influence skills.

These are the goals of a 30-hour course and in-service workshop on interpersonal influence for teachers and administrators. The instructional system was developed by staff members based on reviews of National Training Laboratory materials and other sources. Included are procedures, exercises, films and audiotape cassettes for conducting twenty 90-minute sessions as a week-long workshop or as individual classes scheduled over several weeks. Session topics are:

Session 1 Introduction to Interpersonal Influence

Session 2 The Influence of Forming Groups

Session 3 The Circular Process of Interpersonal Influence

Session 4 Central Needs

Session 5 Defining My Need to Influence

Session 6 Introduction to Face-to-Face Influence

Session 7 Feelings and the Process of Interpersonal Influence

Session 8 Values and Valuing in the Process of Interpersonal Influence

Session 9 Congruence of Intentions and Actions

Session 10 Influence of Nonverbal Behaviors

Session 11 The Helping Relationship

Session 12 Collecting Information About Ways I Influence

Session 13 Identifying My Characteristic Style of Influencing

Session 14 Dual Accountability

Session 15 Collusive Behaviors

The materials have been developed under a contract with the National Institute of Education.

The idea is not too different from Dale Carnegie's idea in *How to Win Friends and Influence People;* however, its scope is far greater and the intended link with the teaching act beyond question. It is, of course, this link that is controversial.

ISSUES OF CONTROL AND INSTRUCTION

The two examples just presented—one derived from an engineering-style "systems theory"; the other, an offshoot of "behavior modification"—have a common intent: increasing the personal power of the teacher. This an an understandable concern when external economic forces cause individual educators to have a sense of powerlessness. But, is this power beneficial? Does teacher power necessarily lead to effectiveness? Is this the right kind of power? At what point does too much of a virtue become a vice?

On the other hand, as represented by the selected examples, programs that have been designed to increase the teacher's authority were not invented *by* teachers but by management *for* teachers. One is led to question whether or not management is, with such tactics, trying to get the teacher's ten-foot "elastic leash" to stretch to twenty feet, to *temporarily* override organizational constraints. Likewise, one may wonder if teacher power is merely an illusion inasmuch as the inventors of the new techniques still remain custodians of the decision-making power of the institution. The new power does not yet have a declared purpose; a greater capability for influence is simply assumed to be better.

The power motive should be suspect; especially when the transfer of power may adversely affect the instructional program. For example, will technique number two indirectly install "affective education" (previously referred to as "values clarification") as an instructional component? And, will technique number one make teacher-controlled learning even more oppressive for the learner than it already is? How can the "survival quotient" of the instructional program be increased?

SEARCH FOR THE SURVIVAL QUOTIENT

What is needed is not an endless documentation of small shifts in practice, but identification of the more significant philosophical stress points. The first step should be to reconsider the *limits of abundance,* meaning institutional resource limits. Not every good thing is attainable. Intellectual horizons can theoretically remain open subject only to the cost of engineering a design for implementation. Nevertheless, many unfortunate social conditions with proven educational remedies will probably become less than urgent priorities.

Frugality is one of the primary, though often poorly stated, motivations of the "back to the fundamentals" movement. If everything desirable is not attainable, then it is logical to select the *most* desirable, postponing everything else. This is a highly prejudicial "adjustment." Administrators and teachers know that some hard decisions will have to be made soon but they do not yet know what they should be. So, they call for "fundamentals" but do not define them; "power," but do not declare an intended use for it; and "accountability," but do not say for what or to whom.

These adjustments are not all bad and do reflect the larger culture's predisposition to want an official, instant, and authoritative "answer" to every social problem. They are a delaying tactic, to be sure, but more importantly, a kind of "search behavior" aimed at crystallizing the public consensus. A case in point is the Supreme Court's arbitration of public morality in such controversial areas as abortion, prayer, and busing. The process is clearly one of *moral invention,* it is an imposition that blurs the distinction between that which is judicial and political. By declaring "answers" that do not yet exist by public consensus, the courts trap educators between a confused clientele and a value definition that is still questionable. They can only question, advocate generalities, invite discussion, and wait for public reaction.

What is the cause of this seemingly pointless behavior and what are its implications for the instructional program's "survival quotient"? Supreme Court judges are being asked for specific answers—and they are giving them. School administrators are being asked specific questions, and thus far, they are still producing vague answers.

When people need answers, but really do not want them from any one source, the prudent public official should respond, not with a specific remedy, but with a controllable decision process. The problem with the instructional program is that it is— not unlike the courts—a *design for answers.* Thus, if it does what comes naturally, it will fall into the same trap as the Supreme Court. *It will select the survival "fundamentals" for people rather than offering a wide selection and letting them choose for themselves.* It will adopt a superficial scientism as a basis for supervision, overtest everything, and force an artificial conformity in the name of "standards."

Alternatively, the schools can be flexible by simply rebuilding the instructional model around three elements:

1. Personal learning that the schools can support as private life choices and not attempt to either influence or monitor
2. Controversies that present cultural alternatives without consensus and that the schools can monitor for process integrity but not conclusions
3. Personal survival skills that can be systematically taught and rigorously evaluated for performance.

Thus redesigned, two-thirds of the school program could bend without breaking as the culture moves away from paternalism in its institutions and substitutes *stable decision and dialogue processes* for definite answers. The "structure for spontaneity" that would be created would make possible the personalization of learning, movement at a sensible pace toward consensus on matters of value, and finally, set the stage for fairly drastic budget cuts without sacrificing the survival of the most vulnerable.

TOWARD AN EMPHASIS ON
THE LEARNING ENVIRONMENT

This unorthodox view of instruction will alienate educators who have spent their lives dignifying teaching through a refinement of technique. It will just as surely distress all who subconsciously assume that the substance of teaching is academic content that is highly stable and largely nonpolitical.

These conditions have long existed, and are familiar to many older teachers still on the job. Interestingly, the "back to the basics" movement has rekindled their memories and the imaginations of younger teachers who find the thought of a more stable body of truth to be personally conforting. Thus, the notion of instruction meaning either "transmission" or "indoctrination" becomes fashionable. And, supervisory techniques, now popularly labeled "staff development," tend to take on the character of the two examples previously given.

These kinds of practices will prevail nevertheless as long as teachers and supervisors continue to advocate technique for its own sake. It would have been easy to fall in line with the popular trend by filling this chapter with a selection from the impressive array of modern "how to" approaches, including interesting new retrieval devices, updated methods for monitoring student progress, and the like. The intent is not to insist that progress has not been made. Rather, it is hoped that the new techniques and technologies can be liberated from the confining tasks to which the new traditionalism in teaching would relegate them.

The root problem is philosophical, raising the question of whether or not this chapter should have dealt with the *facilitation of learning* rather than with the orthodoxy commonly referred to as "the instructional program." The latter focus was selected because it is the operational assumption of most educators, not because it truly represents the potential of the modern teacher.

In conclusion, the concept that might be most helpful for those who are concerned with teacher effectiveness is to *shift the emphasis from teacher behavior to the characteristics of the learning environment,* broadly perceived to include student–student, student–machine, and student–community interactions not necessarily planned by or controlled by the teacher. Only in this manner can the teacher's role expand to deal with all of the student's learning problems.

141

The final key to taking the pressure off school operations, especially where serious discipline problems have surfaced, is to *make a sharp distinction between access structures and power structures.* Students have a legitimate interest in access and would be just as happy to let administrators keep running the establishment if the power of management did not appear to challenge their personal survival. The *administrative perspective needs to be shifted from people control to resource control* to remove the confusion. Examples of this concept at work are numerous. Examine the local supermarket or library. Abrasive relationships would occur only if the market proprietor tried to tell the customer what to eat; likewise, if the librarian decided to select the reader's books.

It is true that the pressure to use the schools as custodial institutions intensifies rather than diminishes when streets become unsafe and jobs are hard to find. However, it is precisely this restrictive function that must be abandoned. Schools should move from the concept of compulsory attendance to voluntary attendance; from uniform standards to personal career and lifestyle decisions; from the selection of access paths for students to the documentation of what happens after they make their own selections. It is not the school's mission to build a new social order. *The forcing of group change is hazardous to individual liberty,* especially when the mandate for change is couched in terms of "the common good." Schools serve best as platforms for debating alternative futures rather than indoctrination centers for any one partisan group. Once students begin to perceive schools as places that do things with them, not to them, much of the dangerous tension should subside. Viewed, instead, as "survival centers," they might even become popular.

The end result of seriously attempting to redesign schools so they can tolerate higher quality learning (in part through better teaching) may well include such related concepts as: (1) the *campusless school* (not at all uncommon in adult education), (2) the *multischool curriculum,* and (3) *multidistrict educational services.* In short, the *working definition of the "curriculum" will likely become personalized paths linking specialized educational service centers.* If the often overactive courts would only stop to consider this, the modern problem of social justice might be most easily and properly solved by switching from buses and racial parity in support of the more sensible goal of *border crossing. It should not be necessary to reshuffle administrative and political jurisdictions to have access.*

The key to peaceful, comfortable, and personally rewarding schooling for all is *access.* A low quality school is one in which normal survival strategies (defined as access paths) are intercepted at the border crossings. Good schools maximize access, poor schools try to "manage" it. All modern schools have no choice but to continue on their present route of specialization, coupled with interjurisdictional compacts, to guarantee that what is needed, wherever it may be, is not blocked arbitrarily. The comprehensive high school is obsolete; its nonterritorial successor is much more superior, requiring only a little more imagination and flexibility to become a truly magnificent invention. In this setting a totally new concept of the instructional program could easily emerge.

SECTION THREE

Survival
Accommodations
of Process and Power

9

Survival Monitors

The monitoring of the educational process is an unquestionable part of intelligent school management. However, it is not intelligent to accidentally or recklessly influence the process being monitored—to induce counterproductive forces as an unregulated side effect of evaluation. The fact is that this happens more often than not.

Open education—the survival model—is both new and highly perishable. The best understood evaluation techniques are outgrowths of behavioristic psychological research and professional experimentation with prescriptive teaching. Neither is more than partially relevant to open education and must, to the extent of obvious differences, be considered potentially dangerous. The selection of a compatible technology for assessing openness is a legitimate question. To advocate a simple application of the full range of known assessment techniques to open phenomena would be naive. Of course, separating the negative options from the supportive techniques is no small feat. We should begin by admitting the limits of everything that is now known, then acknowledging the need for a new open culture evaluation technology that will not degenerate into an antidote to openness for the expedient facilitation of measurement. A few of the old, familiar techniques will be transferrable—but not many.

In this chapter, I have attempted to stimulate the process of invention by posing some of the new questions that are arising as the open education trend accelerates in recognition of its survival capability. Identified are the critical observation points that reveal whether an open program is growing or beginning to falter.

THE MOST DELICATE ELEMENT: TEACHER MORALE

The premise has been that no intervention at all into the educational process is probably better than a bungled attempt. Simple inertia rarely produces brilliant results but neither does it tend to generate sudden disasters. Normal survival behaviors have a way of balancing staff aspirations and anxieties to the point where a tolerable stress level is achieved. It is true that such a standoff can, and often does, accommodate the slow process of institutional obsolescence and eventual self-destruction.

What is most sensitive may not be the same as what is considered most important. But even very small sensitive spots have a way of growing into dangerous infections. The first point to monitor in open programs is faculty morale, that intangible and always sensitive conditioner of everything else related to open programming. Five working components of morale follow.

Perceptions of Personal Trust

The principal is typically the authority figure whose sanction is most sought by teachers. To them, the principal is the symbol of all authority. If the relationship is, additionally, perceived as "personal," whatever level of trust is conveyed becomes doubly important. To be professionally trusted and personally liked contributes toward a high self-image for the teacher. The next step is a considerable intellectual and emotional investment beyond any possible contractual agreement. Personal inventiveness to extend conventional role constraints is the almost inevitable result. Trusted teachers can also transfer trust to their students, almost in the same proportions that they receive it from their own authority figures.

The few exceptions in which "trusted" authoritarian personalities become more autocratic with their own subordinates should be acknowledged. But this exception should not be considered important enough to abandon the general goal of high-trust relationships between teachers and administrators. At any given time, the measure of this important factor is simple. Ask teachers whether they are trusted in general; what they are specifically trusted with; and how they feel about it. Whatever the answers are, they are "objective truth" to them and the only basis for their future behavior. The wise supervisor will listen.

Perceptions of the Impossible

"The community wouldn't go for it." "It violates district guidelines." "We couldn't afford it." "Other teachers would object." "With those kids?" "Interesting, but I don't know how." These are representative of the reasons teachers give for establishing the boundaries of their personal responsibilities. To establish boundaries is understandable, but some forms of delimitation are more stringent than others. The best approach is for teachers to express classroom performance limits in terms of *their own* limits of competence—not in terms of uncontrollable external forces. This requires both a very mature personality and a stable institutional setting.

It is a fact, however, that most modern teachers have much more talent than the school permits them to use. It is simply

149

accurate, not neurotic, for the experienced employee to know many reasons why various kinds of activities will not work. The misleading feature of the teacher's role is its contradictory sense of autonomy coupled with visible proof of its uniformity. Teachers can, it is true, try almost anything. Sustaining the new idea is the problem.

The external reward structure clearly discourages the innovative teacher, very slowly but surely socializing the teacher completely. Given long enough exposure, the teacher's life-style changes to favor less stressful situations and victory for establishment tradition is thus complete. The teacher's "perceptions of the impossible" should thus be monitored for possible constraints on the particular individual. More importantly, the total pattern of constraint, in part subject to administrative alteration, should be watched.

Power to Keep Faith

Open education is an impossible dream unless teachers have a sufficient command of resources to be able to respond intuitively to sudden inspirations from either students or colleagues. This means, not extravagant or unpredictable financial power, but total autonomy within a specified limit. It means more than predetermined spending limits, however, when it is the establishment rule structure, rather than the budget, that must be bent for the welfare of a student.

One does not have to go all the way back to the one-room school to find teachers with the power to commit the school in most significant matters influencing individual learners. However, good examples have become increasingly hard to find. It is not really flattering to the administration that it has succeeded so completely in directly controlling admissions, pupil assignment, testing, academic progression, and reward allocation decisions that once belonged to teachers. It is even frightening to recall that this new power has been largely automated; hence, student survival decisions, once individual counseling judgments, have become unyielding institutional policies and inflexible administrative procedures. Somehow, this unfortunate trend must be reversed.

The teacher who has no power to either control students' impending academic failure or create intellectual opportunity is inadequate for the task of open schooling. Again, all that is needed to monitor this important factor is an occasional sampling of teachers. No one knows where teacher power ends any better than the adults who come through to their students as less than authentic because they are not permitted to speak authoritatively for the school.

Visible Access to Tools

Open programs, by definition, remove as many barriers as possible. But, whatever latitude is granted must be so visible that its constant reaffirmation by teachers is unnecessary. Schools process so many students, so quickly, that teacher-conveyed messages rarely reach everybody. And, when no messages are received, what do students assume? Exactly what they remember from all of the other adult-dominated schools they have attended —namely, that access to everything worth having is through the teacher, and that most special approvals are given one at a time (advance approval is not given for continued privileges).

Direct access is disconcerting to security-minded administrators who remember the turbulent years of not so long ago, and who believe that latent dissent remains. "Limited access keys" issued to teachers are now commonplace, as is the practice of removing teacher control of some of the more attractive technologies of learning (audio-visual tools, cameras, recorders, etc.). True, "loss rates" are slightly higher in open programs but "use rates" are very much higher. The relative loss is thus smaller.

Loss due to criminal intent is almost negligible in many schools. If students believe they are being trusted, they usually respond in a trustworthy manner. If they are only half-trusted, some will steal; others will ignore the resource that the school originally acquired to facilitate their learning. In either case, negative learning is set in motion, so the whole operation drops into the category of false economy and well-intentioned but naive educational accountability.

The needed monitoring process will, therefore, be one that determines whether *maximum purposeful use* is made of the tools of learning. If the students seem to be trying to wear them out, the rating should be high. If secure inventories are maintained but use is minimal, the school is not attending to its primary mission and should be considered a failure.

UNBROKEN INTERDEPENDENCIES

A school cannot be broken down, engineering-style, into definitive "subsystems." Nevertheless, the maintenance of an open program requires that several critical linkages be maintained. One set of options deals with content, another with assessment, a third with data sources, and a fourth with teacher role. Under each heading there are three principal options and it is imperative that school practices remain compatible across the four categories. Number one in column one should match number one in column two, and so on. Table 9.1 should be self-explanatory.

The idea is to maintain authenticity in the school's response to the learner's declared purposes. If, for example, learners want to consider a current social issue that has sharply divided the larger adult community, the school must not evaluate their efforts by using a partisan "objective test." The teacher's role

Table 9.1

Content	Assessment	Learning Resources	Role
stable truth	objective	authoritative	to transmit
contested knowledge	process	multiple competing points of view	to moderate
personal	optional—performance oriented	selected—wide range	to counsel

as transmitter would be inappropriate. Offering constricted or random, learning resources, would also be ineffectual. A deliberate selection of the known competing positions on the issue being studied is required.

Clearly, most of the school's dilemmas arise from the near-institutionalization of certain components. Uniform testing programs, for example, produce sweeping generalizations about the required stability of content in all disciplines. It is irresponsible, however, to ignore the fact that the entire modern world has turned its attention to value redefinitions that cannot be presented without debate. Teacher roles that arbitrarily stop the debate do not close the issue; they only prevent students from participating in it as a part of their formal education.

The three dimensions of each of four curriculum design building blocks should thus be monitored to maintain compatibility. This is essential, regardless of the philosophical bias of the program. The value question is revealed by the distribution pattern of optional resources and can likewise be monitored. It is all made possible by the recognition of the interdependencies that any program deserving survival will maintain deliberately and perpetually.

153

DEACTIVATED DESTRUCT
MECHANISMS

In the early stages of any open program it is necessary to deactivate several critical mechanisms controlled by prescriptive teaching. Without some alteration—at least partial deactivation —it is only a matter of time before the new open program will fail. The reason will be its persistent erosion by management policies more compatible with other values.

Six major destructive mechanisms can be identified. There are others but an endless list would not be helpful. After all, there is a limit to how much people will *stop* doing before a new program is even launched. Such destructive mechanisms come in various degrees and also have a strong tendency to quickly return to their original condition. Thus, constant monitoring is more than desirable; it is imperative. The six major mechanisms destructive to open programming follow.

Unshared Central Authority

Administrators cannot alone create an open school. At best, they can set the stage for their teachers to create it. This requires the ultimate trust of sharing authority with them. How much sharing is a matter of individual choice but it has to be sufficient for teachers to consider it authentic. Current practice is to share authority informally through such devices as coordinator roles, chairmanships, etc. But these roles are instituted for no longer than one contract year. This means that good and bad practices alike automatically revert every summer to total administrative control. Of course, the practice of advancing through the administrative profession by frequent job changes makes new leadership an actual fact every three to five years anyway. Total power for short-term transients thus becomes, perhaps, the greatest deterrent to open education.

A decade of openness would conceivably require enough teacher authority during the first administration to use it as a criterion for the next administrative appointment. Through both terms there would have to be a continuity of leadership in the teacher group—career-oriented, "permanent," teaching personnel with clearly sanctioned supervisory powers. The extent to which this condition would expand, stabilize, or recede would be the first subject to monitor.

Single Criterion Testing

Openness in curriculum design fosters diversity in student and teacher responses. Single criterion testing (usually in verbal ability) is both inhibiting and grossly unfair to those who take open program options most seriously. The minimum adjustment required is the sanctioning of multiple criteria with the intent of legitimizing the full range of human performance. An ideal arrangement would, additionally, reduce the total volume of institutional assessment. In the process *all* testing in certain sensitive areas would be excluded in acknowledgement of the desire not to intrude in the learner's private life. The second monitor would thereby record the degree of deviation from the uniform student role expectancy implied by single-criterion assessment.

Fundamentals First

Discretionary use of school resources has been limited, by tradition, to that portion of an individual's schooling which follows mastery of the "fundamentals." Virtually every academic discipline and skill area operates on the fundamentals, tending to invent more and more as the field of study gains status. There is some kind of cycle at work, however, that has caused the mature disciplines to reverse the trend, defining less content as foundational, and in increasingly less absolute terms. Eventually, it will be discovered that fundamentals do not necessarily come first for any individual learner. Learners may spend their entire lives learning fundamentals and developing performances that, by tradition, would have been considered "elective."

The breakthrough in open school practice is that learners are encouraged to approach any and all disciplines at whatever point their interests and available resources intersect. The content zone can be strictly personal (exploratory) or contested (theoretical), as well as basic (the fundamentals). The open curriculum would sanction an unlimited number of optional approaches, only one of which would make the mastery of fundamentals the prerequisite to a personal choice of content. The third monitor would thereby plot the extent of deviation from the traditional practice of "gatekeeping" academic disciplines through the prescription of fundamental content.

Obsessive Prescriptive Teaching

It has been previously noted that the school's time utilization pattern reveals its real commitment (as distinguished from what educators sometimes advocate but do not practice). The "transmission" concept of the teacher role is evidenced by relatively short time blocks matched with moderate sized classrooms. This is appropriate to some degree in any schedule. An obsession with teacher-dominated learning is evidenced when every teacher, in every discipline, is assigned five periods a day for formal group instruction. This is overcommitment, effectively blocking the personalization of learning in all of its forms. The needed monitor must, therefore, measure the extent of deviation from the schedule that mandates this particular methodological option.

Scheduling Uniformity

This monitoring point also involves the school's master schedule. Flexible teaching requires wide variability in the school's control of the learner's time. The easiest thing for administration is front office control and schoolwide uniformity. Computers applied to this concept can break the uniformity, but not the rigidity. Moving in the opposite direction, the alternative is a "big block" master schedule with decentralized control by teachers of time allocations within designated limits. Open education requires learner control of labs, seminars, studios, independent research—even lectures.

Computers can produce impressive models of time variability—and this can be extremely useful (though most often unnecessary) in exploring the larger dimensions of time spread over the school calendar. Teacher decisions are often expedient; consequently, unplanned variability is the best approach. Good schedules provide the possibility of broken front schedules but do not mandate them. The monitoring point, then, involves two things: (1) the extent of nonuniformity in scheduling, and (2) the source of control for the pattern.

Single Purpose Facilities

It is commonplace to find administrators worrying about optimum utilization of school facilities. This exercise usually leads the concerned parties to equate constant heavy traffic all over with economy—a practice that, unfortunately, requires some considerable manipulation of people and programs. And, in the end, irreparable damage is done.

If there is no place to study except the library, then "independent study" does not really exist. If there are no legitimate social areas, then hallways, restrooms and parked cars quickly

157

become the substitutes. Committee work and special projects of all types require meeting spaces besides those used for large groups. If "cluster space" is not available, the highly productive enterprise teaching method collapses. There is usually no debate; it just disappears as a result of being defined impossible.

There are no general formulas, in spite of the "flexible facility" movement that some people call "open space schools." The device needed would have a more administrative than architectural nature. Administrators would have to stop "scheduling up" more than two-thirds of the building. The protection of this kind of flexibility is, thus, the sixth and final point to be monitored. It is especially important as economic problems cause many to raise questions about the cost of open schools. But refusal to do the wrong thing is sometimes the highest contribution of all.

CONTINGENCY RESPONSE MONITORS

The ability to sustain openness in the curriculum is partly determined by how efficiently unforeseen events are handled. It is not enough to just meet contingencies; they must be responded to in ways that are perceived to be "open." This is not easy because most "emergency" procedures are typically considered most efficient if they are swift and authoritative. "Educational efficiency" at times may be smooth, slow and aimed at intentionally delaying hasty decisions. Nevertheless, there is no excuse for obscure, confusing, ambivalent, sluggish, indifferent, or manipulative responses to educational contingencies. The establishment, unfortunately, does not have a very clean record on this score. Whatever cannot be handled routinely, and in totally predictable ways, is often snarled by administrative inaccessibility or uncertainty.

Categories within which contingencies are most likely to arise can be identified, however, and perhaps these are the logical points to monitor. Some of the major categories are:

1. Guidance service accessibility (location, amount, official attitude; visible roles, including diffused and shared forms)
2. Student perceptions of teacher, counselor, and administrative responsiveness and potential helpfulness when presented with urgent needs
3. Lag time for data printouts on:
   a. individual program status
   b. teacher schedule
   c. space allocations
   d. budget commitments, and
   e. educational tool inventories, also current use and access patterns
4. Availability of administrative decision makers for teachers (stability and clarity, as well as accessibility, of the official authority structure)
5. Extent of "hot line" access to external (beyond the local school or community) sources of contingency assistance to administrators, teachers, and counselors

CHECKS ON AUTOMATIC DECISION MAKING

Automated institutional processes are complicated to install but are thereafter invaluable in facilitating stable, fair, and reliable responses to recurring needs. They have two weaknesses:

1. normal groups are taken into account, not individual deviations

2. they do not anticipate changing social conditions and are thereby subject to accidental irrelevance.

The points to monitor for the maximum protection of open program commitments include the following:

1. *Academic sequences, cycles, and tracks.* Sequences can be helpful but should be kept at a minimum; cycles usually contribute to student knowledge of what is available and thereby facilitate openness; tracks are possibly dangerous and should probably be completely abandoned. Reversals of these conditions should be most carefully evaluated.

2. *Academic admissions ("gate keeping").* All gates should be constantly monitored to determine, not only the characteristics of those who are admitted, but those who are rejected, delayed, or discouraged. Schools have too many gates and gate keepers; open education usually requires a substantial reduction.

3. *Academic retention.* This is a delayed version of gate keeping, one which, for many students, is a perpetual reminder that survival is dependent upon educational authorities. As a general rule, anything beyond openly scheduled periodic performance tests is antithetical to open education. Lingering uncertainly about one's acceptance by a sponsoring institution is both inhibiting and demeaning. On the positive side, performance decisions over a long span of time are more just than total reliance on admission screening.

4. *Appeal processes.* Injustice for some is the inevitable consequence of automatic justice for the many. Consequently, program monitors should focus on the appeal processes. Total error correction will not be the result because those who are most timid and most damaged often do not appeal, they quit. But, appeal processes will be helpful.

   The appeal processes, like a court, culminate in decision. Informal counseling is much less predictable. Of course, the most difficult case of all is the individual who senses trouble ahead and changes direction before colliding with management in any way. This can reflect commendable flexibility and foresight but it can also represent fearful evasion of purpose and responsibility. Both the appeal process and its evasion should be monitored.

5. *The calendar and the schedule.* These two common constraints should be monitored for the staff participation pattern which they sanction and facilitate. Of course, they prohibit some participation too, thus the evolution of informal circumventions of the pattern is also worthy of note. A good working hypothesis is that the strongest controls of open education lie mainly in the administrative calendar. The teacher's schedule may appear to include discretionary time, but rarely is it scheduled so that group action is made easy. If open education practices emerge anyway, administrative endorsement is the only possible positive action. Administrative support is welcome even after the fact, but true "leadership" occurs only when the first step comes from the schedule makers. In the end, good monitors will report calendar and schedule changes designed to further share and reinforce the decision making rights of the total staff.

MONITORING THE PLANNING PROCESS

The way to monitor the planning process is to view it strictly in terms of school improvement enterprises. Projects, like military missions, have specific targets, a designated resource base, and a projected life span. What is planned is clear if one excludes the vague, but common, definitions of planning that make it one and the same with routine lesson preparation. Some even see "planning" as a synonym for "thinking," thereby negating any prospect at all for deliberate monitoring.

The most simple monitoring system would be an uncomplicated log kept by each faculty subgroup that has a planning authorization. Such logs would note project goals, personal assignments, timetables, and criteria for goal attainment. They should *not* be complicated and thereby also become projects. Simple midpoint and terminal notations would suffice to report relative success or failure. Elaborate "research on research" statistical schemes interrupt pragmatic judgments concerning institutional evolution. Likewise, the human relations component of planning should be kept so simple that semitherapeutic goals do not emerge as a result and linger on to compete with the original objectives.

This is not to suggest that either human relations or statistics is unimportant. They have their place but the monitoring process can only remain unobtrusive if the interesting but unnecessary research possibilities are not pursued. Simplicity is the key to broad-based participation, the most important and difficult goal of the planning process. The ultimate requirement is, therefore, the ability to keep important things simple enough for a working level of consensus to be maintained without undue tension. A final caution: good plans not only tolerate but induce a steady stream of reports from minority groups and individual dissenters. No strength exists when the establishment commitment is so strong that the seeds for its eventual reconstruction are not permitted to sprout.

PEOPLE PATHS

The idea that learners leave visible trails to resources that are attractive and essential is an interesting one from the standpoint of unobtrusive monitoring. It is true that traffic patterns tend to be stabilized, largely because of scheduling controls, but also as an expression of whatever freedom of choice is extended to students.

Logs on resource use, perpetually maintained, provide the first clue. The points to monitor include: the library, academic resource centers, shops, studios, laboratories, and social centers. "Sign in" procedures are cumbersome but would be greatly facilitated by access cards that activate electronic recorders giving cumulative resource use profiles automatically and instantly. Supervisors are not concerned with individual selections as such. It is the pattern of group choices that reveals significant social and academic regularities. A monthly, quarterly, or annual report would just be interesting history. The need is for *daily* profiles of resource use and on-request computer printouts for supervisory analysis. Schools tend to change by seasons; for no apparent internal reason they shift from one resource use pattern to another as the school year unfolds. For example, how many experienced teachers would miss their guess on which school month would be the peak use period for the central library? The point is that both traditional and modified patterns are subject to numerical or graphical analysis, thereby inviting decisions on supervisory intervention that will be comprehensive and cooperative. This intervention is, of course, much easier to explain than supervision by hunch, private inspiration, or personal prejudice.

Traffic monitors are as feasible in public buildings as they are on highways, and their use is approximately the same. Even the sampling technique that involves requesting the traveler's destination is transferrable. Schools do occasionally develop traffic jams. However, it is not the traffic itself in which the supervisor should be interested. The focus should be on the reasons for where the students are going and when. The problem then becomes the facilitation of mobility for all legitimate purposes.

People paths can, additionally, be described comprehensively for any one person, by that person. If the samples are carefully drawn (by grade level, career commitments, age groups, etc.) the activities of groups can be deduced from the statements of very few respondents. And, when confirmed by the general traffic count, the result is a solid basis for generalization. Such profiles should, of course, be plotted for the faculty as well as for students to better understand who is accessible to whom and for what purpose.

Having monitored where people are going and why, the next logical question involves their satisfaction with the paths they have chosen (or have been forced into). The question should be couched in terms of success—that is, did the individual actually gain access to the desired resource? Was access gained without an unreasonable expenditure of energy? Good "people path" monitors will, therefore, result in appropriate generalizations on whether or not rewards can be justified in terms of the price of human energy.

MONITORING CHANGING PRIORITIES

Educational goals have been widely misinterpreted by modern school managers. The common error is to present them to communities and faculties as a list to be rearranged in rank order of importance. The bottom of the list is then considered expendable or optional for resource allocations. The problem is that a school's resources are *all* utterly essential for certain learners. There is no top and bottom to the list. It is really a horizontal continuum with all options being equally important. Any deviation from this assumption produces, by arbitrary administrative judgment, "low priority people" (the teachers of the

164

disciplines at the bottom of the list as well as the students who elect their courses).

What *can* be monitored are the changing priorities for resource development. School programs grow on a broken front, responding in part to external political opportunity, need, and pressure. Not every component can command or sustain a major revision or expansion every year, nor should it be expected to. Good plans are more stable than that. Consequently, there is, at any given time, a *resource use pattern* of definitive character that should be its own justification without insult or injury to any faculty member or academic field.

The way to monitor such a phenomenon is *build the big picture first, from the bottom up*. Large institutions are aggregations of decision-making authorizations. Some authorizations may be new, others old; it makes no difference. They have one thing in common—a "territory" within which relatively autonomous adaptive action is necessary. Patterns are evident but the people closest to operational decisions sometimes find them almost invisible. The point of confusion is the simple, unplanned, pragmatic adjustment that is viewed as "common sense" rather than a change in patterned behavior. The components of the pattern that must be monitored are: (1) a status description of program, (2) a recent history of deliberate group-sanctioned program alterations, (3) an enumeration of experimental and inspirational individual initiatives, (4) a cataloging of protest reactions and official responses to them, (5) a listing of administrative reinterpretations of the unit's mission.

The "big picture" of the total institution is a collection of subunit commitments plus the vision of top management. The upper and lower echelons should be in substantial agreement, but in practice, rarely attain concensus. And, it is probably a good thing. There is no reason to assume that there is more wisdom at one level than another. A cancellation effect has to be avoided, however, and this is best accomplished by open communication rather than executive edict. If top management gives itself the same *priority profiling* assignment that it passes on to the levels below, comparisons and contrasts can be made with relative ease. The next step is to monitor the final profile of practice through periodic updating. As indicated earlier, the point to monitor is *developmental priorities* (what is being done not *in* practice, but to *improve* practice) and the significant *changes this makes in the overall resource use pattern.* "Goal analysis" as an abstract study can thereafter be abandoned. It is important to understand the *changes in the access pattern* in educational institutions. This is the ultimate intent of those who like to work from the vantage point of "a philosophy of education." The only difference is that the issue can be faced directly, with education's ever elusive values being deduced from operational decisions rather than verbal speculation.

ATTITUDE AND TRUST MONITORS

Open education is utterly dependent upon positive staff attitudes, and these, in turn, derive from trust. Although fear sometimes distorts attitude reporting, it is not necessary to resort to obscure psychological techniques to ascertain the working level of human relations. The key is the relationship that attitude has to authority. Monitors can simply focus on the following points:

1. Teacher perceptions of the prospects of receiving *personal support* from each of the major authority levels.
2. The *credibility* of the various activity and resource centers as reliable sources of assistance to teachers and students.
3. The *confidence level* that teachers ascribe to discernible groups, both formal and informal. (What is the "real" function of the curriculum council, for example.)

4. "Client group" stereotyping assumptions used as a basis for organizing educational services. This is a little different and probably deserves elaboration. Diverting from public education for a first example, nurses are sometimes told, "Remember, the family of the patient is sick too." This is apparently supposed to elicit compassionate responses and result in good public relations. It does just the opposite, however, by implying that the concern for sick relatives is somehow abnormal if it is expressed in any way short of the medical profession's cool detachment. Their own "survival behavior" thus becomes an accidental working definition of normality.

No one likes to be assumed abnormal or disabled. In school work, the self-fulfilling prophecy is a real phenomenon. Educational examples are endless. Kids from broken homes are disturbed. Blue collar fathers believe in trade schools. Elementary teachers, like their students, are childish. City youngsters are crime prone. Blacks can't learn to read. Administrators are teachers who couldn't teach.

Stereotyping, of course, will continue. Monitors to determine the extent of it would be a waste of time. What is important to isolate is the prejudicial stereotype that either limits educational opportunity for the child or destroys the effectiveness of the teacher, administrator, or supervisor, either individually or collectively. The monitoring system should be especially tuned to pick up adversary relationships beyond normal levels of dissent. At this point, negative attitudes become the hidden curriculum and thereafter supplant or subvert the planned educational program.

To summarize, attitude and trust monitors should be concerned with the reduction of defensive behavior that dissipates professional energy and thereby interferes with the accomplishment of the school's mission. On the positive side, they should highlight attitudes which offer positive reinforcement for open access programming in all its diffused forms.

INTERVENTION MONITORS

Previous mention has been made of "decision-making territories" that are, for all practical purposes, institutional subsystems. These are, additionally, the striking points for intervention aimed at institutional reform. Monitors to detect intervention would seek:

1. an internal source—a group member serving in the role of reform advocate
2. an external local source—a member of the establishment attached to a different decision-making unit
3. an external nonlocal source—a reform advocate on the outside of the institution completely

Intervention is an attempt to modify an existing service or automated institutional response pattern. Under prevailing conditions, it is fairly safe to assume an administrative authorship and protection of current practice, and an *external* desire for modification (teachers are included in this group). Where teachers are fully involved, the desire for change often exceeds administrative resistance, even when vigorously pursued. Good monitors will, therefore, seek out change-related desires that, without effective expression, would backlog faculty dissatisfaction. The same monitoring system can, in the process, make note of intervention failures. Many teachers give up very easily, often with the first raised eyebrow at a cautiously worded hint of a modified practice. Perhaps this trait will soon undergo drastic change as politically oriented teacher group activity replaces the more passive response pattern of the past. For the present, both formal and informal intervention types require systematic monitoring.

In summary, the most important quality controls of open education are noninterventionist. They can also be quite comprehensive. It is unrealistic to think that the extensive practice of monitoring programs with objective tests and quantitative statistics will be replaced. A better balance, however, is a reasonable expectancy.

10

The Power to Change

Not too long ago research revealed that most school superintendents were mere functionaries, responding primarily to external expectancy and pressure on all issues of political, financial, or legal import. This was disconcerting because the educational theory of the time assumed institutional autonomy for schools, and leadership in the superintendency. The former was equated with professionalism, rejecting alternative political models; the latter was flattering to school administrators because of their identification as great leaders. The glamorization of personal charisma as a characteristic of greatness was easier to believe in than the concept of management. Hiding under the contested stereotypes are stable components of leadership. When assembled properly, a theory of power emerges.

THE POWER TRIANGLE

There are three basic components of institutional power—the *position* of authority, the *person* who is the temporary custodian of power, and the *plan* that is being followed for institutional development. The first two components, position and person, seem to be somewhat more familiar than the third planning component if one judges by the western world's first reaction

171

to the long-range plans of communist societies. However, most people no longer associate a given ideology (communism) with what is essentially a neutral process (planning). All societies, for example, must plan for energy allocation whether people want to or not. And, it makes little difference whether a powerful private corporation or a governmental agency does the planning. Once a plan becomes the goal or orientation of the powerful it takes on a power of its own, committing future leaders and future positions as well as current jobs and job holders. Thereafter, it is more properly identified with position and must await the advent of another charismatic leader to once again begin generating new and potentially revolutionary plans.

The components of person, plan, and position are thus related in dynamic tension with each other, not unlike a spring-loaded mechanical device. The spring loading induces alternate dominance in a predictable cycle that begins with a person orientation, moves to a plan orientation, then to a position orientation, recycling thereafter on different time tables—person and plan orientation are always short and spasmodic compared to position orientation—but they are always in this order. Throughout the cycle, the overall character of the institution reflects its particular developmental phase. This image, in turn, colors its priorities, functional definitions of creativity, productivity, accountability, competence, and progress. The Power Triangle is illustrated in Figure 10.1.

During a position orientation the leader:

1. Generally behaves in a value perpetuating way

2. Assumes power to be "in the position"

3. Does not state purposes—is obscure

4. Operates best in a generally static society

5. Operates an oligarchy of autonomous elements

6. Prizes immediate "distinguished" rewards highly

7. Seeks to continue the present orientation of members

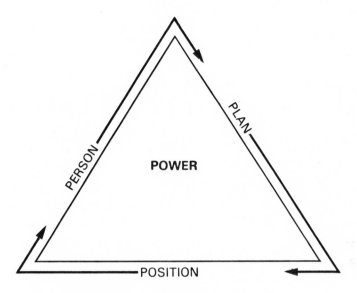

Figure 10.1. *The Power Triangle*

8. Is oriented toward traditional values

9. Is static, backward looking, persistent

10. Permits in-group ethic to differ from general ethic

11. Ignores the competence of all but the most necessary subordinates.

12. Predicts the future on the basis of conformity

13. Prefers many small divisions over centralized strength

The followers:

1. Are basically oriented toward the past

2. Behave in a way not consistent with their stated purposes

3. Are content with deferred rewards

4. Want security based on stability

5. Believe their direction is historically determined

6. Are loyal to the total institution

173

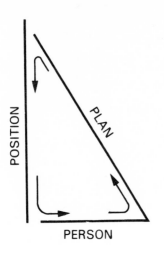

POSITION ORIENTATION
VALUE PERPETUATING
Virtually closed system
Power circular in nature
General bent is backward
Unimportant person
Only internal values circulating
Plan very close to position
Immediate change unlikely

Figure 10.2. *General Characteristics of Position Orientation*

The process:

1. Activates established values
2. Is rational in design but irrational in operation
3. Keeps the decision-making authority uncertain
4. Keeps each internal position virtually autonomous
5. Is deliberately designed to operate elements separately
6. Allows a stable future to be anticipated
7. Keeps routine and ritual relatively "sacred"

During person orientation, the leader:

1. Behaves in a value creating manner
2. Perceives that major power is in one individual
3. Is obscure about real purposes
4. Is dynamic, erratic, expedient
5. Has great audacity in decision making; is individualistic
6. Derives prestige from a belief in general prowess

174

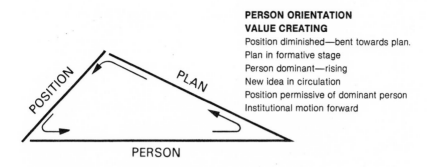

PERSON ORIENTATION
VALUE CREATING
Position diminished—bent towards plan.
Plan in formative stage
Person dominant—rising
New idea in circulation
Position permissive of dominant person
Institutional motion forward

POSITION

PLAN

PERSON

Figure 10.3. *General Characteristics of Person Orientation*

7. Tends toward the irrational in matters related to accepted general ethic
8. Practices administrative effort to reunite the scattered elements of power
9. Derives rewards from direct exercise of power
10. Moves toward plan orientation to consolidate gains
11. Exploits the competencies of others
12. Predicts the future on the basis of change

The followers:

1. Assume power is unified in leader
2. Are primarily loyal to one individual
3. Are pragmatic in terms of leadership purpose
4. Are hopeful but uncertain of future
5. Predict the future as related to a likely successor
6. Derive rewards from decreased responsibility
7. Gain quick rewards for being "loyal lieutenants"

The process:

1. Produces uneasiness at all levels due to the human elements apparent in leadership

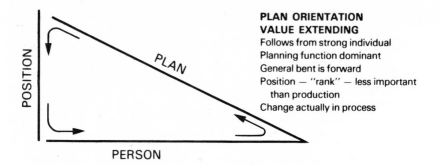

Figure 10.4. *General Characteristics of Plan Orientation*

2. Emphasizes the present; quick rewards
3. Keeps authority certain and quickly administered
4. Causes the power clusters below the top level to be discouraged or destroyed
5. Is forward looking—"soaks up" ideas
6. Produces preliminary planning action
7. Is subject to emotional change

During plan orientation, the leader:

1. Behaves in a value extending manner
2. Assumes power to be a composite
3. States the purpose of the institution
4. Extends and scatters competencies throughout the institution to add to its general strength
5. Derives prestige from specialization
6. Creates a design to operate all elements at maximum
7. Makes decisions through the development of principles
8. Moves positively to new functions
9. Tends toward the rational in terms of general ethic
10. Is creative and evolving but generally internally consistent
11. Uses the present to plan the future
12. "Dissolves" little autonomies by coordination and integration

The followers:

1. Are oriented toward the future
2. Define specific needs in terms of general purposes
3. Have greatest rewards deferred
4. Have productive relationships rewarded
5. Predict a future based upon the plan's success
6. Are loyal to the pattern of ideas

The process:

1. Causes authority to follow function, it is certain and organized
2. Emphasizes the scientific method
3. Is internally oriented to special abilities
4. Produces an ethics change derived from purpose and method
5. Is efficient, pragmatic, subject to rational change
6. Is not sacred—subject to change

INSTITUTIONAL POWER THEORY

The local community has been considered the primary countervailing power that kept professionalized educational leadership in proper alignment with the aspirations and resources of its clientele. The federalization of educational policy was, of course, the trend that eventually made court decisions, congressional legislation, and administrative guidelines for fund distribution more potent than the actions and policy of the once autonomous school board.

As local community powers eroded, school administrators opportunistically opened communication lines with the new nonlocal communities and accelerated in power proportionately. The primary ties between the local community power structure and school administrative authority were thus severely strained though not quite broken. The trappings of a participatory democracy remained but the processes of planning and implementing public policy changed irreversibly. The school administration was clearly in power. Ambivalence could not have been greater among the newly powerful public servants, however, because economic crisis promptly removed about as much power as the collapse of the local community transferred to the superintendency. The mantle of leadership was not a comfortable one, but it did provide a clue to the only useful power theory in school reform—the kind that assumes that the power to be released is *within the institution itself.* Power theory has thus moved full circle, originally assuming institutional self-determination, later capitulating to theories that treated school executives as mere pawns of the more powerful external forces, and finally reinvesting school leaders with organizational powers beyond as well as within their school districts.

PRINCIPAL ORIGINS OF THEORY

There is little that is essentially "educational" in the struggle over the allocation of privilege and the uses or abuses of power as illustrated in previous chapters. Similar behaviors can easily be found in almost any type of institution. Every organization attracts a small number of creative critics, loyal employees who have visions of a better way; a larger number of serious advocates, who are fully committed to the regime in power; and finally, an even bigger group of moderates, who sometimes employ the ultimate power of decision by swinging new policies toward one extreme or the other

The numbers of employees in each category obviously have some significance, but an even more important factor is the intensity of conviction a given group has in the values underlying its position. Clarity of values determines the measurement they will use for assessing prevailing conditions; urgency of reform is, in turn, the result of a discrepancy analysis that judges practice unfavorably.

The search for a more stable explanation of institutional development than the expedient swapping of power by competing factions is a legitimate undertaking for the educator. Political tendencies stem, as noted, from values and behavior predispositions sometimes equated with life styles. These functional roles always have a situational context—a specific institution operating in a given territory for a significant period of time. The time, space, and mission factors are so powerful they virtually guarantee the success of a given leader in one location, or conversely, the failure of the same person in a different locale. Even more important, the point at which the leader appears in the evolution of the employing institution makes a difference. As just illustrated by the tripartite model, a predictable evolutionary cycle can be hypothesized as a basis for the serious attempt to formulate a theory of institutional development. The transiency of top-level educational leadership almost demands the deliberate selection of key personnel on the basis of their life style compatability with prevailing institutional needs. Counterculture institutional leadership can sometimes bend or delay a normal institutional development cycle, but reversals, skips, or arrested motion are unlikely distortions that properly deserve the label of "revolution."

Schools in general show a project tendency—a tendency to experiment. But, once the experiment is over, or the project completed, schools return to normal. A more sophisticated analysis is possible. Suppose that a given school has just passed through a thorough *person orientation* phase (high trust in charismatic leadership), followed by a culminated plan orientation phase (extending the leader's ideas), and is presumed by those involved to be progressing because of the newly planned order. According to the theory of tripartite power, as just presented, the third *position stage* will recycle predictably, accompanied by an inert maturity characterized by a sense of security, complacency, and conformity. Once position is accomplished, pioneers and creative thinkers become relatively less important than in the early stages. They actually tend to obstruct the new bureaucrats or institutionalists who rapidly develop in the new pattern and literally take over. The creative members are either inhibited or intentionally thwarted by the new plurality that often very quickly shifts from a plan to a position orientation, as it gains control and is affected by vested authority as opposed to the natural power of creative members.

The idea is that in its normal sequence the process of institutionalization runs through a creative beginning, a vigorous and shared creative planning stage, and finally, when new roles and functions are defined, into the new position orientation. Routine generally engulfs the energies of the new position holders and they very soon begin to feel secure. A little later their vested authority swells and takes on the semblance of power. They tend to issue "official opinions" that voice their specialty. Conformity to "the plan" seems mandatory and rules and policy supercede thinking, interpretation, and every use of the kind of creativity that produced the new order. The retiring dean of a famous school of education once observed, "As soon as you institutionalize it (any desirable service, practice, or program), you run the danger of making it a walled town that is not nearly so attractive to outstanding people. . . ."

When one observes the extent to which position orientation dominates schools, churches, bureaucratic government, and even service clubs, in most normal times, Robert Ardrey's theory in *The Territorial Imperative* can be interpreted as the biological basis for this type of social action.[1] Ardrey's thesis is that man is a territorial animal, meaning that one primary human drive or instinct is to rule territory. Ardrey further notes that this instinct is of the "open variety," that openness is an innate desire but takes learning to develop.

> When we discuss behavior patterns, such as the territorial, we deal with these open programs of instinct. The disposition to possess a territory is innate. The command to defend it is likewise innate. But its position and borders will be learned. And if one shares it with a mate or a group, one learns likewise whom to tolerate, whom to expel.[2]

Ardrey also discusses what he calls the "amity–enmity equation" in which he postulates that $A = E + h$. That is, that amity equals enmity to the extent that enmity is tempered by a common hazard. Territorial animals defend their territory against all intruders, and this indicates a natural enmity toward their kind. But a common hazard, natural or man-made, reduces enmity and increases amity. He also makes this final point, "Finally we must know that the territorial imperative . . . is the biological law on which we have founded our edifices of human morality."

Society awards positions. It allows certain of its members to hold special positions because of some evidence of their power or value to the group. Such positions in fact do represent at least one aspect of tripartite or composite power. They become "the territory" of position holders, and do in fact represent a staked out domain or stamping ground on which territorial animals are supposed to be invincible. Away from their territory they are as vulnerable as others of the same species. From their positions they may express a certain air of enmity toward

1. Robert Ardrey, *The Territorial Imperative* (New York: Atheneum, 1966).
2. Ibid.

others. When this becomes intolerable to the others, the creative critics come up with ideas.

Viewed in terms of Ardrey's amity–enmity equation, this situation threatens the whole membership. Such common hazards invariably require the position oriented to take some action away from their territory, where their authority or power is diminished by the hazard of new and strange circumstances. This constitutes the culmination of a complete departure from the cycle that any completed plan sets in motion.

It is important that everyone who exercises authority in the schools learns to recognize the principal characteristics of each of the three major orientations because the opportunity for change is always in the next stage of the sequence: position, person, plan, position. If it is true that there is no ultimate escape from oligarchy, or, under the theory of tripartite power, from position orientation, then forward institutional progress can only result from serious attempts to create a self-perpetuating plan orientation.

Only a dedicated individual, or a small group of person-oriented individuals, can break a position orientation. Serious and dedicated planners and a group of plan-oriented followers can turn the substance of a person orientation into institutional practice. Only through the requirement that "position" be controlled by the planning function can any institution avoid the forbidding oligarchic, autocratic strictures of operation under a heavy position orientation.

LEADERSHIP PERSPECTIVE ON PLANNING

Intelligent use of the theory of tripartite power, with its emphasis on the process by which individual ideas become important in institutional development and control, should tend to eliminate to some extent the bureaucratic way of treating individuals as abstractions. As Kierkegaard said, "A major protest of existentialist philosophy is against the effort of Western philosophy to reduce the human being to an abstraction—an essence or universal. The net effect of this is to make man a specimen instead of an individual."

To consider individuality in all its beauty and confusion, in all its errors and accomplishments, and in relation to its necessary existence within a group, is a first duty of planners. Individual effort is still the only creative source of ideas that contributes to progress. Ghiselin reminds us that, "production by a process of purely conscious calculation seems never to occur." He adds:

> Creation begins with a vague even confused excitement, some sort of yearning, hunch, or other proverbial intimation of approaching potential resolution. Not even the most vigorously creative minds always find their way quickly to efficiency. Yet many creative workers have little knowledge of the pertinent materials and would not know where to find them.[3]

It is not easy to invent and to improve, and it is never a certainty that any plan will work or seem acceptable, not if it is really new.

David Riesman, additionally reminds us:

> Movements of thought . . . do not so much reflect the society in which they arise as the account of what that society appears to have left out of account. . . . I believe a contextual analysis is necessary if we as intellectuals are to live in some productive tension with our times and not merely to ride the waves of the past or the future. And it is only through imagination that men become aware of what the world might be; without it, "progress" would become mechanical and trivial.[4]

3. Brewster Ghiselin, ed., *The Creative Process* (New York: New American Library, Mentor Books, 1963).
4. David Riesman, *Constraint and Variety in American Education* (Garden City, N.Y.: Doubleday and Co., 1958).

Parkinson agrees in spirit and insight with the cycle of tripartite power, although his terminology is different. "The story has been told of how monarchy arises, to be superseded by aristocracy, which is replaced by democracy, which ends in dictatorship, which may well be the prelude to monarchy again." History attests to the fact that in every instance some crisis or strong effort to crush human individuality is the spark that sets social change in motion. "New" social, educational, and cultural ideas all have one essential characteristic: they call for a break from tradition or the controls of an oligarchic institution. Any institutional practice that is not perceived by the membership to free and enlarge its opportunity for existence will be certain to alienate strong, creative individuals who will eventually destroy the practice, and replace the practitioners.

The real strength of any institution is in the composite of a competent leadership, a continuous planning function, a sharing of power and authority on the basis of the ability to produce, and in free and dynamic movement of current ideas into the planning mechanism. Overall strength and enduring power is not to be found in either person, plan, or position alone. It is, as stated, in the dynamism, the process, the movement, and the freedom with which the planning operation is able to function as it funnels individual ideas into institutional practices.

SECTION FOUR

Survival Planning Strategies

11

Developmental Planning: A Systems Approach to Survival

The key roles of reformer and catalyst are dependent on an understanding of the planning process. Purpose, structure, strategies, techniques, problems, and potential must be understood as they are related to the development of self-governing open education environments. Effective planning is the vehicle for idea development and implementation. It provides a means of selecting, initiating, controlling and coordinating change action of major proportions. Planning is the only realistic hope the schools have for long-time survival preserving the most essential values.

This chapter focuses on the planning process as a continual decision-making system that coordinates the efforts of a complex organization to satisfy identified needs. Systems theory and techniques are suggested as means of designing a planning model.

This chapter was written by Barry Ersek, Assistant Principal, Alexis I. duPont High School, Wilmington, Delaware, and Vice President, Garnet Valley Board of School Directors, Concordville, Pennsylvania, for the original University of Delaware Seminar on Survival Behavior. Mr. Ersek's contribution to this text is gratefully acknowledged.

The intention is not to offer the ideal model, but rather to suggest design criteria to be used in developing a model that meets the requirements of each local situation.

THE PRESSURES FOR CHANGE

Change occurs in all organizations in spite of the inertia of status quo forces. The pressures that cause change are generated by either internal or external concerns. The internal concerns come from within the organization. They may only be significant to one component of the organization, but if the systematic effects are not considered, the overall performance of the organization can be affected. Internal pressures for change are often hidden by individuals or subgroups if an appropriate forum or receptor is not available to receive legitimate concerns. Consequently, covert change actions are encouraged with no opportunity for coordination. An atmosphere of covert change runs a high risk of destructive collisions from opposing programs.

External pressures come from outside the organization and are usually more apparent. They include state and federal regulations and funding programs, special interest groups, and concerned individuals. Organizations respond to external pressures by accommodation, modification, rejection or defensive action. The hazard of an inappropriate response exists if the planners are incapable of considering the interrelationships among the components of the organization and the relationship between internal and external pressures. This kind of ineffective planning results in random stimulus–response actions that are able to satisfy a few concerns but do not achieve an orderly development based on a stated purpose and defined goals.

These internal and external pressures are listed by Curtis as causing the administrative leadership role to shift from a change orientation to a problem orientation:

As school administrators we are currently problem oriented rather than change oriented, a condition that has been stimulated by the mounting strife that in recent years has engulfed the schools—strife both from the street and from within the school family itself. Neither the superintendent nor the principal need look for his job: it is brought to his desk daily in packages of controversy, delivered personally by both the layman and the professional, without realizing this is a gradual modification in the leadership role.[1]

A change in the leadership role cannot result without an effective planning system. A planning system will help keep the focus on goals and develop coordinated change actions that are compatible with these goals. Consequently, random stimulus–response action will be decreased as the focus moves from problems to purposes.

IMPLEMENTATION PROBLEMS

The pressures for change have provided the impetus for the development of worthwhile programs. However, the program with the greatest potential can become inoperative through poor implementation planning. Implementation problems result from incomplete preparation or personal involvement, poor timing, or limited resources. Consideration of the impact of change on all parts of the organization will help identify constraints in advance and will provide an opportunity to alter the plan to function within these constraints or to modify the organization to receive the change without the limiting effects of excessive restrictions. A common example of incomplete preparation for change is the "program transplant" in which a pro-

1. William H. Curtis, *Educational Resources Management System* (Chicago: Research Corporation of the Association of School Business Officials, 1971), p. 23.

gram that is successful in one school is implemented in the same way in another school without considering the subtle support systems that are essential for its success. Implementation of several innovative programs simultaneously, without knowing how they will function together or in combination with the existing program, leads to staff fatigue due to the stress of change or the destructive competition for available resources.

The problems in the following report by the Center for the Advanced Study of Educational Administration lists the results of incomplete planning. Installation difficulties are given as the reason for the failure of potentially profitable innovations.

> The issue was often one of adoptive failure rather than substantive failure. In the degree this is true, it is impossible even to put the intrinsic worth of an innovation to the test in a field setting. Generally speaking, educators seriously underestimate the enormity of the task of effecting fundamental change in schools, and funding agencies seem to reinforce, indeed, compound the error by imposing time deadlines, evaluation schedules, and budget restrictions which imply that complex organizations can be transformed virtually overnight. Together, the educational planners sometimes act as though all that were required to implement major innovations are serious intentions and a few summer workshops. Such views clearly need modification.[2]

Complex organizations cannot be effectively changed through a simplistic implementation of new programs. The impact of the new program on all components of the organization must be considered to provide an opportunity for it to function effectively. The people affected by the change are an essential factor in the success or failure of the change. They should be involved in the planning so as to better understand the new

2. W. W. Charters, Jr. et al., *The Process of Planned Change in the School's Instructional Organization.* Center for the Advanced Study of Educational Administration, University of Oregon, 1973, pp. 4–5.

190

program and to develop a sense of ownership. Vast amounts of money and considerable effort can be wasted if these factors are not part of the planning process.

A report on the results of using simplistic planning to implement a new program describes a remedial reading program that expended almost one million dollars and underwent almost complete failure.

Nearly one million dollars blown on NYC reading programs. The transition from a centralized to a decentralized school system can create a mighty chasm, New York taxpayers are learning, one into which nearly a million dollars can be tossed and leaving hardly a trace. In a report remarkable for its business, The Urban Ed Inc. described a $998,468 high school remedial reading program in New York City as "poorly planned, undefined, and in effect, barely executed at all." Forty-four high schools were to participate in the program proposed for state funding, but the number was cut to 23 by the time the money arrived. By the time the evaluators arrived, 16 of the 23 schools had never heard of the program, one claimed insufficient time to implement it, six had actually done it and the money was all gone.[3]

This type of simplistic program implementation has very little lasting impact on the learning environment. The money expended was consumed by the organization with little or no impact on the remedial reading needs of schools involved.

Additional examples of implementation problems are given in the case studies covered in *The Process of Planned Change in the School's Instructional Organization.* The report covers four schools that installed differentiated staffing programs. Some of the problems encountered were the incompatibility of change behaviors with structural changes and new problems of adjustment created by the changes in structure. The interdependence of the goals was also listed as a problem:

3. *Report on Education Research* (December 23, 1970): 8.

Progress in the four case-study schools had been far from spectacular. Structural changes had been instituted readily enough, such as employing personnel for new positions, designating teaching teams, appointing team leaders, adjusting pay scales, and so on, but the task of translating formal arrangements into appropriate behaviors proved to be a formidable one for the faculties. The structural alterations themselves created inescapable, new problems of adjustment (for example, learning to work smoothly with a classroom aide), while project activities (workshops, visitors, innumerable meetings) consumed vast amounts of staff time and energy in competition with teachers' central instructional responsibilities. Little time remained for reasoned consideration of the tactics or strategies of change, and by the end of the school year faculties were still seeking the operational meaning of that which they were implementing. As it turned out, two of the schools formally disaffiliated with DS projects at year's end and a third had all but abandoned DS as a goal of its innovative activities.[4]

An important element in accounting for the partial failure (or partial success, depending on one's viewpoint) was the interdependence of the goals. Thus, curriculum development depended on the emergence of viable instructional teams that would serve as centers for teachers and arts specialists to work together in planning. Instructional teams, however, did not emerge during the year.[5]

The above examples illustrate how failure can occur when the systematic effects of change are not considered and staff involvement is inadequate to achieve an understanding of and commitment to the change. The following example from the same source demonstrates complete lack of staff participation in the planning process as it existed in one of four case-study schools involved in the differentiated staffing program.

4. Charters, et al., "The Process of Planned Change in the School's Instructional Organization," p. 8.
5. Ibid., p. 83.

The proposal, however, had not been written as a concrete, detailed specification for an educational program. It was written expressly to solicit financial support from an external agency and emphasized the benefits children would derive from the innovative program rather than details of what the program would be. . . .

It was this lofty statement that served as the guide to action. No "institutional plan" emerged to operationalize its language, nor did the summer workshops deal concretely with how the school would operate under "differentiated staffing" and (an) "arts-centered curriculum." No members of the Stormy Heights staff had a hand in writing the proposal—neither teachers, arts specialists, nor the principal—and the one person who did, the project director, was an outside figure. Yet it was the staff's responsibility to implement the program.

Thus, there was a clear press on the Stormy Heights staff "to change," but in what direction, how much, how? Given the proposal's ambiguity regarding the shape of the future, required changes came to be defined in terms of patterns of roles, activities and norms, known from the past. The staff was obliged to respond to the press to innovate, but the response carried a strong conservative theme. Reactions of staff members involved a tendency that can best be described as "assimilation to the familiar."

The implementation process in Stormy Heights soon became trapped in a vicious circle in which the pursuit of certain goals prevented the attainment of other proposed objectives and in which negative reactions arose among teachers towards those who were perceived as responsible for their plight. Criticism from the outside only heightened the stress under which the staff was already performing. Even by mid-year, teacher resentment was so strong that joint planning, even if the staff's time bind had allowed it, would have been difficult, if not impossible to conduct. The school year ended on this note.[6]

6. Ibid., pp. 75–76.

The implementation problems at Stormy Heights and the ultimate rejection of the change action by the staff were the direct result of having the planning function completed by individuals totally outside the group that was responsible for implementation of the change action. Planning is a people process that cannot function effectively in isolation from the other components of the organization.

SYSTEMS PLANNING TECHNIQUES

The above examples demonstrate a need for a planning process that will provide the means of translating goals into actions that will sustain desirable results. A process is required that is responsive to the interrelationships of a complex organization but maintains a broad perspective of the organization's purpose and its interaction with society's changing needs. A systems model can provide the structure for an effective planning process with these features. The following is a brief introduction to some of the systems planning techniques. Other variations exist and excellent books on applying them to educational organizations are available.

Systems models were developed by the Allies during World War II to analyze various methods of counteracting the German air raids over England. The systems models helped to select the optimum combination of methods to achieve the most efficient use of limited resources. Systems models were further developed by industrial firms as a cost benefit analysis tool and a program planning and control technique. They were also used extensively by NASA to plan and coordinate the complex space program.

The basic functions of a systems model can be represented by eight steps in a systems analysis cycle:

194

1. Determine purpose (reason for being)
2. Select goals (how purpose is to be achieved)
3. Define needs (what needs to be done to better meet the goals)
4. Formulate alternatives (how can needs be satisfied)
5. Analyze and select the "best alternative" (what will achieve the most desirable results for the efforts expended)
6. Develop and implement the "best alternative" (how to install and change action)
7. Evaluate results (assess the change action in terms of the purpose and goals)
8. Recycle and redefine needs based on the evaluation of the change action (recycle into step 1 above—how will the change action satisfy the needs or create new needs)

The systems analysis cycle begins with a statement of purpose for the organization. A complete description of the purpose is provided in the goals. The goals are used in defining the needs and establishing priorities for future action. The needs are the gaps that exist between actual practice and the goals and are used to formulate alternative ways of meeting the goals.

The alternatives can indicate a range and a combination of the three types of projected action. These include innovative action (new programs), expansive action (increase, add on, or fill the gaps in existing programs), or restrictive action (eliminate, regroup, phase out, cut back, or deemphasize present programs). A precaution to remember is that innovative action is the glamour move and is often mistakenly used when expansive or restrictive action may better meet the need. Blind innovation without consideration for the other types of action required to mesh the new with the old may result in isolated innovation with little impact on existing programs, or a hostile reception from the status quo forces. Preparation for desirable interaction between the change action and the existing program is the objective. However, without a minimum amount of room within the existing programs success will be limited, if not precluded.

The alternatives are analyzed in step five and the "best alternative" selected. This alternative is developed and implemented as a change action. The results are then evaluated to determine the effectiveness of the change action and to recycle the information to help redefine the needs.

Figure 11.1 is a graphic representation of a simple model of this systems analysis cycle. Each of the eight steps can be further broken down into subsystems made up of a series of less

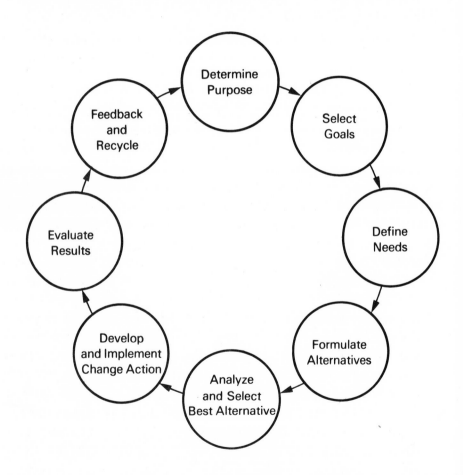

Figure 11.1. *Systems Analysis Cycle*

complex functions forming a network of the individual tasks to be completed.

An example of a subsystem incorporating steps two and three of the systems analysis cycle is illustrated in Figure 11.2, a CPM chart of the Goals Process Project. This example was developed using systems planning to identify the tasks and plot the "best" sequence that could most effectively complete the goals selection and needs assessment steps. This flow chart shows the dependencies and interrelationships of all the tasks of the network. It also lists the group responsible for each task with a projected time line drawn below the tasks. The small flags marked with an "R" are milestone indicators placed at significant points of development. They show when reports are to be submitted to the Board of Education.

The systems approach is incorporated in several other techniques available. The range from ERMS, Educational Resource Management System; PPBS, Program Planning Budgeting System; to PERT, Performance Evaluation Review Technique; and MBO, Management by Objectives.

ERMS is a PPBS method developed for educational organizations. They are both comprehensive decision-making processes that assist at the conceptual as well as the operational planning level. ERMS is a continual planning process that involves the entire organization and the interrelationships of its components.

PERT is similar to CPM. They are operational flow-charting techniques that can involve very detailed network diagrams designed to complete a specific task. They are project control and updating techniques with start and finish dates listed. They are frequently used by the construction industry to plan, coordinate, and update projects using a computer-based model.

Management by objectives can also help to facilitate the use of the ERMS process. It is usually used as an evaluation technique for measuring performance effectiveness in identifying and attaining specific objectives. It complements systems planning processes but it is not used exclusively with them.

198

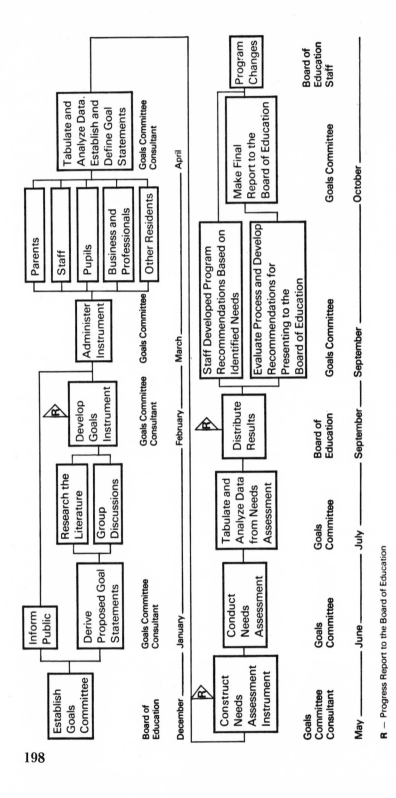

Figure 11.2. *CPM Chart of the Goals Process Project*

R — Progress Report to the Board of Education

ANALYTICAL ATTITUDE OF
SYSTEMS PLANNING

A factor common to all systems process techniques is the analysis attitude required for any system approach to function. This analysis provides a logical procedure of organizing information for the development and selection of alternatives. The analytical attitude is beneficial to systems design. It results from the logical organization of data, development of alternatives, forecasting results of each alternative, and projecting the impact of the change action on other components of the organization to determine the systemic effects.

The analytical activity is a high priority factor in a systems planning process design. A designer can become so involved in the logical layout of a systems network and its mechanical features that the analytical functions are sometimes underestimated. Analytical requirements increase with the degree of creativity or level of judgment desired. It is important to note that the best systems analysis process cannot eliminate poor judgment and that no planning process can effectively make a decision on its own. The process can only help to logically organize information, identify alternatives and project results for the decision makers.

The importance of an analytical attitude in systems design is emphasized by Curtis:

> The analytical activity should allow for the organization and for the examination of information on a regular basis so as to clarify the school district's objectives, and the utility of different ways of achieving them. The level of sophistication which a school district can bring to the analysis of possible alternatives to achieve its objectives is not as important as the adoption of

the "analytical" point of view. That is, the critical message of the ERM System has more to do with an attitude or approach to a school system's decision making than with the adoption of a particular program structure, mathematical enrollment model, or use of advanced quantitative techniques.[7]

This attitude can be described as rational planning based on the logical comparison of alternatives through a highly visible decision making process. Traditional administrative organizations may find the highly visible decision making process uncomfortable. Authoritative planning by a small select group results in a limited analytical function and usually produces "directives from the top" that become inoperative by the time they reach the implementers.

The analytical attitude of systems planning includes high visibility for the decision making process because a broad base of participation is required to effectively gather information and identify alternatives. The analytical attitude causes rational decisions to be made and the process' high visibility encourages an understanding of how and why these decisions are made. Broad based participation also develops a sense of ownership for the participants in decision making. These factors are conducive for establishing a commitment towards the organization's goals and planning decisions. Another benefit of this interaction is that the organization becomes more responsive to the needs of its clients.

OPEN SYSTEMS THEORY

Open systems design is a part of the basic criteria for the development of a responsive planning process. Open systems

7. Curtis, *Educational Resources Management System*, pp. 32–33.

theory views the relationship of an organization with its environment as being in dynamic interaction. This relationship assures responsive action to the changing goals and needs of society. A visible decision-making process is a part of this dynamic interaction. The open systems theory also emphasizes the internal relationships of the organization as being interconnected in a system that functions as a dynamic whole.

Baldridge stresses these features in his explanation of open systems theory.

> Change and dynamism are central to the open systems perspective. Rather than assuming equilibrium or homeostasis—both assumptions that play down the role of change—the open systems approach has adopted a dynamic principle that Buckley calls "morphogenesis." Morphogenesis is the process in which a complex, adaptive system grows and changes in order to confront new goals and organize its efforts more efficiently.[8]

Achieving a functional level of "morphogenesis" as defined by Baldridge and Buckley is the primary objective of an open systems design. This type of adaptive growing system can also be appropriately called an "organic" system.

The learning environment can be viewed as an organic system to exemplify the application of an open systems theory. See Figure 11.3. This example shows the learning style of one learner and how this individual functions within the environment. The large circle represents the total environment from the immediate family to the entire universe. The next largest circle is the learner's area of experience and activity within the total environment. This area begins at the time of conception and continues to grow throughout the learner's life. The growth rate of this area changes at various stages in the individual's

8. J. Victor Baldridge, *Social Science Paradigms and the Study of Complex Organizations,* Research and Development Memorandum no. 76 (Stanford, Calif.: Stanford University, School of Education, September 1971), p. 12.

development. The school's area of the total environment is represented by the three smaller overlapping circles labeled staff, facilities, and programs. The learner's contact with the structured learning environment of the school is shown by the learner's overlap or interface with the school's area.

An objective of open education is to expand the area of influence of the learning interface by encouraging the development of an independent learning style. Open education can achieve this objective by increasing the quality of the learning interface and by decreasing the artificial stress created by unnecessary restrictions in the access procedures to knowledge.

The three symbols in the learner's area of experience and activity help to illustrate the individual learning style. The smallest circle indicates an interest center. Interest centers develop from exposure to and exploration of the total environment. They may be very limited in time or maintained by the learner for life. An interest center becomes more significant when it expands by developing a radiating interface around it, resulting in a learning nucleus. The symbol for the learning nucleus is two small concentric circles with radiating lines around them. When the radiating interface around a learning nucleus overlaps with one or more other learning nuclei areas, a talent cluster develops. The result is a complex learning interface that produces synergistic effects and future growth.

The learning style can be determined by analyzing the frequency, location, and relationships of interest centers, learning nuclei, and talent structures. The illustration in Figure 11.3 shows independent learning because twice as many learning nuclei are outside the school's areas of staff, facilities, and programs. The three talent clusters shown also indicate an independent learning style because one talent cluster, the one on the far right, is completely independent of the school's areas, and another, the one at the top, is only partially dependent on the school's areas. The number of interest centers outside the school's areas also depict an independent learning style.

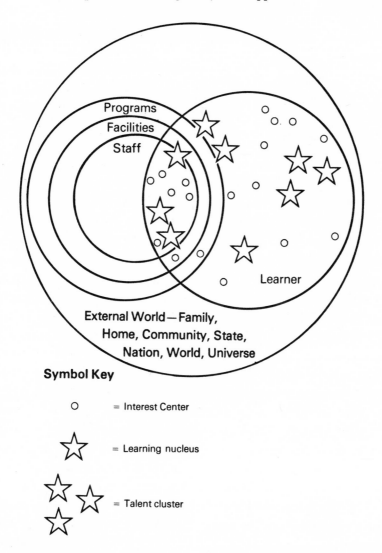

Figure 11.3. *The Learning Environment Viewed as an Organic System*

An example of a dependent learning style would show a high percentage of the learning nuclei in the school's areas. The talent clusters would also be dependent on the school's areas; however, the interest centers might occur in a random pattern.

This example of one application of open systems theory demonstrates a model with several components and complex relationships functioning as a dynamic whole.

DESIGNING A SYSTEMS PLANNING MODEL

Three key factors are required in designing a systems planning model: an understanding of the systems analysis cycle, knowledge of the analytical attitude, and a commitment to open systems theory. The systems analysis cycle provides a basic outline for the construction of the model. The analytical attitude emphasizes the developmental and comparative features required in a planning model. Open systems theory describes the internal and external relationships needed to produce a responsive system that functions as a dynamic whole.

The design and implementation of the planning model should not become an experience for a chosen few. Open communications and involvement of all personnel according to their expertise should begin in the formative stages of the design.

Involvement should include other representatives in addition to the staff design group. The developing trend of establishing the constitutional rights of each learner in functional education requires considering the clients (community, parents, and students) as legitimate participants in the decision-making process. An appropriate role for the clients is also desirable because it helps to keep the system responsive to the needs of the learners.

The formation and operation of the Alexis I. duPont School District's Goals Process Committee, of Greenville, Delaware, is an example of participatory planning with parents, students, teachers, and administrators working together in the formative stages of developing a process to determine the district's goals. The committee was appointed by the Alexis I. duPont Board of Education and charged with the task of recommending

> whether or not the school district should engage in a project to establish and evaluate its educational purposes, and if so, what process should be used.[9]

The committee spent six months studying goal development processes and made the following recommendations in its December 1973 report to the Board of Education.

A. That goals be established and prioritized
B. That the process focus on learner goals, but not at the exclusion of other goals
C. That the process include a needs assessment
D. That the total community be involved
E. That a budget be established for accomplishing this task
F. That a Goals Committee be established:
    1. That this Committee consist of twenty-five members, including citizens, teachers, students, and administrators
    2. That members of the existing Goals Process Committee be invited to serve on the Goals Committee
    3. That community representation be the prime consideration in determining membership

Some criteria for selection are geographics, recent high school graduates, citizens living in the district who have no children in the schools, school principals, teachers, college-bound students, and vocational students.

9. "A Report from the Goals Process Committee to the Alexis I. duPont Board of Education," Alexis I. duPont School District, Greenville, Delaware (December 18, 1973), pp. 1–2.

The committee agrees that goals are a necessary first step in developing a self-improving educational system. The broad involvement of staff and community in developing these goals, will establish a level of expectation and a need for continuous product evaluation.

The process selected by the committee was developed into a CPM flow chart using systems planning. See Figure 11.2, the CPM chart of the Goals Committee. The tasks were identified and the most effective sequence was developed to complete the first two steps of the systems analysis cycle. The CPM technique was used because the tasks could be organized on a time line. The completed chart shows a logical network of the tasks and their interrelationships.

This example shows one attempt at the necessary first step in designing a developmental planning system model for the unique characteristics of a school district. Each organization should design its own model to function within its environment. Transplanted planning models run the same high rejection risk that exists with program transplants. The key factor in any model is the analytical attitude required to develop and select alternatives and to achieve a systemic perspective for the participants in the planning process.

Changing to a systems planning model requires preparation as well as the involvement of the organization's members. The potential stress of the change may be controlled by open internal and external communications for developing the model and designing a gradual implementation of one phase at a time so it can self-correct or be adjusted to mesh with the organization. It may take three to five years to design the model, develop the operational expertise, and complete the implementation. The mistake is often made of expecting completion of the total cycle of planning, implementing, and evaluating a new procedure or program in a ten-month school year. Some change actions are not given a fair chance to succeed when they are forced to occur in such a limited time frame.

The basic purpose of a systems approach and its benefit realized by investing time and effort in its development is well summarized by McManama:

> We look to a system for solutions when we are confronted with a problem which is too complex to respond to lineal analysis. When the interrelationships are complex, when the expertise of several disciplines must be combined toward the solution of a problem, when functions occur simultaneously or when feedback correction is essential, a systems approach will most likely provide the best solution and the effort expended in analyzing and designing a system will be well spent.[10]

The design and operation of a developmental planning system through broad based participation cannot eliminate mistakes, but it can efficiently and effectively organize information in a logical format so as to identify alternatives for the decision makers. The desired result is a responsive educational system that seeks solutions to the learner's needs in a changing society.

10. John McManama, *Systems Analysis for Effective School Administration* (West Nyack, N.Y.: Parker Publishing, 1971), p. 51.

12

The Human Side of Survival Planning

Planning, properly executed, serves as a basis for a healthy organization. Contrary to popular opinion, planning does not require expensive and sophisticated techniques or equipment. In fact, the most critical aspects of effective planning are the humanistic elements that relate to the planners and those individuals affected by the plan. Failure to weigh and evaluate both aspects of the human side of planning will lead to serious problems, for example: (1) inadequate and unrealistic input of information; (2) lack of real support throughout the organization, from inception to implementation and evaluation of the plan; and (3) unconscious and deliberate attempts to sabotage the effectiveness of the plan. All this can occur in an organization that is producing in every other respect.

This chapter deals with "the people" involved in planning. It draws heavily on concepts and principles from the field of management that, although universal in nature, are particularly appropriate in the field of education. Most of the pitfalls of

This chapter was written by Robert Barker, Director of Personnel and Business Services, Lincoln University, Pennsylvania, as part of the original "Survival Behavior" Seminar at the University of Delaware. Professor Barker's contribution to this book is gratefully acknowledged.

planning can be traced to "who" the planner failed to consider. While the primary objective here is to identify and expose areas where planning becomes sidetracked or bogged down; the material is deliberately presented in a prescriptive manner. The contention is that the administrators will find at least one reference to their repertoire of practices, and if honesty prevails, to real shortcomings in their approaches to planning. Hopefully, some questions will be raised that until now have been ignored, or asked and not answered. Self-analysis and self-criticism represent the best means for effective management of an organization. The ability to realistically interact with other people represents the key to effectiveness in all planning processes.

Although it is technologically expedient, there is something distasteful about the attempts of planners to "handle all variables" in one plan or model that deals with the attitudes and behavior of people. Conceptually, one is thereby misled into believing that people are merely objects on some type of game board to be set in place and moved by the planner, according to the plan. Any plan, directly or indirectly, affects someone, somewhere. Herein lies the planner's greatest pitfall; the failure to consider the systemic effects of the plan as it relates to the lives of people. There is nothing wrong with planning—the problem can always be traced to the planners. Administrators simply fail to recognize that what is really important is the planning process and not the plan itself.

DEALING WITH UNCERTAINTY

How can someone function without planning? The answer is that one cannot. It is a matter of letting the future take its course, or influencing the outcome. There is no question that planning is an effective way for administrators to deal with the future and its uncertainties. This does not mean that they control, or have to control, the future in order to be effective. All they need do is to guide its course and be prepared for predictable and unpredictable events. The closer the plan is to their immediate work situations, the greater their degree of control over the results. A teacher planning and implementing a new curriculum within the classroom will exert a maximum influence over its results, not necessarily positive. The teacher's influence over other teachers attempting the same curriculum in their respective classrooms may be, and probably is, minimal. The farther the plan is removed from planners, the less their degree of control over the outcome.

Proper timing is a crucial ingredient in good planning. Knowing when to revise and introduce a curriculum is just as important as the content of the revision. Introducing a student class schedule that calls for "open mods" and a heavy amount of "independent study" before the students are ready for it can be catastrophic, as was the case in many high schools in the early 1970s. The students lacking the academic preparation for this type of freedom, and in most cases the maturity to handle it, badly misused it. Consequently, the master plan for such scheduling was suddenly dropped and the schools returned to the more rigid and structured program. The potential benefits from the innovative curriculum were forgotten because the plan failed. Another example that relates planning control to good timing concerns the introduction of a school referendum for financing a new school building. All the research, planning, and politicking is useless if the referendum is scheduled for public approval in the middle of a local economic downturn; particularly a downturn that has a serious effect on unemployment in the area. You cannot expect people to voluntarily increase their taxes when they are out of work.

When one stops to think about it, some things can be planned and some things have to be planned for. One can plan the construction of a new school building. The type of structure, the materials to be used in its construction, and the layout of the rooms in accordance with a planned curriculum, can all be carefully planned. But it is another matter to predict such things as the availability of required staff, building materials, and certainly not last or least, the weather. It is this problem of planning *for things* that gives most individuals the greatest amount of trouble. For some people it is the reason that they avoid planning altogether.

To many people planning is an uncomfortable task—uncomfortable in the sense that they lack complete information for formulating the best plan. Of course, if they had complete information regarding the future, there would be no need for a plan. They would simply describe what is going to happen. Management theorists and practitioners have generally given up on the idea of "maximization"; reaching some optimum level of achievement, normally expressed in terms of dollar profit. Instead they have turned to a concept formulated by March and Simon known as "satisficing." Realizing that all, or perfect, information is never available, management attempts to achieve satisfactory levels of performance—high levels, but levels that are attainable. As March and Simon stated:

> Most human decision making, whether individual or organizational, is concerned with the discovery and selection of satisfactory alternatives; only in exceptional cases is it concerned with the discovery and selection of optimal alternatives. To optimize requires processes several orders of magnitude more complex than those required to satisfice. An example is the difference between searching a haystack to find the sharpest needle in it and searching the haystack to find a needle sharp enough to sew with.[1]

The best opportunities for action can slip by if administrators wait for the information they think they need to complete

1. James G. March and Herbert A. Simon, *Organizations* (New York: Wiley, 1958), p. 7.

a plan to suddenly appear. Planners who will not move ahead and refuse to act because they do not have complete information are not real planners. Furthermore, with this type of attitude toward risk, the organization will be sluggish, unmotivated, conservative, and unexciting. Most important, the educational programs will suffer.

Because there is a degree of uncertainty in achieving a goal as planned, one must be prepared to deal with the statistical concept of subjective probability. If individuals are willing to spend all that time putting a plan together, including hours of research and study, then they should be willing and able to attach a probability-of-success factor to any goal or planned result. They must ask themselves, "What is the degree of certainty that such and such will happen? Eighty-five percent? Ninety-five percent? Ninety-eight percent?" The probability-of-success factor that they use represents their best evaluation of the situation and is, therefore, a subjective probability statement. When submitting a plan to higher authority or to a committee for its consideration and action, it is essential that they qualify the proposal with their best estimate of its chances for success. There are distinct psychological advantages to forewarning all parties concerned of the inherent risk or uncertainty of attaining a goal as planned. Finally, probability statements are useful in evaluating alternative plans, or subplans within a master plan. Although Plan A may achieve its goal in one-half the time, it may represent a real longshot. But if time is crucial, an administrator may just be willing to accept such a risk and move ahead with it.

Every plan should carry a set of alternatives or subplans to accommodate predicted and unpredicted changes. How does one accommodate something if they cannot predict it? There is no real way to allow for something that was never expected to happen. A "margin of error" or "enough room to maneuver" is simply built in to accommodate the unexpected. The better a planner is, the smaller the allowed margin of error. One thing is certain about a forecast—it will usually be wrong. The same thing is true about planning; it will not be 100 percent on target. As indicated previously, people will avoid planning because of all the uncertainties. Actually, it is the fear of making a mistake that prevents many administrators from engaging in the planning process, particularly as it refers to long-range goals. They do not realize that having no plan is worse than having a plan that misses its mark. For one thing, a plan always serves as an objective tool for evaluating the past and making important adjustments for future courses of action. Also, a plan allows for adjustment as the plan unfolds, thereby preventing little mistakes from escalating into serious and very costly errors.

As a personal, psychological element, the degree of risk taking varies from individual to individual. If school executives reflect a fixation for complete accuracy in the set goals, they will limit the freedom with which people plan in their organization. They will also limit their own freedom. On the other hand, if they are willing to deal with and attempt to minimize uncertainty, an atmosphere of conscientiously creative planning can exist. Risk avoidance and the fear of making mistakes can also result in restrictive planning whereby the planner will safely plan one day or one week at a time. Extreme risk minimization usually means losing control of situations before they happen. One would simply be dealing with events as they happened on a daily basis. Consequently, cautious planners would probably spend most of their time "putting out fires."

Striving for perfection is one thing; demanding it is another matter. A negative atmosphere will prevail among personnel throughout the organization simply because of the fear of not reaching the pinnacle and making mistakes along the way. School executives will set the tone for the type and amount of planning that goes on under their span of control. Overzealousness, impatience, and unnecessary interference on their part will stifle the process. They can initiate and direct the planning process, but they must not control it. Issuing commands, setting unrealistic deadlines, and critically evaluating individual progress at every opportunity will ruin the project. Not only will the process be smoother and more effective with a minimum of executive interference, but with realistic deadlines, adjusted when necessary, tension and high pressure will be avoided. School executives should realize that the real value of planning is in the process of creating plans and not only in the results.

A PLANNING ATTITUDE

The positive belief in the value of the planning process must touch all levels of the administrative hierarchy whether line or staff. All too frequently only the top administrative positions engage in planning. And, all too frequently only their staff is involved. In management circles the distinction between line and staff is purposeful and functionally important. A line position is always directly related to the accomplishment of the organization's objectives. In a firm manufacturing a physical product, line positions are those involved in the production and sale of the product, and therefore, directly related to profit. A staff member assists line personnel in the accomplishment of their duties. As an example, the efficiency studies of the industrial engineer (staff) are conducted to assist the production superintendent (line) in doing a better job. However, actual implementation of any recommendations stemming from such a study will depend on acceptance of these recommendations by the superintendent and other manufacturing personnel. On a strictly formal organizational basis, line has the real authority while staff acts in a purely advisory role.

It follows from this that any planning that is done in the school system must involve line personnel—the superintendent, the principal, the teacher. One of the popular, yet most self-defeating approaches to planning is the assignment of the planning function to a staff planner or planning group. Totally divorced from the essential support of the principal and the teacher, plans are developed, but never implemented. They are suspiciously rejected because they are suddenly thrust upon those individuals expected to adopt them; or they are totally unrealistic, having been developed in theoretical rather than practical terms. As stated previously, for any plan to succeed it must (1) have the support and total endorsement of top administration, (2) represent the integrated effort of line and staff positions, and (3) elicit the support of relevant subordinate positions throughout the organization.

Bureaucracies, or formal organizations, can exist on rules and procedures designed to guarantee their survival from one day to the next. Anything that suggests change or looks into the future is seldom seriously considered. In many cases new plans are feared by members of the organization because of their possible effects on job routine and job security—two facets of employment that sometimes appear of equal significance for the bureaucrat. In this type of atmosphere the first and most important step in planning is never taken, namely, recognizing and supporting *the need to plan.* In such an environment the standard prologue to a discussion of the proposed plan begins and ends with the statement, "It'll never work here."

If it is true that people in general, and employees in a bureaucracy in particular, resist change, how can an organization such as the school establish a system for effective and meaningful change through planning? The answer lies in the establishment of a *planning capability.* To begin with, as just mentioned, top administrators must hold a positive belief in the value of the planning process. Take for example, the school superintendent who is an advocate of planning; his or her first task is to convince key subordinates to adopt a similar attitude and sense of commitment. There are at least four ways that this can be accomplished: (1) set the example that will teach and persuade; (2) send key personnel to in-service workshops or special training conferences; (3) fire or transfer out unqualified personnel; and (4) hire or transfer in trainable personnel, or individuals who already possess the needed qualifications.

Determining a planning capability requires a clear perception of the depth of an organization and its personnel. A positive attitude is that every individual in the organization is important. There is nothing wrong with a humanistic philosophy provided it does not prevent raising the question, "Is the person qualified to assume more responsibility and a higher position?" Without actually picking a successor for every position in the organization, an intelligent appraisal can be made of how much depth and strength exists among current personnel. Take a good hard look at the assistant principal. Is this person qualified to assume the principal's position? If not, why not?

Depth in the organization is directly related to planning continuity. A five-year plan, designed and implemented by a superintendent–planner for the first two years of the plan's existence, only to be inherited by a successor who endorses neither the plan nor the planning process, will quickly be destroyed. Without continuity, which only depth in the organization can provide, planning merely becomes a short-term exercise and ego-gratification device for the individual currently in control. Personnel turnover, particularly at higher levels in the organization can produce this type of disastrous effect. In some cases it is advisable for the planner to actually consider the length of the plan, or number of years to effectively complete it, in terms of the length of the planner's contract. On a practical level there is wisdom in setting a planning target date in accordance with one's expected length of service, provided goals can be legitimately placed within a time constraint. Such a procedure does enable the planner to personally set up and achieve specific objectives. Insofar as the continuity and life of the organization exceeds that of the planner, however, this procedure is not always in the best interest of the organization. For example, a plan that involves an evaluation and long-range study of the organization should be conducted on a continuous basis with only interim goals set on a short-term timetable. The overall plan and its evaluation should be perpetual and not cut off simply because there is a change in leadership.

An effective planning capability also depends on the right *type* of personnel in the organization, specifically individuals with the proper *traits*. Manager–planners must develop or possess the ability to think and act in terms of the logical sequencing of events. Prior to the development and popularization of such concepts as systems and critical-path analysis, good managers were already conducting mental and paper-and-pencil models for purposes of solving problems, both long and short-term. In spite of the advent of the computer, planning still calls for a mental systems analysis of the problem and possible courses of action leading to a solution.

Planning also requires an intense devotion to detail. Although "brainstorming" can be extremely successful in creating unique and innovative ideas and even the construction of an exploratory planning model, actual planning calls for methodical attention to all the possible variables that may come into play as the plan progresses. It is a long distance from the generation of the initial idea to the successful implementation of that idea. A major portion of the necessary detail deals with the systemic effects created by the plan itself, whereby the effects of one course of action must be measured, or at least considered, in terms of agents in the surrounding environment such as the school, the school district, and the community.

An obvious, yet often overlooked, criterion for effective planning is the personal trait of maturity. Maturity, in this case, is not a function of age. It is a state of mind that (1) is receptive to new ideas; (2) supplements and willingly substitutes the better ideas of others for its own; (3) promotes an enthusiastic sense of cooperation among personnel; (4) appreciates and listens attentively to another point of view; and (5) endorses the most work-

218

able plan instead of always demanding "what's best for the organization." A significant test of maturity occurs at a time of crisis. Does behavior actually generate more pressure? Does emotionalism replace logical thinking? Mental inconsistencies of this type only deepen the crisis and damage the unity of purpose that has been built up among subordinates and colleagues.

There is always the danger of the plan becoming an entity in and of itself. The phenomenon can occur at almost any stage in the planning process. In the initial stages of creation and formulation, the plan assumes the character of a "mission" or a 'pilgrimage" that the school district is destined to follow. Normally, the extent of the semireligious fervor is determined by the highest ranking school officer that is involved in the process—namely the school superintendent. In the data gathering phase of the project, if there are any data to be obtained, the plan comes alive as the data originally gathered to be used as the basis for conclusions, are substituted for and analyzed apart from the sources from which they were obtained. By placing an unquestioned faith in the validity of the instrument used for gathering the data, a questionnaire for example, the tabulations and cross tabulations quickly become divorced from the sources, the respondents.

In addition, marginal numerical differences between tabulated categories automatically become the basis for making definite and absolute distinctions in what people actually think and believe. This author had the opportunity to review the statistical summary of results derived from questionnaires used as part of a plan to study educational goals in a school district. Educational objectives that had been scored by parents, teachers, students and district personnel, were to be ranked or put on a priority basis according to their respective scores. The ranking of the top five was accomplished with numerical differences of less than one whole number between objectives. In order words, goal number one was established because it received a composite score of 34.85; while goal number two assumed its rank because it scored 34.25. One researcher proudly exclaimed, "This is where the people are telling us to put the emphasis."

It was stated earlier that long-range plans involving organizational self-evaluation should outlive the administrator in charge, in order to provide a sense of planning continuity. However, a plan that becomes totally detached from its author and generates standard operating procedures, also assumes an identity, or at least the rules and procedures do. This phenomenon is typical in a bureaucracy whereby personnel methodically and indifferently follow the prescribed patterns of behavior. The planner, the reason for the plan, and in some cases, even the goals that the plan originally set out to accomplish are forgotten. Instead, established procedures serve as criteria for current and future actions by the organization—also serving as constraints for any future planning. A very significant point is that plans and actions can be made within or outside the existing structure, as long as it is remembered that someone, sometime, established the existing structure, and it can be changed.

PARTICIPATORY PLANNING

There is some truth in the principle that any attitude or position taken by top management will affect the lower levels of the organization. However, this principle does not guarantee that management's plans will be accepted, or even implemented, by its subordinates. It was suggested earlier that the resistance to change can be overcome through the establishment of a *planning capability*. Complementary to the idea of having a sufficient number of qualified personnel throughout the organization is the recommendation that the personnel *participate* in the planning and decision-making process. In management circles this concept is referred to as "participatory management." Stated in simple terms, people better understand and are less likely to object to something they helped put together. In academic terms it means that the risk of nonacceptance is minimized when those people to be affected by the plan or decision are involved in the planning or decision-making process.

To be assured of a maximum amount of legitimate and meaningful acceptance of management decisions, the participatory program must be a conscious effort on the part of the administration. Top administrators must endorse its implementation, and follow it to its ultimate conclusion. It is not a program for the direct involvement of all personnel, all of the time. It is a program in which personnel are selected to participate because they, or the group they represent, will be directly affected by the plan or decision; and, they are capable of making a contribution to the problem at hand. The same personnel do not participate in all the projects. However, depending on the individual's need to be involved and the degree of the individual's expertise, a maximum number of employees are given the opportunity to participate. Finally, involving the right people will not only lead to a better solution, it will produce a spirit of organizational unity of purpose.

Although a popular and widely publicized concept, participatory management is not as much in use as organizations would have us believe. Just as many administrators would have us believe they maintain an "open door" policy, upon investigation it may become immediately apparent that it is an organizational policy in name only. Similarly, in participatory management, many organizations are involving certain personnel in the planning process, but not in the decision-making process. Herein lies the significant difference and the point at which effective utilization of the concept breaks down. Seeking advice and counsel from subordinates is one thing; granting them the authority to implement decisions is another matter and is something that is avoided.

The reluctance to grant or delegate authority is a human as well as an organizational problem. In the latter case, if explicit job descriptions are not drawn up and the organization is improperly staffed, delegation of authority will only make the situation worse. But given an ideal organizational set up, human reluctance to delegate can also stop the process dead in its tracks. The human reluctance to delegate can be a function of the administrator's desire to take credit for all the successes and hide all the failures; and related to this, the administrator's fear of being blamed for any mistakes or failures rightly belonging to other members of the organization. Naturally, as top administrator, he must bear the final responsibility for the delegation of authority and its results—good and bad. Even with the best staffs, managers rationalize their solo decision-making process by claiming they can get the job done faster and better by handling it themselves. They actually create the belief in their minds that subordinates cannot be counted on to make the most important decisions.

And so the participatory approach breaks down. Involved in the planning, employees are not asked to participate in the implementation of the plan. Indeed, it is hardly management's intention to allow involved personnel to actually spend the money that was budgeted for the planned program. Why not give specified personnel the authority to approve and sign all necessary purchase orders? If the plan involves a new curriculum, the teacher should help construct it, draw up the budget, and spend the money for the needed equipment and materials. Then the employee would be involved in planning, have a stake in the project, and could be held accountable for the results. This is participatory planning.

Plans that are ill-conceived and that ignore, deliberately or otherwise, members of the constituency not only run the risk of nonacceptance but actually serve as the basis for grievances or issues that must be resolved through some form of arbitration. Recent experiences have shown that students and teachers alike are demanding full consideration of their points of view. Through the years of great unrest on the school or college campus during the late 1960s and early 1970s, school administrators yielded, however reluctantly, to interference by "outsiders" in the schools' planning and decision-making processes. Because of the unfortunate violence that occurred, many schools and colleges met the demands, not because the administrators wanted to, or felt it wise, but because they had no other choice.

Since the period of violence has waned, school administrators have had the opportunity to build the planning and decision-making machinery that will prevent future confrontations. To date, however, there is little evidence that administrators have learned anything from the past. In fact, the gap between teachers and the administration becomes wider and wider. Administrators continue to hold to the same structure, with minor modifications and a brand new procedural label. Because the same people who *planned* and *decided* before are now responsible for engendering the "new curriculum" the classic example of "old wine in new bottles" applies. There are new names for old courses, or at best, new course content with students subjected to the same academic rules and regulations as before. It is the nature of the input that makes a plan workable. Therefore, it is imperative that whenever and wherever possible educational administrators consult with their constituency.

Not to be confused with participatory decision making is the process referred to as "groupthink." This is a procedure whereby the administrator responsible for making the final decisions on projects recruits, on a permanent basis, the services of a variety of individuals from within as well as outside the organization. Eventually all individuals on the "outside" team may become employed by the organization on a regular basis. In some cases the decision-making unit is simply composed of the central administrator and members of his or her immediate staff. Seeking the collective wisdom of high caliber personnel representing several fields of specialization, while not a form of participatory management, is an intelligent way for obtaining input essential to the success of any plan. However, its permanency leads to some serious pitfalls for the decision maker.

Under participatory management, the criteria for selecting personnel to participate were: they, or the group they represent will be directly affected by the plan or decision; and, they are capable of making a contribution to the problem at hand. But when establishing some form of braintrust for decision making, management only becomes concerned with the criteria for making a contribution. Psychology has shown that people of the same point of view deliberately gravitate toward each other for the sole reason of reinforcement of their point of view. Of course making decisions entirely within the administrator's immediate staff almost guarantees concurrence, especially when two or three staff members are selected from the rest because of the way they "work so well together." A perfect example of the latter case is the way in which decisions were made in the administration of President Nixon under the "groupthink" of Haldeman, Ehrlichman, Mitchell and Dean.

Irving L. Janis, professor of psychology at Yale University, describes the "groupthink" process in the following manner:

An illusion of invulnerability, shared by most or all the members, which creates excessive optimism and encourages taking extreme risks;

Collective efforts to rationalize in order to discount warnings which might lead the members to reconsider their assumptions before they recommit themselves to their past policy decisions;

An unquestioned belief in the group's inherent morality, inclining the members to ignore the ethical or moral consequences of their decisions;

Stereotyped views of rivals and enemies as too evil to warrant genuine attempts to negotiate, or as too weak and stupid to counter whatever risky attempts are made to defeat their purposes;

Direct pressure on any member who expresses strong arguments against any of the group's stereotypes, illusions or commitments, making clear that this type of dissent is contrary to what is expected of all loyal members;

Self-censorship of deviations from the apparent group consensus, reflecting each member's inclination to minimize to himself the importance of his doubts and counterarguments;

A shared illusion of unanimity concerning judgments conforming to the majority view (partly resulting from self-censorship of deviations, augmented by the false assumption that silence means consent);

The emergence of self-appointed mindguards—members who protect the group from adverse information that might shatter their shared complacency about the effectiveness and morality of their decisions.[2]

Janis summarizes his analysis by stating that "The more amiability and esprit de corps among the members of a policy-making in-group, the greater is the danger that independent critical thinking will be replaced by groupthink, which is likely to result in irrational and dehumanizing actions directed against out-groups." [3] A strong recommendation would be to carefully read and analyze the above eight points in an attempt to purge the planning decision-making process as it exists within our school or school district. What Janis is saying is true.

OVERPLANNING: A PAPER KINGDOM

According to Parkinson's law, work expands in relation to the time allotted to it. In other words, jobs that can easily be done

2. Irving Janis, *Victims of Groupthink* (Boston: Houghton Mifflin, 1972), p. 34.
3. Ibid., p. 35.

in one hour will take two hours if the employee is given two hours to complete the task. And so it is with planning; the amount of time spent in planning will depend on how much time one is willing to devote to it. Administrators tend to fall at both ends of the planning–time spectrum. Either they do not plan at all, or they spend all of their time planning, sometimes to the total exclusion of making decisions. This part of the chapter is concerned with the administrator who overplans and literally builds a paper kingdom.

One reason overplanning occurs involves the ego gratification of the planner. For some administrators a sense of power is derived from rallying personnel to one's side and preparing plans that represent a form of empire building. By the same token, some administrators become engaged in what might be termed "arrogance planning"; picking plans or parts of plans that appeal to their egos, fit their preconceived idea of what is best for the organization, and are easily understood. This last point is more significant than it might seem at first glance. Time and time again a plan will be vetoed simply because top management did not understand its merits or appreciate its real value.

Administrators become victims of overplanning without realizing it. Administrators operating under a concept of "mission planning" are so involved with the planning process that it never occurs to them to take stock of their *total effectiveness* in the organization. In such cases, an objective, self-job-analysis would show that a reallocation of time and effort is necessary. In all probability the discovery will be made that the area of personnel relations has suffered the greatest amount of neglect.

Earlier it was stated that in an organization there is always the danger of the plan becoming an entity in and of itself, with the plan assuming the character of a mission or a pilgrimage that the school or school district is *destined to follow*. In such situations overplanning is bound to occur. In fact, ego-gratification is so prevalent that the completed plan becomes a legacy that is to be left to the organization by the administrator–planner. However, the plan will outlive their terms of office only if it remains effective, and its effectiveness depends on their having successors who share their belief in planning. There is one other way for the plan to carry on in their absence—in a bureaucracy a plan can generate standard operating procedures for years to come. But when this process occurs, it is likely to be dysfunctional to the organization and, consequently of no great credit to its author. Furthermore, in such cases, as mentioned before, the author's name becomes totally detached from the plan and the procedures it has generated.

Another major cause of overplanning is the administrative failure to deal only with what is significant. In management jargon, the administrator must learn to operate under the "management-by-exception" principle, delegating run-of-the-mill, day-to-day operating chores (which includes some planning) to his subordinates. Any planning that top administration is involved in should only be of major proportions. The task or enterprise that is under investigation should be significant to the viability of the total organization. And if there is more than one plan under consideration, or a set of related plans, each plan must be of equal importance. If any single plan is less important than the others, it too should be delegated to a subordinate. This leaves top administration to create only those plans of major importance that are commensurate with their responsibility.

Another reason for the problem of overplanning is the failure to locate and research plans that have been made in the past, assessing their success or failure, and utilizing this information for any planning currently under consideration. In the first place, the discovery may occur that a plan, similar to the one proposed, is already in effect. In a large organization this is not as unlikely as it seems, since plans often fail to cross departmental lines or levels in the hierarchy. If a similar plan is currently functional, unnecessary duplication can be avoided. In the second place, if the plan has been tried before and failed, knowledge of how and why it failed can prevent making the same mistake twice. In both cases time and manpower will not be wasted.

Overplanning is also the result of creating the need for a plan, or requiring a plan, to solve every problem that arises. Ironically, plans frequently become substitutes for decision making. One plan after another is compiled with absolutely no attention given to making specific recommendations for action, no follow-through to insure action was taken, and therefore, no evaluation to measure success or failure. Designed as an academic exercise, committee reports and data analyses are neatly catalogued and filed, probably never to be used again.

Seldom considered is the cost of the planning process; and it should go without saying that the cost of a "paper kingdom" can be excessive. Just how expensive is a moot point, since few organizations have actually estimated the cost, for example, of designing and implementing a new curriculum. Relevant cost accounting procedures have only recently been accepted in educational administration and seldom applied to the planning process. Nevertheless, the expense is real, both in terms of teacher and staff time, consultant's fees, special materials, secretarial supplies, postage and travel. Estimating, in advance, the cost of a plan, or putting it another way, how much one is willing to spend on a plan, is one way of deciding whether or not the plan is worth it. It is also a way of evaluating the relative merits of several plans in a situation where choices must be made.

HUMAN RESOURCES:
A PLANNING PRIORITY

It is frequently said that social skills need to catch up with technology. Presented as a warning to society in general, the advice is very relevant to the administration of a school. Computers are the constant targets of our critical humor regarding the relationship of man and machines. The efficiency of computers and computer programs cannot be ignored. But efficiency for efficiency's sake is a poor principle to follow. The real emphasis should be placed on the efficient use of human resources. Efficiency in this case includes the mental, emotional, as well as physical aspects of human behavior. It is not meant to imply, in any way, that man be equated with the machine. Available technology and technological procedures should be selected that best complement the individual's mental and physical capacity for work.

Scientific management as introduced by Frederick Taylor in the early 1900s concentrated on routinization and specialization to achieve the "one best way" to complete a task. All elements of the job were carefully studied and outlined to establish definite standards of efficiency and to insure job-method consistency regardless of the employee involved. Raymond E. Callahan in *Education and the Cult of Efficiency* provides us with a well-documented and interesting account of the impact of scientific management in education from 1910–1930 during the peak of its popularity.[4] Callahan's book treats of educational administrators adopting and applying a method derived and designed outside the field of education to the scheduling of courses and classrooms in a school district. Because the scientific management concept overlooked the mental or emotional part of work, it eventually was modified by its proponents in industry, but not until several school districts had expended time, money, and manpower on a method that substituted the relative cost efficiency of "pupil recitation units" as the criterion for learning.

Systems analysis, a management planning tool currently in use, presents a scientific management technique with many of

---

4. Raymond E. Callahan, *Education and the Cult of Efficiency* (Chicago: University of Chicago Press, 1962).

the expected traits—routinization, specialization, and "the one best way," referred to as the Critical Path Method. The use of such planning techniques is recommended, since a scientific approach, properly used, can assist the administrator–planner in identifying, incorporating, and understanding the significant role played by human resources in the preparation of a master plan. But whether one uses Management by Objectives (MBO), Program, Evaluation, and Review Technique (PERT), or the Critical Path Method (CPM), there is a need for constant reminders that these are merely decision-making tools and should not serve as the constraint under which all other decisions are made. Because something is the next logical step according to a model, does not make it the most realistic move in view of an event that has occurred unexpectedly, or will occur as a result of taking the step. If faced with sufficient adverse reaction from a constituency, one may decide that the planning model needs to be put aside, substituting in its place a plan that is less structured and more informal in its approach. Myopic fixation on one planning method can cut off a larger view of the surrounding world.

It has been a major contention throughout this chapter that success *in the planning process* is the prerequisite to successful implementation of the plan. The ability of administrators to raise the right questions for establishing the most appropriate planning method will help avoid the pitfalls of individual self-righteousness and the groupthink syndrome.

Management Strategies with a Survival Orientation

13

Trusted Systems of Self-Management

Before people started putting so much trust in their institutions they managed to make sound decisions and feel reasonably comfortable about them. Sociologists of an earlier time looked for the "real power" in the "informal leadership structure" rather than in the institutions proper. Everyone wanted "good people" in office—meaning honest and predictable individuals—but they did not find it necessary to ascribe "leadership" to every public servant. The "change agent" concept would have been decidedly frightening. They understood responsible custodianship but still looked to themselves for bedrock security-giving decisions, including the right to decide when public services needed extending, updating, constricting, or terminating.

THE TRANSFER OF POWER

When and why the usurpation of citizenship privilege (of self-governance) occurred remains debatable because it is not completely clear whether autonomy was stolen or given away. Regardless, it was lost as the presumption of the "right to decide" shifted from the private to the public sector. The "back to the basics" movement is probably the most widely understood battle cry to reverse the source of ultimate control; however, large numbers of citizens in the "under thirty" category confuse the issue by remembering only the guarantees of the welfare state as dependable sources of personal security. A generation gap does exist but an even more important, and encouraging, fact is a pervasive distrust of authority and a tendency to selectively build new informal interdependencies.

The planning function, advocated in the previous chapter, is a double-edged sword. Plans can be made in the public arena for the purpose of reinforcing personal freedom; conversely, they can be elaborate (though often well intentioned) conspiracies to deactivate private decision making in favor of some loftier concept of "justice" or "progress." Legal assaults on suburban independence, for example, manage to "solve" social problems by putting them in larger containers. Similarly, if one school system has more real or imagined glamor than another, combine them and the "dilution effect" will spread around both the deficiencies and the merits. This is such a powerful trend at present that a countermove to shrink legal jurisdictions seems almost impossible. However, there is an encouraging new awareness of the inefficiency and corruptibility of most forms of "bigness."

Monitoring the shifting public attitude is more subtle than the often misleading public opinion poll. For example, did multiple academy awards go to the movie *One Flew Over the Cuckoo's Nest* because of Jack Nicholson's acting, or was it because of the fine documentation of the potentially devastating impact of equating normality with conformity in public service institutions, in this instance mental health?

Another barometer of a resurgent self-reliance is the paperback press. Paul and Ann Erlich in *The End of Affluence* state:

A phrase now often heard from the lips of politicians is that we must "restore faith in our leaders." We disagree. Rather than "restore faith," we must *utterly destroy the last remnants of it.* We can't afford to put faith in people who *must* present a false impression to the public. Americans must learn to have faith in themselves and to monitor the behavior of politicians continuously and with great skepticism. Independent thought and eternal vigilance must always be the price for preserving democracy. A political leader may earn a degree of trust from his or her constituents on the basis of performance—but total unquestioning *faith* in political leaders must always lead in the end to fascism. Indeed, such faith in *any* leaders—military, business, religious, scientific—will only make the next decades more perilous.[1]

HYPOTHESIZING "BALANCED POWER"

Ten years earlier a more scholarly work by Peter Blau anticipated public retaliation as the response to exploitative leadership:

> The oppressive use of power, as defined by social norms of justice, may engender active opposition to it. The unfair exercise of power tends to evoke anger and a desire to retaliate for the exploitations suffered. Serious deprivations experienced in a collective situation may produce a social surplus by giving rise to a revolutionary ideology, since such ideals make men less dependent on material rewards and thus free their energies to oppose existing powers.[2]

1. Paul Erlich and Ann H. Erlich, *The End of Affluence* (New York: Ballantine Books, Random House, 1974), pp. 145–6.
2. Peter Blau, *Exchange and Power in Social Life* (New York: John Wiley, 1964), p. xix.

Underlying this comment is not only the issue of "trust" but the equating of trust with a "balance of power" notion not unlike some of the assumptions made by foreign policy planners. This preceded the revealing Arab oil embargo which, by creating a countervailing power base, forced new trust (or nontrust) relationships throughout the industrial world. It also preceded, but not by much, the cynical proposition of B. F. Skinner that the only system of social control that can really be trusted is "beyond (concepts of) freedom and dignity." Skinner's case is that behavior should respond to whatever "environmental contingencies" are perceived as positive reinforcements. Concepts such as "freedom" are thought to be both vague and deceptive.

BACK TO SELF-POLICING

A sociological pioneer of a different breed appeared on the scene in the early 1960s when Jane Jacobs published her classic, *The Death and Life of Great American Cities*.[3] Of particular significance was her analysis of safety on the sidewalks and streets of New York. In essence she equated safety with informal and voluntary behaviors rather than the visions of urban planners or surveillance by public functionaries. Self-appointed "natural proprietors" of the streets were characterized as more potent in keeping the peace than the police; diversified high use of public areas signaled more security than hidden courtyards, sheltered play areas, and territorial fencing; and the "hired neighborhoods" of doormen, building superintendents, and nursemaids were seen as a precarious last base that could easily collapse with economic decline.

3. Jane Jacobs, *The Death and Life of Great American Cities* (New York: Vintage Books, Alfred A. Knopf and Random House, 1963).

With her faith in the "invisible hands" of the self-policing many, author Jacobs harked back to some of the original free enterprise assumptions but simultaneously updated them beyond the current overconfidence of urban planners and politicians in their drawingboard models of idealized human interactions.

THE MINIMAL STATE

Philosophy follows reality, explaining rather than projecting, rationalizing rather than regulating, and in general documenting the value underpinnings of what will later be accepted as history. The single decade separating Jacobs' work from Robert Nozick's provocative theory of the "minimal state" in *Anarchy, State and Utopia,* is really an amazingly short span of time for a brilliant minority report to receive the stabilizing backup of classical philosophy.[4]

Nozick's list of possible invisible hands models, of course, placed Jacobs' urban behavior analysis in its proper perspective as just one dimension of the problem, number eight in the following enumeration of sixteen:

1. Explanations within evolutionary theory (via random mutation, natural selection, genetic drift, and so on) of traits of organisms and populations. (James Crow and Motoo Kimura survey mathematical formulations in *An Introduction to Population Genetics Theory* [New York: Harper & Row, 1970].)

2. Explanations within ecology of the regulation of animal populations. (See Lawrence Slobodkin, *Growth and Reg-*

4. Robert Nozick, *Anarchy, State and Utopia* (New York: Basic Books, 1974).

ulation of Animal Populations [New York: Holt, Rinehart and Winston, 1966] for a survey.)

3. Thomas Schelling's explanatory model (*American Economic Review*, May 1969, pp. 488–493) showing how extreme residential segregation patterns are producible by individuals who do not desire this but want, for example, to live in neighborhoods 55 percent of whose populations is in their own group, and who switch their place of residence to achieve their goal.

4. Certain operant-conditioning explanations of various complicated patterns of behavior.

5. Richard Herrnstein's discussion of the genetic factors in a society's pattern of class stratification (*I.Q. in the Meritocracy*, Atlantic Monthly Press, 1973).

6. Discussions of how economic calculation is accomplished in markets. (See Ludwig von Mises, *Socialism*, Part II, *Human Action*. Chapters 4, 7–9.)

7. Microeconomic explanations of the effects of outside intervention in a market, and of the establishment and nature of the new equilibria.

8. Jane Jacobs' explanation of what makes some parts of cities safe in *The Death and Life of Great American Cities* (New York: Random House, 1961).

9. The Austrian theory of the trade cycle.

10. Karl Deutsch and William Madow's observation that in an organization with a large number of important decisions (which can later be evaluated for correctness) to be made among few alternatives, if large numbers of people have a chance to say which way the decision should be made, a number of persons will gain reputations as sage advisers, even if all randomly decide what advice to offer. ("Note on the Appearance of Wisdom in Large Bureaucratic Organizations," *Behavioral Science*, January 1961, pp. 72–78.)

11. The patterns arising through the operation of a modification of Frederick Frey's modification of the Peter Principle: people have risen three levels beyond their level of competence by the time their incompetence is detected.

12. Roberta Wohlstetter's explanation (*Pearl Harbor: Warning and Decision* (Stanford: University Press, 1962) contra the "conspiracy" theorists, of why the United States didn't act on the evidence it possessed indicating a Japanese attack forthcoming on Pearl Harbor.

13. That explanation of "the intellectual preeminence of the Jews" that focuses on the great number of the most intelligent male Catholics who, for centuries, had no children, in contrast to the encouragement given rabbis to marry and reproduce.

14. The theory of how public goods aren't supplied solely by individual action.

15. Armen Alchian's pointing to a different invisible hand (in our later terminology, a filter) than does Adam Smith ("Uncertainty, Evolution, and Economic Theory," *Journal of Political Economy,* 1950, pp. 211–221).

16. F. A. Hayek's explanation of how social cooperation utilizes more knowledge than any individual possesses, through people adjusting their activities on the basis of how other people's similarly adjusted activities affect their local situations and through following examples they are presented with, and thereby creates new institutional forms, general modes of a behavior, and so on (*The Constitution of Liberty,* chap. 2).[5]

THE TRUST FACTOR
IN PLANNING

Planning is a presumptive autocratic act which, when done on a governmental level, makes decisions for even the unborn. The more insecure people feel the more they compulsively attempt to stabilize something. If they rule out subservience to all-power-

5. Ibid., pp. 20–21.

ful leaders, the only remaining option is obedience to the intellect—and the result is some form of plan. The issue is, of course, *when to stop planning for others* on the assumption that personal plans contain more wisdom in critical areas of private choice than any master plan could possibly envision or absorb. The gap between essential governmental planning and millions of private survival strategies is the fascinating *territory of non-decision covered by generalized folk wisdom.* This is not faith in anarchy; rather, it recognizes a confidence-inducing *dynamic tension among a variety of forces* that creates *enough stability for private plans to succeed* more than they fail. The problem with the so-called "planned societies" is that, once destroyed, the accountability factor in folk wisdom can never be fully equaled by even the most brilliant official planners. Yet, this trade is sometimes made when public disenchantment with private processes catches up with latent plans of public authority.

The easiest way to show that individuals have not completely lost their faith in self-management is through a few examples, followed by a general categorization of some of the healthier systems of informal control. The examples now follow:

CASE ONE

Trusted Systems of Self-Management: Self-Regulation and Safety via the Citizen's Band Radio

Craig. R. Wilson
Director of Tennis Education
Houston Indoor Tennis

Breaker one nine . . . (Channel 19)

Go ahead breaker. . . .

Good buddy, you got the one Robin Hood here going up this ol' East coast. . . . What's your 10–20 (location) and destination today? Come on.

Mr. Robin, you've got the one Wildfire going by mile marker two seven and we're headed up to that ol' Sugar Town (Savannah). 10–4.

OK Wildfire, Robin Hood just went by two eight, so I'll run that front door for a while. . . .

240

You keep an eye over your shoulder for me and we'll keep modulating as we go. 10–4.

That's a big 10–4 Robin Hood. . . . We'll be 10–10 and listening in. . . . We've got the Orange Juice behind us so Wildfire will stay in the rocking chair, you stay on the front, keeping the bugs off your bumper and the Bears (police) off your . . . tail. 10–4.

How about you Juice? . . . Wildfire and me are going to put that hammer down for a while, so lay that pedal on the metal, and let's go. 10–4.

The popularization of the citizen's band radio has become an important sociological phenomenon. Effective communication among people has always been the primary reason for the success man has enjoyed when attempting to act cooperatively. The advent of the CB radio is an informal example of this and its success lies primarily on bypassing the established institutions of highway regulation. The Highway Patrol, for example, would state that highway safety is best maintained through rigid maintenance of the 55 mile an hour speed limit, and it is for this reason that they spend thousands of man hours and dollars giving tickets to those who break the institutionalized rule. It is a rule, a Smoky's absolute, that becomes for each new trooper more

habitual to enforce than anything else. Truckers in the United States have a job to do that relies on two things, one of which is speed (which the police oppose), and another which is safety. With the citizen's band radio, the trucker can accomplish both of these job prerequisites, even though they sometimes accomplish those goals, technically speaking, outside of the law.

How about you North bound ninety five. . . .

You got a north bounder here, good buddy. . . . I'm Robin leader in front of the rocking chair with Wildfire, Orange Juice, Haystack, and K. W Cowboy on the back door. 10–4.

Robin Hood, you've got a double barreled picture taker (radar) at mile marker five eight, so break it down when you get up that way. 10–4.

That is a big 10–4 good buddy. . . . We do appreciate that modulation. . . . You've got a four wheeler on the side at three eight but he is clean. . . . You have a safe trip and a good day. 10–4.

We'll do it, Robin Hood. . . . Keep running that good front door and we'll see you on the flip flop (back down the coast). 10–4.

Essentially, CB communication is an ever moving community of friends. They are people whose real name you rarely know but who operate under the philosophy of help your fellow man; for like the universal law of karma states, we often do "reap what we sow." Truckers are all living witnesses to this axiom, for with their radios, they take care of themselves by taking care of others.

The safety factor that truckers employ is not restricted to avoiding Smoky Bears and Tijuana Taxis (police). As they drive late into the night, they watch carefully for careless drivers, road obstructions, and inclement weather. They are able to know ahead of time about patches of fog that might hinder early morning driving, an icy bridge, a wreck that has tied up traffic, a trucker on the side who might need help, as well as the aversion to all truckers, Smoky, the proverbial bear. While the range of a CB radio is only about five miles, it is amazing how fast and far any news over the air will travel. Very often truckers will know hundreds of miles ahead about the most current situation. There are, in addition to the moving transmissions, periodic base stations along the way that some CBers install in their homes and prepare truckers passing through for the ever-changing environment.

Breaker one nine. . . .

Go ahead one nine. . . .
This is Diamond Jim looking for a North bounder on this ol' nine five. . . .
You got him. . . . This is the one and only Silver Bullet. 10–4.

Silver Bullet and Diamond Jim carry on for a few minutes, after which it is discovered that the Bullet is going to pass within twenty miles of a small Georgia town that has a special cigar store stocking Mr. Diamond's favorite cigar. Silver Bullet pulls to the median, gets five dollars from Jim, goes twenty miles out of his way to pick up the cigars, and leaves them in a locker at the Savannah bus station with a nickel change on top. CB communication often transcends the traditional boundaries of friendship. The most certain thing of all however, is that Silver Bullet and many others like him occupy a permanent place within the significantly growing community of trust. The truck driver is not the lonely individual with a white line as his only companion. The radio is an extension of the self, and the bonds of communication and good will form a network of safety for all. Safety through self-regulation is a reality—and it works.

Trusted Systems of Self-Management: Oystering

George Cook
High School Principal
Eastern Shore of Maryland

There is a long tradition of professional oystering in the Chesapeake Bay and with the exception of the use of gasoline engines instead of sails, the ways and means of catching oysters have not changed for two hundred years.

The gear needed by an oysterman (tonger) in order to work efficiently is very simple—no complicated equipment is needed. He needs an open boat, several pairs of tongs of different lengths, and a culling board. The oysterman leaves his port in the early winter morning, ice and weather permitting, and chooses a place in the river or bay where he has learned from long experience that oysters are likely to be found. It is an unwritten law that oystermen respect the rights of other oystermen if they are oystering in that area first. There is a story told about a young, eager oysterman who anchored so close to another oysterman that the shearing of his boat drove the other oysterman off. The oysterman that was about to be driven away got down off the workboard, hung up the pair of tongs he was using, and walked aft to his anchor line. He looked at the man who had sheared him off his patch and he said, "Cap'n, I'm about to pull my line in and take up my anchor. I'm going to cut you in half and I hope there won't be no hard feelings."

Once the oysterman has caught what he feels is an adequate day's catch he will pull up anchor and head for a buy boat or a packing house. The choice is his as to when to pull anchor except for emergencies or weather conditions. The choice to sell to a buy boat or to any of the many packing houses located all over the bay is also strictly his. The multiplicity of buyers means a fair price to the tonger since each buyer is competing with the others. A trustworthy captain of a buy boat and packing house owner generally builds up a clientele, a string of twenty or thirty boats that can be depended upon to sell their catch to him. A single packing house, for example, dominating a larger area of water and the sale outlet for a fleet of workboats, is subject to a nearly irresistible temptation—price cutting.

Oystermen usually sell to the buyer who pays the most per bushel of oysters. In the selling process the packer or captain of the buy boat lowers from the boom an iron measure, exactly one and three-tenths of a United States bushel. This measure has holes in its bottom to drain water from the wet shells of oysters as it is filled. The oysterman shovels his oysters into the bucket until it is filled and the moment that iron measure rests on the floorboards or ceiling of a workboat, a conflict of interest begins. The buyer wants as many oysters in the bucket as possible, after all, he is paying for them. The oysterman has every intention of shoveling in as few oysters as he can, he has worked all day for those oysters. The result of this tug and pull is that some tongers have acquired a high and polished state of proficiency in loading a tub. It is best to put the oysters in lightly, leaving plenty of air space between the shells. It is said that some Queen Anne's County men could shovel an iron tub full of eggs without cracking one of them.

Expert shoveling is not thought of by oystermen as being dishonest; it is simply proficient, one of the many skills needed by a successful tonger.

The oysterman is his own boss. Not everyone is happy in that condition but there are a few people everywhere who would never be happy in any other situation, and among them are oystermen. Definitely, those who like the water are fond of its freedom. Freedom is a relative matter and we are all bound by economic laws, but there are few trades freer than that of the oysterman. He owns his own boat and gear. There is no one on God's earth to say he must go out at a certain time of day or wait for the whistle before quitting. He can come in if he doesn't like the weather or stay out depending on his own wishes and his own judgements.

In his work, the oysterman is delivered from the rat's maze of uncertainty. The villains and the heroes of his story are concise; the issues are clearly cut. Either he has the courage to endure or he has not. Either he can apply accumulated knowledge intelligently in a trying task calling for will power and the desire not to be defeated, or he cannot. He knows his villains well enough. Wind, sea, tide and weather alternately defeat him and are conquered by him and both praise and blame are equally easy to apportion. When he wins, he feels a stronger sense of satisfaction than most of us ever have occasion to know. The basic lines of his contest are clean, clear and uncluttered.

What is not evident to an outsider is the almost passionate involvement by oystermen in their trade. Everything to do with oysters from tonging to marketing is, to them, a subject of most interest, even after many years on the water. They are genuinely and always interested in every possible aspect of their work, near or remote. As an illustration of the general concern among oystermen for every facet of their trade, it is interesting to note that tongers, on a voluntary basis and without pay, tong and transplant thousands of bushels of overcrowded oysters to have better growing grounds yearly.

Generally speaking, tongers realize that next year's harvest depends upon leaving behind this year's small oysters and they behave accordingly.

Independence is fostered by the job itself. A life lived mostly alone on wide stretches of water under all conditions of sea and weather creates a self-dependence impossible to those masses crammed into cities, exurbs, and suburbs. If an oysterman's motor catches fire, he cannot call the fire department. He must cope with the matter himself and it is likely to be one hell of a long swim if he doesn't. If his boat goes dead in a gale and wallows dangerously in a heavy trough, he must be able to handle the crisis or drown. If his gear breaks he mends it or loses time at work. He cannot draw new tools from the storeroom clerk. Every oysterman must develop self-reliance and determination.

Oystermen, in general, willingly help one another. This spirit extends even to pleasure craft and pleasure boatmen. Water is an unstable and frequently dangerous element where help may at any time be needed, a fact even more pressing and obvious in the case of professional oystermen who must earn their living in all weather. There is an unspoken bond created through the hardships endured and dangers overcome in a common trade, even though rivalry among individuals and groups may run high.

Generally speaking, oystermen are not law haters. They are law interpreters. If they find a law to be good and reasonable, they will abide by it, though not to a foolish extent. These men do not take easily to harsh, arbitrary, and foolishly rigorous application of the law. Above all, oystermen like one of their own to enforce the law. In the first place, oystermen distrust foreigners; that is, any man not born and bred on the eastern shore. In the second place, a shoreman, preferably one who is a resident of the same county where he works, will know the local conditions and local men. He will be in a better position to act efficiently, yet without foolish letter-of-the-law, blanket blindness.

Oystermen are the most opinionated, confident, critical, conservative, and independent group of men I have ever known. Nothing you do will entirely please them; and nothing you do will visably impress them. They may very well be the last living specimens of an almost extinct species: the independent, individual personality.

In conclusion, the oyster business is unique in scope fostering both independence and competitive spirits. The lines of communication and authority are written in the long tradition. The very nature of the trade nurtures concern for the safety and well being for fellow workers.

There are many invisible hands at work in the oyster business: ice covered creeks opened, boats pumped out, bow lines unfouled, markers put on dangerous bars, floating objects towed ashore and many others.

Compared to oystermen many city dwellers have lost the desire to be independent. It is not their fault. They are served on the one hand and actively discouraged from self-help on the other. If you find a need for some improvement in or around your home, do not try to do it yourself. You will be discouraged. Obtaining a permit is complex, ridiculous, and discouraging. Human beings, through their complex society, have lost their initiative to help themselves and consequently have lost their desire to perform their roles as invisible hands.

SELF-REGULATION PROTOTYPES

The examples just cited represent two important categories of self-governing behavior—technological (the CB radios), and occupational (the oystermen). The former is an "open" system; the latter, "closed." One is nonterritorial; the other, tied to a specific natural resource. The first is new—as new as the technology that facilitated the creation of its unique communications network; the second, very old and provincial. Many factors are involved but the most important is always the one that would collapse the community if removed. For example, without their radios, the truckers would be unlikely to sustain their present activities through occasional truck stops and telephones. Similarly, if pollution destroys the oyster, the water occupations will die along with the osprey. Both systems are therefore vulnerable to outside interference, such as legislation governing access to two-way radios or regulations opening fishing grounds to water sports or pollution-prone industries.

The most common characteristic of all forms of self-government is probably its tragic level of vulnerability to legal invasion. Another category of self-governance that represents this might be called "temporary interdependence," as illustrated by the safety and security record of camp grounds throughout the country. The technology of camping is wide ranging, covering the gap between a backpacker's pup tent and the millionaire's land yacht. It is an essentially "open" system, requiring mainly desire and mobility. Access to common facilities is devoid of social class impediments. Wealth, race, education, religion, occupation, age, sex—all of the common differentiators of status are neutralized. Yet, the temporary condition of equalized risk makes the camp ground one of the safest places on earth. People look out for each other as a survival necessity, effectively controlling all forms of interpersonal crime without police protection or managerial control. Sadly, this condition is changing rapidly due to legal prohibitions against overnight stops at highway rest sites, or open country roadsides. This seemingly logical regulation of public land use in the name of litter control, safety, and sanitation has produced police harassment of all who do not enter a formal campground where registration and service fees are accompanied by the uniform regulation of behavior.

Still another category of self-governance might be labeled as "isolated by choice." The Amish religious community is a highly visible example. Many of the same controlling characteristics also apply to other religious orders, communes, and also in some degree, to the geographical isolation of Appalachian Mountain communities. The idea here is that withdrawal from the larger community is an intentional continued separation being considered essential for the achievement of a higher objective. Once accepted, this overriding goal becomes the taproot of self-governance.

"Accidents of history" might well be a fifth category of self-governance, some types of which appear to live "within the law"; others, beyond it. The multicultural Jewish faith, an example of the former, seems capable of rising above even national identity to form a nonterritorial sense of community rarely achieved by other religious orders. The state of Israel added the territorial dimension but it was not required for the crucial trait of voluntary discipline to emerge.

Similar only in its cross-cultural discipline is the Mafia. The key factor in the shadow government of crime is the reordering of allegiances to place "family" above "state." Once done, freedom from common restraints is one result; the other is acceptance of an in-group discipline that makes no pretense about being either democratic or legal.

Thus, the Mafia and organized religion have in common a self-policing component which may or may not be legal, moral, or just. This latter point is necessary in order to avoid the mistake of assuming that self-regulation is always the preferred option. However, more errors have undoubtedly been made in the arbitrary destruction of self-governing groups (because they are politically unsuitable) than in the overacceptance of them. Nevertheless, one must eventually examine the intent and impact of any group that demands and achieves autonomy.

A final category of self-management deserves special mention, and can be placed under a heading of "life styles for sale," referring to the interdependent, compressed, and comprehensive community life in condominiums, retirement homes, and occasionally in apartment complexes. When these institutions become unsafe they are usually very dangerous indeed. However, when the intensified interdependence of the vertical community has the effect of extending self-discipline and the mutual help concept of the family, the results can be impressive. Then, security does not derive from double-locked doors, TV scanners, doormen, and lighted parking lots. People take care of each other in many different ways—even including limited nursing care, informal counseling, shared transportation, barter-type continuing education, and recreation; consequently, a price tag could never be put on it.

In summary, current living for most people is heavily dependent upon a *complex collection of basically uncoordinated subsystems of self-regulation.* In the panic created by a troubled economy, it is easy to forget the volunteer fire department, the local charities, the often silent but always potent private foundations, community services that survive only through volunteer leaders, and the stretching of family budgets to perform a banking function for the temporarily delayed generation of young job seekers. The list could continue, including of course, the endless number of commercial services that a free market rewards but refuses to mandate. Superimpose this fabric on the six categories of self-regulation presented—(1) technological, (2) occupational, (3) temporary interdependence, (4) isolated by choice, (5) accidents of history, and (6) life styles for sale—and the private side of life still looms large in relation to the public dimension. Since everyone "plays his trump cards" when threatened, it seems logical that increased self-reliance would be the long-term remedy for reducing economic casualties. The serious possibility still exists, however, that a panic-induced loss of faith in self-regulation will irreparably damage the concept of a free culture supported by institutions that know their proper limits and steadfastly stay within them.

14

Frustration with Organizational Constraints

Teachers have been criticized for their lack of initiative in the creation and implementation of change in the school. Similarly they are criticized for their refusal to accept the changes designed and implemented in their behalf by administrative experts. Teacher-initiated change, the most productive kind, is lacking in schools today. The teacher-designed innovations that do occur remain concealed and unshared by the teachers themselves, while various forms of administered change are never accepted or adopted.

This type of teacher behavior is symptomatic of an organizational deficiency. Under the present organizational setup, the teacher is placed in a subordinate relationship beneath several echelons of administrative personnel at the school, district, and state levels. Consequently, the real control of educational standards remains a centralized administrative function.

Ironically, the teacher's sphere of control at the classroom level has remained intact. Teachers, unwilling to be managed, have successfully ignored and avoided administrative intrusions into their domain. They are participating in what can best be characterized as the *silent revolution*. Herein lies the crux of the problem; although teachers are not in an organizational position of authority to initiate and implement change, they are able to block change that emanates from any other point in the system.

SEARCH FOR AN ALTERNATIVE MODEL

There may be a need to consider an alternative organizational model for the management of our schools—perhaps one that elevates the teacher to a professional status and defines the teacher's role as coequal to that of the administrator. Recognition for the basic idea to adopt a new model must go to Brubaker and Nelson in their recent book, *Creative Survival in Educational Bureaucracies*.[1]

Of central importance in the new model is the locus of control for decisions regarding curriculum and instruction.[2] The proposed model rearranges the existing structure and redefines the functional roles of teacher and administrator. It places the responsibility and the authority for curriculum and instruction in the hands of the teacher and assigns the responsibility and the authority to the administrators for such matters as fiscal control, transportation, building and grounds, and management of support personnel. There are now two distinct organizational

1. Dale L. Brubaker and Roland H. Nelson, Jr., *Creative Survival in Educational Bureaucracies* (Berkeley: Mc Cutchan Publishing Corporation, 1974).
2. A key argument in this analysis is that the responsibility for the development of curriculum and instruction belongs to the teacher. A corresponding shift in the locus of control will result in the deregulation of curriculum and instruction.

"sides of the house," academic and nonacademic. Figure 14.1 shows the basic diagram of the new model.

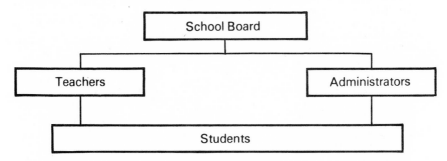

Figure 14.1. *The Brubaker–Nelson Model*

Radical theorizing of this type serves mainly to expose the degree of frustration with conventional constraints. It also provides cautious appraisals of possible break-out points. With this qualification, the examination of the Brubaker–Nelson model continues.

On a conceptual level the model calls for a real strengthening of the traditional relationships between teacher, student, and parent as "partners" in the learning process. Having the authority to function as the key agent of change in curriculum and instruction, the teacher would then presumably be directly accountable to the student and parent for what happens in the classroom.

As the organizational diagram indicates, the formal relationships between the students, teachers, administrators, and school board members are also extremely important. In order to adequately explain the nature of these relationships it would be appropriate to include at this point the analogous model of the hospital as presented by Brubaker and Nelson.

An example of reconciliation between the bureaucratic and professional models is found in public hospitals. The public hospital is dependent on the local and/or state, and/or federal governments for support, and is accountable to those governments for compliance with their rules and regulations. At the same time, the public hospital provides treatment for its patients within a model more professional than bureaucratic. The medical profession decides who can practice in the hospital, what treatments are appropriate for what patients, and the competence of their colleagues, the medical doctors. The nonprofessional staff of the hospital—nurses, technicians, and aides —are typically organized bureaucratically and are governed by professional decisions made by medical doctors.[3]

The above description requires further explanation. Under the hospital model the professionals, the doctors, are granted permission to practice in a hospital by a medical review board of that hospital. (The review board is comprised entirely of doctors). Once having received permission to practice, a doctor's performance is seldom questioned by the review board unless it is an obvious case of malpractice—legal or ethical. The doctors are protected against censure from their colleagues. There is little, if anything, that the hospital's board of directors or administration can do to prevent a doctor from continuing to practice in the hospital. Similarly, aside from actual legal judgments against doctors, there is little their patients can do to prevent them from continuing to practice in or out of the hospital. Accountability is badly needed in this system.

The same measure of accountability is needed in the organizational system of the schools. Teachers, just as doctors, need to be "responsive to their clients as far as the general results of their services, such as curing disease and maintenance of health, but their patients cannot dictate how such services will be applied to reach these general ends." [4]

A possible modification of the Brubaker and Nelson model

3. Brubaker and Nelson, *Creative Survival in Educational Bureaucracies*, p. 71.
4. Ibid., p. 72.

254

may be needed. As reflected in the organizational diagram, under the dual, coequal, organizational format, the teachers as well as the administrators report to the school board, under the condition that the board membership is composed of students, parents, teachers, and administrators. Reporting to a "board of directors" is a recommended variation from the hospital model for two reasons. First, to elevate the teacher to professional status and, at the same time, to break all formal ties with the rest of the organization would only serve to reinforce the adversary relationship that currently exists between the teachers' union and the administration. Secondly, a mechanism must exist for removing a teacher from a given school because of ineptness or unprofessional conduct—a problem that would also be dealt with by the teacher's professional peer group organization. In the creation of any organization it is important to remember that accountability without authority results in frustration, and authority without accountability is the basis for dictatorship.

Brubaker and Nelson's description of the student–parent role is inconcise. While arguing for a more autonomous and more professional role for teachers, they go on to say:

> All this does not mean that students, parents, and citizens should not actively participate in establishing the objectives of the schools. It *does* mean that the means for reaching those objectives should primarily be the concern of professionals, the teachers, otherwise teachers will continue to play their present role as bureaucratic functionaries who are in effect midwives for public reaction.[5]

It seems logical that students, parents, and citizens not only participate in establishing objectives, but that they retain an ultimate measure of control over the entire educational process.

5. Ibid., p. 73.

Admittedly, the proposed model goes one giant step beyond the system often referred to as "participatory management." Direct or indirect, formal or informal, teacher participation in educational decision making has not worked for the simple reason that it has never been considered a major responsibility by the teachers. At best it has been considered merely as an opportunity to contribute, usually in a once-a-year in-service workshop or departmental faculty meeting jammed between the end of a hectic school day and responsibilities on the athletic field or at home. Furthermore, because the teachers are not participating on a coequal status with members of the administration, they also view the process as manipulative. They merely go through the motions, and quickly lose interest in the whole "team effort." Therefore, the professional model is not merely an extension of participatory management; it is a substitute. The professional model advocates self-management and self-regulation. These are its distinctive characteristics.

School teachers have long sought true professional status in education. Unable to achieve this status within the school organization they have turned to the union to gain collective recognition. However, rather than improving their professional status, the union has contributed to their adversary relationship with school administrators as mentioned earlier. Creating the organizational mechanism for self-management, not unionism, is the first step that must be taken if teachers are to achieve the status they deserve and desire. Admittedly not all teachers are professionally prepared to assume decision-making roles. Some teachers are in the process of upgrading their knowledge and skills through a university program of professional development. Others would have to undertake such a program. Still others would be forced to leave the teaching field entirely due to a lack of training.

The current system under which teachers are managed is professionally delimited for many and perhaps even psychologically destructive for others. As in other organizations that function under the pyramid-type model, subordinate positions and their corresponding job descriptions simply are not comprehensive enough. Teachers are greatly underutilized. They are viewed by administrators as a functional part of the bureaucratic machinery designed to move students through the educational process by sorting, classifying, teaching, and testing.

Creating a position of professional status for the teacher within the proposed organizational framework could create a more positive psychological climate essential to individual professional growth. Formal educational programs would likely be demanded by teachers because of their value in upgrading teacher competence. Currently, many teachers accumulate course credit hours simply because of the correlation with salary increments. Under the proposed system, teachers could possibly move toward an enlarged sense of accountability to themselves and their clients.

Under the new model teachers are viewed as specialists, supported by an educational background and teaching experience that provides them with the necessary amount of knowledge, expertise, and competence. Placing teachers in a professional role increases the demands placed on them by students and parents. It also increases and intensifies the standards and objectives they set for themselves.

A unique reward system corresponding to the proposed model would be required to make the system work. As noted above, intrinsic rewards, i.e., job satisfaction, should increase under the positive psychological climate, inducing teachers to rise to the occasion when the responsibility for the development of curriculum and instruction is passed into their hands. In the same manner, extrinsic rewards, i.e., salary, could be directly related to their ability to satisfy teaching standards and meet educational objectives.

When this would happen is highly speculative and ultimately dependent upon examining the constraints that different environments place upon radical reorganization proposals.

COMPARATIVE CONSTRAINTS

An issue of *Education USA* presents an argument for so-called "teacher centers," not exactly the same thing as the Brubaker–Nelson plan but probably philosophically close. The purpose of the teacher centers was said to be ". . . to restore the initiative of the teacher in the learning process." [6] The full story has been reported in *Supporting the Learning Teacher*:

> Teacher centers in England, according to the preface, "are a kind of local club where teachers receive support from each other" and public funds for outside advisors. There are more than 600 centers in England, and while the movement is much newer in this country, four states already have mandated them and there are several major pilot studies under way. The book is a collection of articles and essays on teacher centers in both countries, and includes descriptions of specific centers. It concludes, however, with a prediction that most teacher centers "will die on the vine" unless the power relationships of teachers, administrators and communities can be successfully compromised.[7]

If the successful compromise of power relationships is the ultimate survival option (for "teacher centers") in the relatively supportive climate in England, it is important not to underestimate the formidable difficulties that United States tradition would magnify. The following structural comparison of the two countries for purposes of analyzing the possibilities for "open education" (the spawning ground of teacher centers) is illustrative:

6. *Education USA* 18, no. 27 (March 1, 1976): 158.
7. Marilyn Hapgood, ed., *Supporting the Learning Teacher* (New York: Agathon Press, 1976).

England

The British form of government is more centralized than ours; therefore, there is less local or community pressure on the school.

Teacher training is narrow, technical, and is continuous from preservice to inservice.

Headmasters are chosen because they have demonstrated outstanding teaching ability. They need not take any further course work to qualify.

Buildings are small, providing facilitation of communication among staff members.

Headmasters usually spend some time each day working with children.

Funds for materials are spent on art and craft supplies, manipulative materials and basic tools.

Equipment is bought for use by the whole school even though it may be housed in a particular classroom.

Most of the library books are distributed throughout the buildings and catalogs are kept in a central place so the books can be located if needed.

United States

In the United States the local school board is elected by the community and the public has easy access to state and local political figures, therefore, pressure is often placed upon the school.

Teacher training is often theoretical, broad, and does not extend beyond the preservice stage.

Principals are chosen for their ability to be managers. They must have courses in administration to qualify.

Buildings are large and some staff members may seldom see each other.

Principals almost never provide instruction for pupils.

Funds for materials are spent on audiovisual hardware, commercial curriculum systems of texts and ditto sheets.

Similar equipment is purchased for each classroom and seldom shared with any other room.

Most of the library books are kept in one room and used by the children for a limited time period.

England

In-service is almost always outside of school hours and teachers are not paid for attending. Some teachers spend the whole weekend, including Sunday, at workshops, for which there are waiting lists.

Substitute teachers are seldom hired as the headmaster fills in for the teacher.

Children begin school during the three month period in which they become five. They move from school into junior school in the same manner when they turn eight.

Many schools have mixed-age groups that span a three to four year range. Movement from one classroom in the school to another is done if deemed necessary for child or teacher adjustment.

Because of multiage grouping the child will often have the same teacher for two or three years.

Many teachers spend only an estimated ten percent to twenty percent of each day talking to the whole class.

All display on walls and bulletin boards are made by the children.

United States

In-service time is regulated by union contract. It may occur in the evenings but very seldom on weekends.

Substitutes are hired and the principal covers a classroom only in an emergency.

Children begin school in September of the year they turn five and move from one grade to another each year.

All schools separate children in grades according to age and the span is of two years. Movement from one classroom to another is almost never done.

The child has a new teacher each year.

In many United States classrooms, fifty percent to sixty percent of class time is teacher dominated.

Much of bulletin board spaces are used for teacher made or commercial exhibits.

England

The child has his own locker for outerwear but no desk of his own.

When the child has acquired the basic communication skills he begins to choose many of his own study topics.

Pupils are well behaved, courteous, and busy and appear quite happy.

Teachers and headmasters are very supportive of the child and his work. They seldom make marks on the child's papers but instead record needed corrections in their own record books to be discussed with the child later.

Instruction is in small groups or individualized or the teacher is available for consultation.

By British law, the entire school population must come together once a day for "corporate worship." It is usually a general assembly period, often carried out by the children.

United States

In most classrooms children are assigned a seat that in many cases is the same all year, unless they talk to their neighbors too often.

Only rarely are pupils allowed to choose study topics and usually these choices are bound by the theme the teacher has presented.

Teachers complain about the "behavior" problems in their classes. Children are often sitting with nothing to do or are busy at tasks that bore them.

Most teachers are not aware of how to use positive reinforcement with their students. Papers are heavily marked with red pencil, and the child must make corrections.

At least half of the instruction is with the whole group except in the area of reading.

The school rarely gathers as a body and when it does it is for a formal program of some sort.

261

England

The children seem to respect the art objects or models the teacher has displayed. They appear to take good care of materials and equipment.

A close working relationship exists between the headmaster and teachers.

The professional staff seems to be dedicated to the job of teaching and there is a feeling of commitment to the new ideas and methods.

There are no paraprofessionals except connected with food service and custodial work.

Classes often number close to forty children. Teachers are asking for class size reduction.

United States

Teachers complain that they cannot put valuable things on display because the children often break or steal them.

There seems to be a gap between United States principals and their teachers and it appears to be widening with the growth of unionism.

Very few teachers seem to have a commitment to their work and they use certain methods because they have been told to use them.

An increasing number of classes have teacher aides, some on a full time basis.

Classes are usually under thirty children. Teachers are asking for smaller classes.

The contribution of this comparative outline of educational structures in England and the United States by Judith Meyers, of the Delaware Department of Public Instruction, is gratefully acknowledged.

Three conditions are undoubtedly related to a teacher self-government, namely:

1. The distance of the central authority for curriculum decision making from the classroom (a measure of bureaucratization)
2. The presence or absence of a leadership echelon *just above the classroom level* that has a *teacher* point of view
3. The identification of open education with personnel (a spirit) as opposed to facilities (the "open space" school)—something teachers do versus something administrators do

The organizational obstacles to open education in United States schools are formidable but not beyond alteration. Item 2 above is probably the most promising breakthrough point. The teaming of teachers for purposes of planning and self-supervision continues to fail more than it succeeds, typically being defeated by "redepartmentalization" proposals. Ill-conceived team composition—with everyone having essentially the same, rather than different, talents—accounts for still more setbacks. Finally, management's perception of a loss of control destroys any remaining possibilities for teaming. It comes down to the point, ultimately, of a clash between collaborative teacher-group authority and the delegated authority of the principal. The rates of teacher turnover annually increase despite the most sincere delegations of authority, leaving the principal with a group of half-teams requiring reconstituting and retraining before anything can happen. A few years of this and the line of least resistance is to simply announce that team teaching is a failure, requiring the reinstitution of the long familiar academic department. The critical need appears to be *an organizational arrangement that can handle transient members with ease*—recruiting, indoctrinating, assigning, and evaluating rapid-turnover personnel without letting responsibility for the team's basic functions revert to the principal. Obviously, some kind of distinction needs to be made between career personnel and probationary appointments, the former being fully empowered by title, salary, and contract to perform many of the functions now associated with the principalship.

No organization can be self-correcting unless it is structured around its most stable elements. Contrary to popular opinion, the local school system is not too stable; it is rather decidedly unstable. The problem is the dislocation of power from the most stable personnel. The tenure system is illustrative. In rank order of transiency (from the most to the least transient), the profession looks like this:

1. probationary teachers
2. superintendents
3. principals
4. regular teachers (3–10 years)
5. supervisors
6. career teachers (with tenure)
7. rule structure custodians—career secretaries, financial clerks, personnel officers, etc.

Superintendents are very powerful *but only for a very short time*. Principals typically serve under two or more superintendents within the same district before they are caught up in pyramid climbing themselves. They soon learn that they will get their own way in the end if they obey superintendents' directives one at a time (rather than using their own initiative to further the intent of the new policy and thereby incur a personal obligation to it). Career teachers will sometimes claim that they have "trained" two or more principals—using the "soft" approach, of course, where "this is how we have always done it" arguments prevail. It is usually a standoff, however. In time, principals thwart teacher initiatives with their own version of school policy—meaning the stable (recurring) operations from which they acquire their own security.

Supervisors, by being out of the direct line of fire, can often be almost as long-tenured as the senior teachers (and the superintendent's secretary). The potential for long-term power can be seen in this role. Unfortunately, it is typically the result of many supervisors staying at their jobs longer than other contenders rather than because they possess the critical competencies.

But this is the needed element to build on. Supervision can be considered a special kind of program management with a long-term community commitment that also possesses critical competencies related to career teacher input to instructional policy. If this role could be properly developed, principals and superintendents could come and go and the schools could still retain enough stability to keep reasonably up-to-date. Under such conditions, updating into a significant open education trend would not be an impossible thought.

RULE STRUCTURE RECONSTRUCTION

As suggested in previous chapters, bureaucracies rely heavily upon their rule structures even more so than upon their employees. If your operation is repetitive, it makes little sense to approach each new step as if it were being taken for the first time. Programming the whole operation is much less wasteful of employee energy and the openness of the plan lets everyone know exactly what is expected of the total group. Moreover, such an arrangement is especially useful if temporary employees are involved, such as teachers who plan to contract their services for only one year. The writer is acquainted with an especially clever director of pupil personnel and guidance services who, when faced with the problem of spending a year residence to complete his doctorate, actually programmed his office operation for an entire year. He was so successful that only occasional consultation with the employees was necessary to keep the district's testing and counseling service intact and on schedule. His presence was not needed because all of the big decisions had been anticipated and made in advance. Operations personnel had only to follow the chartered time line to make their respective contributions in the proper sequence and manner.

A self-correcting curriculum is enhanced, rather than destroyed, by a judicious use of this technique. If routine operations are openly declared, then "creativity" in that area becomes the redesigning of the entire programmed service. This is a bigger and more important task than trying to alter a repetitive process by changing, one piece at a time, whatever small operation one may have temporary control over. Moreover, such changes, though brilliant in their own right, may easily make the larger machine malfunction.

The other half of the coin is, of course, to make wise decisions on what is *not* to be programmed. The goal is not to program as much as possible, but only what is optimized by this procedure. Some of the remaining tasks may approach optimization by group consensus, others by the mild conflict that goes with trying out competitive ideas simultaneously, and still others by private inspiration.

The reconstruction process in education is, thus, a matter of not making a mechanical monster out of the rule structure. And, neither is it a question of destroying as much of the rule structure as possible. The differentiation of decision making and personnel talents is the goal. If this is correctly accomplished, the organization becomes capable of "course correction" whenever the institution begins to wander off course, not after it has failed.

THE DEVELOPMENT
EXPECTANCY

Teacher autonomy requires a proper attitude toward development work in education. Indeed, it is essential if employees are to feel free to engage themselves in the updating process without waiting for specific management assignments. Teachers who constantly look to principals for reassurance still believe that "a better way" is already known and that some kind of hide and seek game is being used to test their insight and dedication. The resultant activity is wasteful of everyone's time and certainly frustrating for the teachers.

The common teacher–leader (often equated with supervision) error is to issue a general invitation for faculty creativity. At first glance, this is flattering to all and does release a certain amount of thwarted or latent inventiveness. The problem is that any organization that uses contract rules as its basis for organization magnifies "territorial" identification. The understanding is that the general invitation to creativity does *not* cross jurisdictional lines; otherwise, defense mechanisms are triggered that rapidly become more destructive than the original invitation was helpful.

The easiest way out of the dilemma is to tie official requests for development activity to specific projects—to determine the feasibility of . . ., to evaluate, to ascertain, to survey, to select, to redefine, to establish, to institute, etc. The rule is that if a teacher does not know when the assigned task is complete, then the original task plan was too general. Perpetual non-specific charges rarely produce satisfactory results compared to forthright mission assignments. Of course, the ultimate goal is to get everyone involved in defining the needed missions. As long as supervisory personnel have to invent them, only the smallest success can be claimed. Priorities are involved in task selection once the total employee group starts to contribute. Some people's nominated tasks will take precedence over others—not an easy thing to accept but it is an invaluable lesson in the management of always limited resources. Supervisors cannot arbitrarily reject anyone's serious suggestion if they intend to invite that particular employee to contribute again. A sensible response would begin with the modest assumption that the teacher *might* be right, despite the supervisor's initial wariness. This, in turn, leads to further exploration, additional hearings, perhaps experimental tryouts. ("I have some doubts about it working, but I could be wrong. Let's see what you can do with it. I'll help all I can, or just get out of your way if that's helpful.") The guideline is to give the conscientious employee the benefit of the doubt.

Finally, the development expectancy is strengthened by candidness at the outset concerning the areas of potential development that the management team has already claimed. If clearly and honestly defined, all of the remainder should be within the teachers' realm. And, this is all that most creative people need to know.

MANEUVERABILITY IN RESOURCE CONTROL

The schools do not lack money—but they do have a shortage of *uncommitted* money. The one-year budget cycle, alone, negates sensible planning for multiyear projects because so few things of great importance can be squeezed into the 180-day span. Line item and state-level accounting procedures further restrict administrative options. The federal government remains fixated with the economies of "target group" funding (notwithstanding recurring interest in consolidated block grants to states). This means, in more familiar terms, that appropriations will be earmarked for the presumed benefit of specific groups of students. The judgment of the highest and most remote political office is thus substituted for the opinions of the two lower levels of control that have the most direct knowledge of local needs and options. The end result is practically no flexibility. With everything but petty cash already committed, even the most inspired teacher eventually despairs of taking personal initiatives. It will, incidentally, never be known just how large the hidden personal subsidy of educational development is when choices have to be made between project abandonment and the use of the teacher's own funds.

The solution is noncategorical funding from the upper levels of government, especially in research and development.

If this cannot be arranged, the only remaining alternative is the use of local funds in such a manner that specified amounts of money are available to teachers virtually for the asking. The temptation to bureaucratize even small development accounts is great, with local curriculum councils soliciting and evaluating teacher-initiated project proposals almost in the same manner as the federal government does. But, this must be resisted; otherwise, the schools will have no prospect at all of being routinely updated.

WIDE-RANGE COMMUNICATIONS

"A good school can be measured by the size of its telephone bill," a knowledgeable superintendent once commented. Even before the energy crisis, this was the fastest way to communicate; now it may be the only way. Schools do, in fact, change through the imitation of their contacts. But, they do *not* typically imitate their neighbors. Neither do they take very seriously the results obtained by spending more money than they can command, or the sociological advantage of having a privileged student body to represent as well as teach. Schools are imitative of only those schools that are already similar; consequently, the points of contact are scattered and often far removed.

The open line to the larger professional community is invaluable; for some, it is truly a lifeline. The technology for communication via closed-circuit television is available but not yet utilized. Perhaps someday it will be. Likewise, universal "on request" sharing of such revealing documents as master schedules, student choice profiles, and staffing and budgeting variations would be quite feasible if computer and copy machine capabilities were tapped. All that is needed is a "communications fund" of realistic proportions.

ACCESS TO THE WORLD
OF COMMERCE

Teachers are not primarily writers or publishers, but they can, and should, try to develop some of their own teaching materials. But to expect significant authorship from teachers is quite unreasonable. Even the number of university authors is low and largely attributable to special research professorships and released-time arrangements, neither of which the public schools have taken seriously (and properly so).

Role differentiation in teaching has other dimensions from which a school can benefit. One is the constant screening, evaluation, and selection of those kinds of teaching–learning aids that can be purchased. This is no small task, requiring the creation of communications channels with the publishing industry that do not currently favor all sections of the country equally. Staying up-to-date in New England is much easier than in the South, for example, due to the concentration of commercial sales representatives there.

Self-correcting curriculum processes do not require instant responsiveness to the national market. On the other hand, no one would suggest that ignorance of the nonlocal alternatives is beneficial. Of course, knowledge of alternatives accomplishes little if access to them is lacking. It would be expensive, but a considerable gain in curricular openness can easily be achieved by making an overabundance of software available. When the visible learner options clearly supersede traditional teacher selections and prescriptions, it is only a matter of time before clever students will find ways to avoid existing obstacles, one being the lethargic or resistent teacher. Initial teacher distress typically gives way to enthusiasm as students begin to take on the updating process as one of their most personal obligations. When this

happens, the self-educating student becomes the logical extension of the self-correcting curriculum.

POWER AND CONFLICT MODEL

Thus far, the desirability, and the difficulty, of teacher autonomy
has been described as a standoff. What is advocated is not what
is practiced; consequently, the search for more useful models
must continue. One source is the academic world of colleges
and universities because of the imitative practices that result
from teacher training in this environment.

As colleges and universities are observed today in times of
grave fiscal hardship, it is clear that a *bureaucratic model* is at
work. This model of organization stresses maximum efficiency
achieved through hierarchical chains of command. The model
has systems of formal communication, formal policies and rules,
salary plans, and promotion schemes based on certain criteria.
All of these characteristics stress the structure of the institution
but provide little or no information about the human processes
and nonformal forms of power and influence that, in fact, shape
the policy decisions of the institution thereby giving a quality
of life to them.

If the bureaucratic model does not completely depict the
current scene, neither does the *community of scholars* model.
John Millet of the Ohio system described the university as a
community of scholars who work on the basis of consensus among
professionals who have legitimate authority by nature of their
competence and who are relatively free from organizational constraints. Surely this is no longer true.

Victor Baldridge's analysis of power and conflict in the university is probably closer to the truth, as he calls attention to
three characteristics of institutions:

1. *Policy Formulation*—The process of setting long-range goals and arranging basic decision-making structures

2. *Conflict Processes*—The conflicts between diverse interest groups trying to influence policy decisions

3. *Change Dynamics*—The dynamic forces that shape the campus and that can lead to change in policy formations [8]

If the university is viewed from the perspective of a *political model*, fragmentations within the university community are immediately noted. The university is composed of many interest groups, each with its own goals, values, and purposes. These groups are necessarily in conflict, each trying to achieve some advantage over the others, especially in the struggle for favorable budgetary consideration. In one sense, such conflicts are natural and employees should expect to participate in them. It is often from such conflicts that positive institutional changes occur in time. Perhaps all that could be reasonably asked is that such conflicts be kept open so that all groups have a chance to have input according to their biases—to be contestants in the full sense of the term.

Acts of power and influence go through a complex, and sometimes very private political process until policies are shaped, reshaped, and forged out of the competing claims of multiple interest groups. Figure 14.2 summarizes the components of a simple political model.

The political model has several stages that center on policy-forming processes, i.e., decisions and policies that commit the institution to major goals, strategies for goal achievement, and in general, set the long-range future of the institution. Thus, because of their great importance, policy decisions become

8. J. Victor Baldridge, *Power and Conflict in the University* (New York: Wiley, 1971), p. 3.

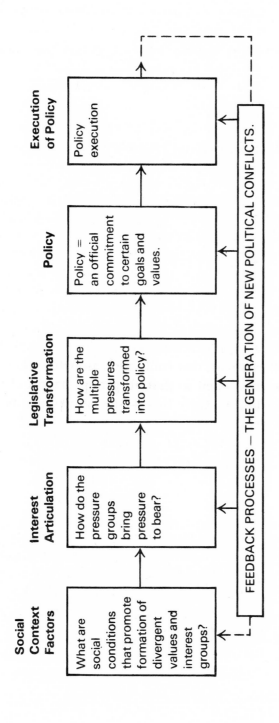

Figure 14.2. *A Simple Political Model.* Adapted from J. Victor Baldridge, *Power and Conflict in the University* (New York: John Wiley & Sons, 1971) by permission of the publisher.

sources of conflict as the special interest groups try to influence them. The political model has five characteristics:

1. *Social Contest*—Many groups with basically different styles and political interests engage in conflict. The university is a complex, pluralistic social system. The interest groups are also pressured from sources within and outside of the university.

2. *Interest Articulation*—Groups must translate their goals, values, and interests into *effective* influence on the policy formulation processes. The goal is to receive favorable action from the legislative decision-making body. How does a group exert its influence? What promises or threats can the group make? How does the group translate its goals and needs into political capital? These are the key questions.

3. *Legislative Transformation*—How do the decision makers process the pressures and conflicts brought to bear on them? Policies, of course, tend to reflect effective interest group pressure. The task of the decision makers is to translate conflict into politically feasible policy.

4. *Policy*—The decision is the end result. Conflicts have been confronted or ignored and compromises have been reached. These policy decisions set institutional actions, goals, and values.

5. *Execution of Policy*—Policies and decisions are implemented and the major losers may start a new battle and try to force a new round of interest articulation and negotiations, if it is politically sane to do so. The execution of the policy may cause reactions that generate new tensions, new vested interests, and new conflicts.

Many university components give the impression of being ineffective in this political process. They simply are not contestants in many cases. Much of the time the conflicts are unknown to the rank and file because they are private and held in academic councils or in administrative chambers.

STRUCTURAL FLAWS:
UNCERTAIN REMEDIES

Low priority programs, always vulnerable, exist on every campus. A student counseling center is a good example. Clearly, if major decisions are to be made unilaterally by the most powerful—and if a hierarchy of relative value is arbitrarily applied to the various academic programs and services—justice has no meaning apart from power theory. You are right if you win, wrong if you lose.

The flaw is structural because the democratization of participation is too difficult. Bureaucratic authority and colleague authority still exist, somewhat uncomfortably, side by side, the former winning most of the battles when funds run short. There is a missing ingredient. If bureaucratic authority belongs to administrators, and colleague authority to teachers, then student authority and trustee authority must also have a place. Together they may be labeled lay authority. Don Adams sees the trend as follows:

> As conflict between bureaucratic and colleague authority grows, what happens to the notion that schools should be controlled by the public? Increasing either bureaucratic or colleague authority will produce the potential for increased conflict between school personnel and laymen. The conflict between bureaucratic authority and colleague authority is an intrainstitutional conflict, and an important one. But an increase in *either* of these constitutes a decline of de facto trustee authority, even though a general belief in trustee authority may continue. Thus it may well be that the whole notion of authority as a public trust will become mere ritual, while the bureaucrats and the professionals contend over control of the schools. In the meantime, bureaucrats, teachers, and the public are likely to repeat the ritual of authority as public trust. It is as if both

275

the educator–bureaucrats and the teachers are asking who are the best trustees of education, with neither group seriously considering the possibility that for *some educational questions* perhaps the public is the best holder of the public trust. The failure to consider this possibility may be one of the major reasons that educational professionalism is sometimes viewed by the public as a kind of paternalism.[9]

John Dewey's faith in lay involvement was best expressed with an analogy:

The man who wears the shoe knows best that it pinches and where it pinches, even if the expert shoemaker is the best judge of how the trouble is to be remedied.[10]

The term "folk wisdom" has been used in this manuscript to say essentially the same thing. The lay person's feeling about any public institution's impact on his or her private life may be nonspecific but this does not make it less real or less legitimate. Indeed, the more that power drifts into the hands of internal management, the greater the need for an alert, always half-suspicious, clientele. Power shifts result, perhaps inevitably, in information dislocations—that is, withheld facts that might cast doubt on the credibility of the new power figures. The public could, therefore, easily become progressively ignorant of internal processes, more and more vague in the focusing of client concerns, thus fostering even more managerial arrogance, additional knowledge constrictions, more alienation, and eventually revolution or oppression.

Any large scale alternative requires taking a new look at the total decision-making system, especially the power bases that legitimatize participation. However, whether such a far-

9. Don Adams, *Schooling and Social Change in Modern America* (New York: David McKay Co., 1972), p. 236.
10. John Dewey, *The Public and Its Problems* (New York: Henry Holt, 1927), p. 127.

reaching reexamination can be internally sponsored during a period of economic unrest is uncertain.

In conclusion, almost everyone realizes the structural impediments to increasing teacher effectiveness. These blocks are somehow linked more with issues of power than matters of curriculum and instruction. Power reallocations can be proposed by outsiders but to get the holders of power to voluntarily share their privileged position with others seems close to impossible. If this is the unhappy conclusion that one is forced to accept, then the search should begin immediately for remedies within the bureaucracy rather than alternatives to it.

SECTION SIX

Survival-Focused Supervision

15

The High-Access Leadership Persuasion

Once the desirability of creating an open institution as a planned survival behavior has been assumed, the supervisor's "mission" definition becomes crucial. It makes no difference whether it is self-defined or administratively prescribed, the direction of activity should never compromise the goal of perpetual openness. And, neither should its focus be on anything less central than the curriculum.

GESTURES OF INTENT

Small, deliberate supervisory acts, designed to reveal the sanctioned adminstrative direction, are effective for releasing teacher initiative. A school district, for example, once hired a principal with uncommon vision for its new high school. Within a month of the appointment and before a single teacher had reported for work, the principal made a public announcement of two characteristics of a new "open" curriculum. First, grades of D and F would be dropped from report cards, and a simple system of A, B, C, and Incomplete would be substituted. Secondly, partial credit would be given quarterly for any conventional 36-week course, with students being allowed drop–add privileges on request. Thus, simultaneously, a 100 percent success policy was adopted, and the major rule structure impediments to personalized programming were removed.

The principal's larger plan envisioned movement toward "performance testing" but it was not necessary to say that. It was logical as one of the major options in working off Incomplete grades. The plan further anticipated new importance for student evaluation of teaching (exercised through the quarterly drop option) but the principal did not need to threaten insecure teachers with such a controversial idea. Instead, a case was based on the desirable increase in exploratory choices for students. The stage was simultaneously set for future short-term courses to crack some of the previously impervious 36-week sequences, but the necessity for making specific recommendations for any given academic discipline was deferred pending teacher involvement. Students who would have normally felt tension as a result of having to take too much in too short a time suddenly saw a badly needed safety valve in the pressure cooker. Likewise, students who wanted to explore new fields but feared failure now had a safe method of exploration. The result was solid support from parents, students, and teachers. Open education, by those two small but significant clues, was to mean more importance, more maneuverability, and less extraneous pressure for everyone. With this kind of start everything to follow had more than a fair prospect of success.

At the same time, another principal opened school with the announcement that the former principal had gone too far in the master schedule. Therefore, to "combat permissiveness" every student would be solidly scheduled with 45-minute, 36-week courses. It was called "high density" scheduling. Additionally, the principal invited community support for a schoolwide testing program designed to guarantee "accountability" in teaching. Suffice it to say, the second principal tipped off personal priorities and intentions just as surely as the first. The difference was a determination to arrest the open education trend and to do so in the name of progress.

The clues to an open education commitment are numerous; the example cited is only one possibility. The important thing is to remove as much ascribed or actual ambiguity as possible from the supervisory commitment to open education. And, the sooner the better, preferably in the supervisor's first year. The "future shock" years shorten everyone's timetables, imposing a need for earlier and more intense teacher involvement in actual program development. The luxury that no one can ever again afford is years of political shadowboxing with supervisors and administrators who have only half-hearted commitments to the democratization of access.

LIMITING THE POSSIBLE
TO THE DESIRABLE

Until recently, what was possible in educational planning was always somewhat less than what was desirable. Try as they might, the educators' practical capabilities remained less than their dreams. Sometimes the idealism in their culture led them to err in their designs on the captive student but their own impotence usually prevented effective follow-through. Educators and their innocent clients were saved by their own incompetencies, not the institutional guarantees of student rights and respect for community prerogatives.

Now, in several crucial areas the techniques and technologies of educational imposition are frightfully effective. Prescriptive teaching against the will of the learner is currently more possible than desirable. Likewise, the regulation of literacy and career tracks from ages six to sixteen is a social class determinant of such power that many educators will not even discuss it, let alone test it as a research hypothesis.

Several of the factors that have combined to increase the relative power of the educator are:

1. The general transfer of home responsibilities to public agencies of all sorts, particularly functions related to the socialization of the child

2. The nationalization of educational goals, especially those with economic implications

3. The application of information-gathering and processing technologies to the monitoring and eventual control of individual progress through the educational system

4. The emergence of a breed of educator who sees nothing wrong with the deliberate modification of someone else's behavior

5. Subtle but significant shifts in the educational power structure that have the net effect of diluting the discretionary power of the individual teacher

6. The externalization (to local schools) of testing and evaluation procedures

7. The commercialization of comprehensive curriculum packages designed to stabilize school programs, irrespective of teacher turnover—a practice sometimes referred to as "teacher proofing"

8. The conceptualization of the school as an educational "factory" to which the "systems analysis" type of management theory is alleged to be applicable

The supervisor who wishes to foster open education cannot alone reverse such powerful trends. However, much can be gained by habitually stating curriculum problems as questions of desirability. "Yes, we could do that, but should we?" The weak link in the establishment is the absence of an educational counterpart of the constitution. Few "rights" are guaranteed but bureaucratically awarded "privileges" abound. To date, the civil liberties movement has been the dominant force in strengthening the "rights" category. When the internal leadership of education takes over, many things not possible through the courts can be brought to pass. The general idea will be to give the student and his parents increasing powers of decision at critical turning points in student development. Such a trend can be thought of as "deschooling." The idea is to deliberately back off from the traditional school controls—not recklessly or totally, but thoughtfully and selectively. It is not known what would be most effective; nevertheless, it is certain that self-control cannot significantly increase until automatic adult regulations recede. In this case, we can do more for open education by doing less for establishment perpetuation. Artistry in leadership will make the retreat look like what it truly is, an advance of significant proportions.

CONTENT AS A MOVING TARGET

For too long, supervisors have divided into two camps on the question of academic content. The first group supports content for its own sake; the second, the process of learning it. Both are half right.

Content and process have always been opposite sides of the same coin and completely dependent upon each other. The supervisor's dilemma stems not from attempts to separate them but from the fact that content comes in different forms—stable, contested, and hypothetical—as noted earlier.

School tradition has made the progressively false assumption that all content is stable. The story of the speed of change is simple but profound:

1. More is known (the "knowledge explosion") but less, much less, is known *for sure.*
2. The most stable knowledge is in the form of multidisciplinary theories quite *un*representative of the traditional clusters of content that make up the public school curriculum.
3. Schools have grossly inadequate precedents and procedures for handling contested and exploratory knowledge; the time allocations required to begin working on the problem necessitate markedly shrinking the prescriptive transmission of knowledge presumed to be stable.

Thus, once again, doing less of something familiar is the only realistic approach to getting started on something better—something more relevant for purposes of increasing student access to both emerging, new knowledge and the most efficient processes for keeping it current.

For some incomprehensible reason, a number of tried and proven means of increasing access to changing academic content are not even being employed experimentally in the public schools. What are practiced are prescriptive sequences coded to career tracks, tempered by a relatively small provision for "elective" additions to the required fundamentals. Overlooked are counterparts of college courses bearing such labels as "special problems," "readings and research," "special topics," "institutes," "forums," "thesis," and "independent study." Not as completely omitted—but almost—are the familiar unstructured studio and laboratory courses. In the aggregate, these are the most widely understood approaches to legitimate new knowledge through student and teacher curiosity and initiative. Typically, this dimension of knowledge is some type of minority report. It is often personal, untested, controversial, and sometimes even false or foolish. And, the process of legitimation does not require administrative sanction in advance, or after-the-fact review. It is assumed to have instant merit as a result of the presumed rights of its authors—the directly involved teachers and students.

The fact that public school administrators and supervisors have not seen fit to trust teachers and students to this degree is obvious— even though it is a rare university that has withdrawn or corrupted such privileges. Supervisors interested in open education should find it most profitable to find out how many of their teachers have personally experienced such arrangements and might be willing to initiate a similar innovation for the benefit of their current students. The results could be strikingly successful since a degree of accidental oppression is involved in the denial of the scholars' traditional right to contribute to the knowledge they are trying to disseminate.

RANDOMNESS AND ACCESS: A DELICATE RELATIONSHIP

It should have been no surprise that the first breakthrough in open education took the form of the short-term course. The level of commitment in all disciplines to long prescribed sequences could have produced no other result, and it is still a secure start in the direction of open education.

Breaking the 36-week calendar into 9-week courses, at least in part, instantly creates many of the advantages of the quarter-system college. In fact, this has been so successful that it may not be long before some secondary schools go all the way. Re-registering students by quarters is infinitely easier than combining year-long prescriptive courses with short-term electives; consequently, there are expedient as well as theoretical reasons for moving toward this particular form of openness.

It is important to remember, however, that unlimited randomness eventually becomes self-defeating. The super highway analogy is probably still accurate. Too many on ramps and uncontrollable traffic jams defeat the purpose of swift access. The same is true of the sheer volume of voluntary travelers, all trying to go somewhere at the same time and blindly competing for space for their private purposes. The paradox of the horsepower rating of the modern car negatively correlating with the effective speed of mass travel probably has some hidden implication for the way in which schools handle the ultimate randomness of personalized learning.

For the present, the most important generalizations include the following:

1. Traditional overcommitments to content sequencing make short-term elective programming both desirable and safe.
2. Increased student choices require stable alternatives publicized well in advance. The idea of repetitive recycling of certain basic content areas is thus a positive principle. No one time span is necessarily better than another. Some things should be recycled annually; others, more frequently. Cycles within cycles are a definite possibility and should be experimented with freely.
3. Prescriptive teaching balanced with guaranteed randomness is the only way to protect the equally important goals of personal life style support and cultural continuity.
4. The randomness implied by the concept of "personalized learning"—a practice in which one is a step closer to learner independence than "individualized teaching"—requires policy safeguards beyond simply designating some courses "required" and others "elective." The principle in need of support is the right of both students and teachers to institute and pursue private purposes within institutional limits because undeclared boundaries always leave the learner (whether student or teacher) vulnerable to the whims of a nervous administration when personal activities become controversial.

288

SIMPLIFICATION AND
ACCOMPLISHMENT

Access to time—the most scarce and valuable of all resources—will always be a central concern of the educator. Yet, this concern has created a serious secondary problem of politicized master schedule allocations. The pattern has been simplicity itself—within two categories, "basic" and "enrichment," every student and each academic discipline receives the same amount. This is necessarily illogical, ignoring the uniqueness of both the disciplines of knowledge and the students who strive to master them. It is a great compromise that uniformly negates excellence.

One of the major sources of public school mediocrity is undoubtedly the unstated prohibition of student interest levels. To produce "well-rounded" individuals has long been a goal of the schools. Many have championed excellence at the same time but few have admitted that the one is often achieved at the expense of the other.

The supervisory problem is to devise a workable policy to sanction more concentration on high achievement than is now possible. Call it "total emersion," "saturation scheduling," or simply "majors," the technique means studying fewer things at any given time and doing it in as much depth as possible. The logic is sound, because of the large amount of competition that typical learners encounter when five or more adult authority figures simultaneously expect their undivided attention. A simple expedient for raising students' achievement scores would be to pick their long suit, reduce the scheduled competition with it, and then let them set their own timetables for performance demonstrations. Schools typically do just the opposite, namely, diagnose the students' primary weaknesses and prescribe remedial work under direct teacher supervision. The former technique is both popular and effective; the latter, psychologically destructive and intellectually disappointing.

Simplicity is such an obvious solution that one wonders about the extremely complex schedules, plans, and programs that tempt some supervisors. The "Stanford Flexible Modular Schedule" was a computer creation in this category. It was one of the best of its time although it never was flexible after the master schedule was finally cleared of conflicts and adopted. And, there were even more complex schemes that aimed at computer management of individualized instruction. Those who implemented such devices made one big mistake—they sought increased options and access through prescription rather than simplicity. Open access supervisors will sometimes use even the most sophisticated technology, but they will always direct their thinking toward simplicity. Much progress can be made in the human manipulation of human environments. A good test is in the form of two questions: "Can we do it ourselves?" and "Can we change our minds without spending money or asking permission?" When the questions can be answered in the affirmative, the plan is simple enough to work. Everything else being equal, this characteristic can alone increase access for both learners and teachers.

DIVERSITY WITHOUT ANARCHY

Most supervisors try to convince teachers of the merits of individuality, but they are usually not believed. The reason is that the recommendation always assumes teacher initiative will remain within the context of district policy, the decision-making power formally delegated to teachers, and a general concurrence of the community.

The fact is that bureaucratic organizations, the schools included, derive a large measure of their stability through uniform employee roles. Such job descriptions are perceived to represent a "fair" allocation of responsibility to equally paid workers. The "single salary schedule" is a part of the picture. Other factors are uniform requirements of teaching hours (classes per day), student load (a fixed teacher–student ratio), and courses of study supervised from the district office. The increasingly prevalent inclusion of these and related factors in union contracts, of course, further rigidifies an already difficult system.

Experienced supervisors also know that the authorization for their classroom intervention more often than not derives from a concern for more, not less, uniformity and compliance. The best example is the common attempt to relate individual teacher lesson plans to schoolwide and interschool "scope and sequence" outlines. Intergrade-level testing likewise tends to produce achievement norms from which deviation is considered serious enough to warrant a supervisory investigation.

The traditions and the current political pressures are wrong. The situation must somehow be reversed if teachers are to start believing the forward-looking supervisors who have tried to encourage personal creativity in the face of overwhelming odds. It begins with open and frank discussions with administrators concerning the degree of diversity in teacher behavior the administrators can personally tolerate before becoming nervous enough to intervene. A second useful step is to make it quite clear that an increase in teacher autonomy includes at least three things: (1) the right to make mistakes without administrative reprisal (having been wrong is enough of a penalty); (2) the right to become more "traditional" (even though the supervisor would prefer more openness); and (3) the right of non-participation. It is important that a "broken front" approach, voluntarily sustained, be the official policy for all activities initiated by teachers beyond their contract obligations.

Supervisors can sometimes bring about a general reduction in teacher role expectancy, both formal and informal, without having to specify and justify how the new classroom freedom will be used. Stated positively, this comes out to be the granting of authority for a desired increase in teacher autonomy. It amounts to taking some of the "laws" off of the books in recognition of the almost ludicrous fact that school rule structures have tended to be cumulative from one administration to another, thereby making practically everything potentially "illegal." This type of teacher vulnerability is little different from the vulnerability of students. Both groups have unprotected civil liberties at stake. Good faith can correct a part of the problem but a deliberate deletion of contradictory, confusing, and obsolete behavioral controls is also necessary. The proper tone of the reform movement should be in the spirit of a "Teachers Bill of Rights." It can be positive because the stabilization of personal autonomy is threatening only to those who have an improper and exaggerated concern for the prerogatives and privileges of an abstract "establishment." The best school is the one in which morale and trust is so high that teaching and administrative personnel alike honestly believe that there is no such thing as "an establishment."

TECHNOLOGIES OF INDEPENDENCE

Changing people is a largely futile effort, but it nevertheless lingers on as a goal of many supervisors. The logic of this persuasion is that the teacher *is* the curriculum; therefore, curriculum "improvement" requires teacher change. Who decides what change is needed? If the answer is typical, it will be one of the school's authority figures, rarely the teacher himself.

Supervisors who prefer to relate to their teachers in a less manipulative manner have another option. They can focus on changing, not people, but people's access to the tools of self-development. Admittedly, it is a "soft" technology that the supervisor can alter by unilateral decision, but consistency in its use for open purposes can yield very beneficial results. The simple expedients are many. For example, it makes a big difference when special funds are turned over to teachers for purposes of creating "branch library" resource centers suitable for independent and cooperative study in their respective disciplines. When reading materials are both directly accessible and varied, the uses teachers will make of them with students are likely to be responsible—and open.

Supervisors can also influence the access of teachers to the modern tools of data analysis and control. The range is from photocopy equipment to computer profiles of student progress. Things that can be monitored and studied can also be rearranged and revised. Invention starts sometimes not because it is mandated, but because it becomes technologically feasible. Most school faculties are surrounded by the tools of modern management and planning but find that they, individually, cannot even get something typed, let alone computed.

The opposite side of the technology question is the availability of technicians. Expensive? Beyond the power of the supervisor? Maybe. Yet, it is also true that the school has long been afraid to permit students to share in the operation of the business that attempts to educate them. Student apprentices are a part of the American tradition, but in only some places. Hospitals and various agriculture, trade, and industrial schools have many student apprentices. The point is not that the arts and the humanities should necessarily follow the few examples that can be drawn from the sciences—and, incidentally, one room schools—it is, rather, that such role changes are within the power of the supervisor to question if not institute. Teaching roles are not presently differentiated as they are in practically every other business (such as the medical clinic). Careful analysis of the institutions that have moved toward higher levels of interdependent specialization (role differentiation) have almost universally tied their new roles to new tools. With this in mind, the interested supervisor can readily extend this small list of examples into a long list of realistic possibilities.

Schools have command of the world's most complete collection of modern technology. They procured it for teaching purposes and thereafter parceled it out to nearly autonomous departments. They forgot that the same tools could be used across departmental lines to enhance their own internal efficiency. Supervisors can extend the planning invitations that have the power to make many teachers more effective—and they will not, in the process, have to decide how to remake the teachers who volunteer to participate. By treating teachers in the true spirit of open education, treating students the same way will appear both feasible and noncoercive.

EVALUATION WITHOUT INTIMIDATION

Evaluation, as reflected in school tradition, is an external judgment. If students are evaluated, teachers do it. If teachers are the object, supervisors, administrators, or paid reviewers evaluate them. As a general practice, it is subject to gross error because the control of purpose and procedure by target groups tends to generate suspicion, private resistance, and ultimately misinterpretation.

Self-evaluation is frequently advocated; indeed, the entire machinery of school accreditation is based upon this principle. Nevertheless, the fact that schools deal with large groups makes them particularly vulnerable to standardized testing and the norms it presumes. It is, thus, not easy for the more simple or personal evaluations—or even the "executive appraisals"—to have an equal impact. An authoritarian tradition, coupled with a large-group testing technology, could hardly yield anything else.

Open education cannot be generated through this kind of evaluation. Openness requires maximum individual control and as much compatibility as possible between the teachers' necessarily diversified purposes and the assessment methodology that is employed to determine the extent of personal achievement. This is most difficult, perhaps even impossible.

Is the answer to have no evaluation at all? This is hardly defensible. The most fashionable recent proposal has been the comprehensive accountability model, but this is faltering too.

The general facts are:

1. The schools now suffer from too much, not too little, evaluation; existing programs should be deliberately streamlined, especially those dependent upon extensive standardized testing.

2. The most effective evaluation is done once a clear school improvement "mission" has been declared and attempted; the involved parties should request evaluation when they feel it can be useful in further planning. Monitoring from higher authority levels is legitimate but should be nonobtrusive and always open.

3. Authorized evaluation should focus on specific authority delegations for the accomplishment of approved missions; in short, the persons responsible for the key controls of program quality. These persons are rarely teachers.

4. The input–output logic of the fashionable systems analysis models implies teacher blame for inadequate student achievement well beyond any possible intervention by the teacher. Such procedures are therefore inappropriate and harmful; they should be summarily discontinued.

5. Perpetual monitoring of the educational environment is desirable; however, unobtrusive methods that do not intervene in the learning process need to be invented. Few such procedures now exist.

6. Supervisors should never use teacher, student, or program evaluations for purposes of intentional behavior modification; a cooperative colleague orientation is far more conducive to effective planning than any form of intimidation, no matter how cleverly administered.

IN-SERVICE EDUCATION AND THE PLANNING PROCESS

Teacher involvement in curriculum development is usually described as in-service education. Financial provisions for this activity are meager, about a week per year being average. Proportioning these funds throughout the school year is a real dilemma for supervisors. How much is possible in less than a week? Hardly anything of a genuinely crucial nature can be considered. Thus, the question of how to give participants a sense of accomplishment remains. (Note that the *sense* of accomplishment is considered important, the real accomplishment having been acknowledged.)

One way to stay ahead of the problem is to establish committees. But, what will they be asked to do? If the answer is to "define the problems," you get one thing. If it is to "adopt a new program," a slight variation results. Either way, when the large group assembles, two things are a foregone conclusion:

1. The conference content can only be (a) informational, or (b) an invitation to participate in program implementation.

2. Regarding strategy, a sense of identification with the total school system will be balanced against a provision for direct personal involvement; ritual and conversation will be about equally important.

Alternatives to existing priorities, purposes, rule-structure prohibitions, establishment organization, authority distribution, and employee expectancy (rewards and punishments) are lacking. In practical terms, it means that master schedules cannot be rerun, budgets cannot be revised, teacher contracts cannot be reissued. The concerns of administration, finance, and law thus remain above and beyond the grasp of teachers. It is not surprising then that a ritualistic pattern emerges as the best answer for everybody.

However, the schools still require planning for curriculum updating. And, since only the slowest and least consequential changes can be imposed upon teachers, some plan of involvement that can be considered continuous must be invented. This requires a degree of staff reorganization on all levels and new agreements regarding faculty authorizations. Supervisors who initiate dialogue leading toward this end may well be more beneficial for the schools than the most elaborate in-service format. As things now stand, there is little reason to expect open education to emerge from a process that is essentially closed.

BALANCING THE BIG CONTROL LEVERS

The foregoing entry points, along with others of a similar vein, are typically used by supervisors intuitively and selectively without too much question about the disappointing results these often produce. There is a better way—one that is subject to self-discovery by trying different settings on the big "control levers" that govern the establishment. These levers can be defined differently but six labels are often used for practical purposes, namely: (1) time, (2) space, (3) technology, (4) talent, (5) authority, and (6) academic territories.

The school bureaucracy is like a giant locomotive, already in motion. Generally, repairs are made in the barn, not on the run. Only emergency adjustments are really welcome then. The machine has, at any given time, discernible speed, power, a communications system, a timetable, safety and security provisions, and a clear differentiation of authority appropriate for high-speed, operational decision making. Personnel roles are almost 100 percent implementation-oriented. Nobody in this kind of enterprise wants a "creative" brakeman—only a completely reliable one. And, even the engineer is not supposed to relocate the track.

The only realistic opportunity to "improve" our hypothetical railroad is when the model changes; meanwhile, maintenance and good human relations are assumed to be the backbone of an efficient service. The engineer has already picked a setting for the six big levers and, to him, they are comfortably balanced. A change in one, he knows from long experience, requires an adjustment in the other five. He does not necessarily fear or resist new settings, but he is fully aware of the effects of imbalance. He just wants to be sure that the full impact of any proposed alteration is understood in advance.

Applying the analogy to schools, we readily see that it fits only in part. For example, many of our teachers are, in fact, like conductors. If told be to "creative" in the name of open education, they have serious reservations about the recommendation—and, they are right. Likewise, schools have about as much reliance on external pressures for reform as railroads. The containerization of freight and the piggybacking of trucks are two inventions that have helped to revitalize railroad economics. But where did these ideas come from? And, how could the timing

298

have been so wrong as to allow major railroads to fall into re-
ceivership before high-magnitude inventions even started occurring. Teachers, like engineers, have not been led to believe
that they are being paid to propose changes involving roles other
than their own—in short, to regenerate the institution proper,
as opposed to competently or even creatively performing a given
role. For fear of meddling, inventive behavior, though not
totally curtailed, is decidedly restricted. The result is small inventions but not of the sort needed.

The analogy begins to break down when we realize that
school administrators do have the power to arrest obsolescence
(unlike the railroad engineer). Most do not choose to exercise
the privilege, but they have it nevertheless. The schools do not
have special designers waiting to update the equipment, or cost
accountants worrying about economic problems. When the
schools are in a planning stage, the principal, the superintendent,
and the supervisor—the operations team—simply change hats
and become architects, engineers, and economists. They do not
have to subvert a planning and management team; they *are* that
team.

*The message for supervision is to raise the sights of this role
from mere instructional improvement (upgrading teaching methods) to curriculum design—and, to do so in harmony with the
administration so that diversionary questions of power and
privilege are minimized.* Realistically, some of the unfortunate
realities of power explored in the first chapter of this book can
be expected to cloud the issue. The hope is, however, that a
cooperative resetting of the six big control levers of program
design can be negotiated. Only in this manner can the school
retain responsible control of its own future.

The latitude for invention is limitless and it is not the function of this chapter to try to mastermind the future. Incidentally,
neither is it the destiny of the supervisor to become an apostle
of futurism. Setting the stage for such planning, yes; controlling
the unpredictable outcome of it, no.

A few examples can be given, however, to illustrate the wide open field for invention that the open education movement invites.

1. A master-charge-type "access card" can be issued to students for selectively retrieving, without administrative impediment, such useful tools of learning as typewriters, computers, shops, and laboratories. Performance qualifications could, of course, precede the issuance of the access card, as well as meeting any other relevant criteria such as age or grade level. (Note how this idea affects the three big levers of "talent," "technology," and "authority" simultaneously, making its consideration quite impossible under conventional planning authorizations.)

2. It is possible to repackage content imitating the supermarket that has some things in king-size boxes, others in medium or small sizes, and even more in open barrels for custom orders. At present, practically everything in the educational supermarket is packaged in king sizes, making much inaccessible or inappropriate for many. (Note how this idea would affect the two levers of "academic territories" and "time," meaning that authority to change the schedule and to approach all major teaching departments on an in-service basis would be prerequisite to even entertaining the idea.)

3. Prescriptive teaching could be constricted to no more than half the available teaching–learning time in order to make room for the neglected dimensions of content that are either contested or exploratory? Conceivably, this would produce secondary schools not too different from the open-campus, quarter-system junior college. (Note: this affects all six control levers, making its consideration quite impossible except under a superintendent's personal order, one that would force him to become chief inventor to get things started.)

The planning deadlock really can be broken but the evidence to prove it is scant. The expansion mood of the sixties failed by using project money to do all new program planning above and beyond permanent budgets, thereby causing the new program to fail when funds expired. The later accountability thrust shrank everything but reconstructed nothing. The next attempt could use permanent funds to create a planning function that can last long enough to see some of the bigger and better reform possibilities become public policy. Supervisors have no mandate to take on a burden of this magnitude, but their lives might be interesting indeed if they did.

16

Programmatic Conversions for Open Access

More often than not content and subject matter are regarded as synonymous, and the two are used interchangeably throughout educational literature. In this chapter, however, a much more comprehensive meaning will be assumed for content, one approaching the more common definitions of program or curriculum.

When the limited meaning of content is accepted, it becomes easy to argue that content is what is found in textbooks, and it is precisely this point of view that has led supervisors and teachers into the nebulousness that sometimes characterizes program development. The mere availability of information does not constitute a program of learning. In a real sense, Carlyle's observation that a university is a collection of books is at best a deceptive understatement.

In the broad view, and this is the outlook we must take if

This chapter was written by Professor Donald Butcofsky for the first Survival Behavior Seminar at the University of Delaware. His contribution to this book is gratefully acknowledged.

we are sincere about open access learning, content involves at least three highly interrelated components. The first of these, and unquestionably the most important, are objectives that are value statements about learning. Objectives, rather than subject matter, give learning its identity by their anticipation and control of changes in the ways in which the learner thinks, feels, and acts.

If objectives indicate what should occur, methodology, the second component, specifies how it shall occur both quantitatively and qualitatively. Methodology is in effect a strategy for the constructive reduction of tensions that have been created in the learner by the objectives. Stated another way, methodology gives learners an operational means of overcoming the frustration of not knowing in a manner that is consistent with their needs, motivations, and capabilities.

To this point, content has been described in the abstract terminology of objectives and methods. The tripartite nature of content is completed by the learning materials or resources that add the final and necessary element of substance. From this substance is drawn the experience or the reordering of experience that was identified by the objectives and structured by the methodology. In this sense, the teachers are as much a learning resource as are also books, films, and tapes, so long as they serve as facilitators of learning.

Learning resources are as extensive as the world is wide. In *As You Like It* we find the exiled Duke aptly observing that we find ". . . tongues in trees, books in brooks, sermons in stones and good in everything." Thomas Huxley was inspired by a piece of chalk and Newton saw in the fall of an apple an explanation for the ordering of the universe.

Content then extends beyond the limiting confinement of subject matter to include objectives, methods, and materials, and it is from the latter component that we derive subject matter, which is often only of incidental worth to the learner. The constructive changes that occur in the learner's thinking, feeling, and acting are the most important outcome.

The concept of content that has been developed to this point is illustrated in Figure 16.1. The slightly overlapping circles represent the three components. Content as a balanced system is represented by the larger circle.

CONVERSION AS A RENEWAL PROCESS

That our educational enterprise has fallen on hard times is well documented, and the need for general upgrading requires little

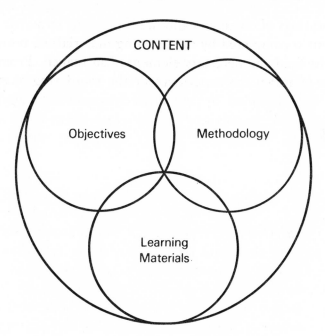

Figure 16.1. *Content as a Balanced System*

if any supportive argument. As John Gardner has pointed out, institutions as well as their individual members must carefully cultivate a capacity for self-renewal if they are to retain their vigor and purpose in an ever-changing world.[1] Obsolescence is the certain fate of those who cannot recognize the need for change or else who, in the recognition of the need, find themselves unable to act. A resolute commitment to openness offers the educational enterprise the opportunity to make and keep its function dynamic and emergent.

The essential nature of open access conversion is such that, taking the comprehensive view of content, change can be soundly and systematically affected. Open access action operates from a values matrix in recognition of the fact that learning objectives are value judgments that indicate what is of real worth to the learner. If our collective objectives in education today were to be put to the test of this single but fundamentally important criterion, the results would be catastrophic.

But open access is not a revolutionary concept that advocates total and immediate change. Conversions in the open mode will always be relative rather than absolute. What would be radical change in one situation would perhaps amount to little more than minor change in another. Variables such as attitudes and resources will influence the nature and extent of change. The matter is clearly not one of all or nothing.

OPEN PROGRAM CRITERIA

Legitimate conversions must adhere to the rubric of openness. There is no latitude here for closed-door planning sessions, rever-

1. John W. Gardner, *Self-renewal, the Individual and the Innovative Society* (New York: Harper and Row, 1964).

ence for the status quo, deference to a favored few, or for public relations gimmicks. Openness implies both honesty and sincerity. Open program development involves the following conditions:

1. Conversions should be designed to meet the needs and expectations of all learners, who are in turn given equal opportunity to participate in the planning, implementation, and evaluation of the changes that affect them.

2. Conversions should make adequate provision for building and bolstering the learning self-concept through assured success.

3. Conversions should provide multiple points of entry and exit so that learners can start and finish at levels that are consistent with their self-declared goals.

4. Conversions should provide flexible time frames for learning so that adjustments can be made for variable conditions of need, motivation, and capability.

5. Conversions should offer guidelines that enable learners to develop and maintain a style and pace of learning that is best suited to their unique goals and aptitudes.

6. Conversions should encourage open teaching as well as open learning by providing for maximum utilization of teacher knowledge and talent.

7. Conversions should be indigenous to a particular school or learning environment in recognition of local needs, resources, and attitudes.

But the intent is not to advocate openness through a closed list of criteria. Open learning by its very nature is emergent and therefore receptive to opportunities for self-renewal. A movement that issues a descriptive statement of itself in definitive terms has taken the first step into obsolescence.

OPEN ACCESS LEARNING IN OPERATION

Two programs in widely separated geographical areas offer an opportunity for the analysis of conversion in progress. Each is a wholly indigenous development that reflects the recognition of local needs, resources, and attitudes. Each has made a resolute commitment to the eradication of traditional restraints to open learning. One is The Tatnall School in Wilmington, Delaware. The other is Pope John XXIII High School in Elgin, Nebraska.

The Tatnall Nova system has discarded the traditional 36-week, 180-day school term for a unique distribution of time that provides a high degree of both horizontal and vertical planning flexibility. The year is divided horizontally into nine Novas, each of which consists of twenty-two uninterrupted teaching days. The year also includes two mini-Novas, which are short teaching terms of eight days each.

The summer session at Tatnall begins with a mini-Nova which is followed by Novas A and B, giving it a total of fifty-two teaching days. Novas C, D, and E make up the fall session, with a total of sixty-six teaching days. The winter session includes Nova F, the second mini-Nova, and Nova G, for a total of fifty-two teaching days. Finally, the year ends with Novas H and I in the spring session, with a total of forty-four teaching days, giving the full year a total of 214 teaching days. Provision is made for special event days, and the students are given all of the traditional recess periods. Seven Novas and one mini-Nova represent an academic year, with attendance required only during Novas A and G. This provision gives both students and faculty a number of options for planning an academic year.

Vertical time allotments are made in Nova units and result in an almost endless variety of combinations. A unit is equivalent to five hours of instruction distributed over one Nova or twenty-two days. A three-unit time frame, which consists of forty minutes of daily instruction, is the smallest offered and is reserved for exposure or minor courses involving no homework and for nonathletic extracurricular activities. The units increase in increments of three, with each increment resulting in an additional forty minutes of daily instruction. The 18-unit time frame is reserved for total immersion courses on campus. A 21-unit time frame is used for off-campus total immersion learning, that may take place anywhere including foreign countries. During each Nova, students are required to complete a minimum of eighteen units, with the maximum being twenty-one.

The eight-day mini-Novas function on independent schedules. Students may elect from one to seven courses, with a minimum of six and a maximum of seven units. The mini-Nova offers enrichment experiences that are not part of the basic curriculum. These range from Outward Bound activities in Vermont to field trips or on-campus activities.

Through the Nova system, Tatnall students have access to time frames that are best suited to their individual interests and aptitudes. For example, an above average student can complete a full year of mathematics in just two Novas of six units each. Similar adjustments can be made for those whose rates or styles of learning require more time or different instructional approaches. Dead time has been practically eliminated from the school day. Study halls have been eliminated, and unstructured time occurs only as its need is indicated. As a result, students spend ten percent more time in class, not including the additional 150 to 195 hours that are available during the school year for enrichment activities. They also have the option of attending classes on a twelve month basis if they so desire, or they can design a seven-Nova year around the two required Novas. Extended absences can also be made up more conveniently, and there is an option for retaking only a portion of a Nova.

Better use has been made of both space and equipment because of their continuous utilization in a twelve-month year along with the fact that fewer courses are in operation at any given time. The effect of this dispersion has been reflected in a substantial increase in course offerings without any increase in the size of the faculty. Greater use has also been made of part-time faculty who bring new expertise from regional business and industry.

One headmaster expressed the spirit of the Nova: "The ideal of education is to help each student make maximum use of his potential. To accomplish this, courses and schedules should be developed around the needs of students—but there are obvious difficulties. Students learn at differing rates of speed; some courses cover more complicated materials than others; some students absorb new ideas quickly, while others, who may learn as much in the end, need more time to do so. A course ought to last as long as it takes for a particular group of students to acquire what they need."

While the variable time frame is perhaps the most visible aspect of the Nova, its effect goes far beyond the mere scheduling of classes. More important are the fundamental changes that it has effected in the total instructional program at Tatnall, particularly with respect to the unique learning needs of the individual student. Most scheduling changes are nominal with the only apparent outcome being that of administrative convenience. The nova has facilitated a legitimate content conversion that should receive the most serious consideration of those who earnestly search for means to revitalize the process of education.

The program at Pope John XXIII High School has been developing on a somewhat more limited scale than that at Tatnall. This content conversion in science and mathematics was implemented through a design team composed of students, faculty, and administrators who did their preliminary planning during a one-week suspension of classes at the beginning of the school year.

As proposed changes took form, nearly all mathematics students were placed in independent study. Scheduled small group meetings were held twice weekly along with subsequent small group meetings that were essentially individualized laboratory periods. The nature and extent of the laboratory meetings were principally determined by the students with faculty guidance when it was needed or requested. Problem solutions were made available for immediate feedback on progress, while weekly quizzes and periodic evaluation of notebooks provided data on individual progress. Student interaction was developed through informal, small group discussion with an instructor or an advanced student available for consultation.

Two open access courses became fully active, one in algebra–trigonometry and the other in physical science. LAP's (learning activity packages) were developed to guide students through a basic text. Each LAP offered the student a set of behavioral objectives: a pre-test; an outline of content, skills, and concepts to be developed; references to available resources; specifications for assigned and optional learning experiences; self-tests; and quest activities suggesting areas of enrichment, depth development, or related study. Each student moved through the LAP at the pace best suited to individual need and rate of learning. When the students were ready, they scheduled individual examinations with an instructor. Credit was granted when the work was completed at an acceptable performance level.

Students who finish their LAP's early are permitted to select additional enrichment activities, begin the next course, or terminate study for the year. A student who does not complete a designated program within the school year is given partial credit and is allowed to complete the program during the following year.

Variations of these techniques appeared eventually in all six mathematics courses and all seven science courses. A geology course was made up of selected instructional modules, each designed for one week and supported by a wide variety of learning materials, with tests administered at the end of each weekly module. Students in Harvard Project Physics and Math IV opted traditional instruction with a higher degree of teacher control.

Perhaps the most significant feature of the Pope John program is its development of the LAP as a means of implementing content conversion within a conventional class schedule and within only a part of the total curriculum. The LAP can be integrated into almost any learning program with minimal risk. It can, if caution is the watchword, be introduced on a limited basis by one teacher in a single class. Even such a modest start could pave the way for more comprehensive change over a period of time. As was noted previously, open access is not an all or nothing proposition.

CONSERVATIVE CONVERSION STRATEGIES

Resistance to change is part of the human condition, and large scale content conversion is advisable only under the most favorable conditions conducive to almost total student and faculty support. Anything less than that introduces a risk factor that does not argue well for success at the very outset of the program. The Pope John conversion demonstrates due regard for this factor.

The learning activity package has already been cited as a conservative means of implementing content conversion. Mastery learning and contract learning are two additional strategies that function on a minimal risk basis. Like the LAP, neither requires the sudden or extensive change that is threatening to the student or the teacher.

Mastery learning functions with many of the basic assumptions of open access learning, and its application carries with it many of the features of the learning activity package. Mastery learning, as sometimes described, is both a philosophy about schooling and an associated set of instructional strategies whereby the philosophy can be implemented in the classroom. This philosophy asserts that under appropriate instructional conditions virtually all students can and will learn most of what they are taught.

Mastery learning can take place in a group as well as on an individual basis. In either case, individualized learning is the primary goal, and it is achieved through immediate corrective procedures for learning difficulties when and where they occur, and through the implementation of objectives that clearly identify areas of learning along with levels of expectation. With these conditions, the teacher assumes the competence to guarantee success for each student.

Based on the Bloom working model that discards the notion that there need be a high correlation between achievement and aptitude, mastery learning seeks to equalize the opportunity for achievement through adjustments in instruction. These adjustments compensate for differences in aptitude or rate of learning within a given time frame. Consequently, the number of students who attain the mastery level will be significantly in excess of that which is statistically predictable through the self-fulfilling prophecy of the normal curve. Stated yet another way, through mastery learning, all or nearly all the students in a given class can meet the performance criteria for a final grade of A. This, in fact, has to be the assumption at the outset.

In planning for mastery learning, teachers first need to determine what is meant by mastery in the course they are teaching. When this has been adequately defined, course objectives are developed as a means of giving identity to the desired learning. Next, with the objectives clearly in mind, the teacher develops a final examination that encompasses all the important achievement criteria. This instrument will determine the extent to which each student has achieved mastery by the end of the course. If the whole plan is well executed, the final evaluation should reveal an extremely high number of students who are functioning at or above the previously determined mastery level.

The next step in the procedure divides the course content into a sequence of related learning units that could take the form of learning activity packages. Feedback-corrective procedures are developed for each unit, and these represent the most important components of the mastery learning strategy. It is through them that the teacher is able to monitor instructional effectiveness so that it can be supplemented or modified to meet the unique needs of the individual learner.

The corrective-feedback component is an ungraded diagnostic-progress test that is used to obtain a prescriptive evaluation of learner needs at the conclusion of each unit. And for each item in this test, assuming a very high degree of test validity, the teacher provides alternative learning modes or corrective activities that teach the identified material in new or different ways. Preliminary practice in the use of unit correctives should be offered at the beginning of the course so that students will know how to use them later on.

The first unit is taught according to the teacher's usual method for group-based learning, and when it is completed the first diagnostic progress test is administered to determine how many of the students have achieved unit mastery. Those who have scored below the criterion level are then referred to the specific correctives that have been identified through item analysis of the test. Students who undertake corrective work are expected to do so on their own time but with as much individual encouragement and help as the teacher can give them. Often students who have attained the mastery level can be helpful to those who have not. This cycle is repeated with each unit until the course has been completed.

On the basis of a fairly large body of research, it appears that mastery learning is superior to conventional group-based learning both in the amount learned and in the development and maintenance of a positive self-concept in the learner. Among its many apparent values, it also gives teachers an evaluation of their effectiveness in the planning and implementation of learning in the classroom.

The most flexible conversion strategy developing individualized content is the teacher–student contract. These contracts are documents that establish specifications with respect to objectives, working conditions, methods of working, learning activities, provisions for the application or demonstration of learning, and terminal evaluation procedures within a given time frame. They are entirely custom designed for the individual learner, and their effect is to place the student in learning conditions that are most favorable for success.

Authorities have noted that contracting as a mode of instruction is not a total replacement of conventional teaching. Teachers, by subjective trial and error, should select which portion of the knowledge and skills will be most effectively taught through contracting. Diagnostic efforts with cumulative folders, preliminary observations, and testing will indicate where pupils are. There is no shortage of information as to the logical sequence of knowledge and skill development. Teachers are equipped to make judgments as to what is psychologically appropriate for the age level of students entrusted to them.

In the initiation of a contract system within a class it is usually better for the teacher to assume the major portion of the responsibility for the development of learning specifications. Then as familiarity with the procedure develops, increasingly more responsibility can be shifted over to the individual student.

Most assignments that are made in teaching are in reality implied contracts. The shift to written sets of learning specifications is only a matter of refinement and individualization in explicit terms. The contract gives learning a sharper focus, a more pointed direction, and identifies the learning mode that will be most profitable for the student.

The performance specifications can and usually do vary considerably from student to student. However, with few exceptions, short contracts of a week or less seem to work better. The short contract is not overwhelming in its demands and at the same time it tends to discourage procrastination. But the duration is a matter for negotiation based on the teacher's knowledge of the students and the students' knowledge of themselves. The overriding consideration in contract development is that of establishing the most favorable learning conditions for the individual student. Contracts can be sequential or one-time enrichment or reinforcement experiences. Their possibilities are limitless in the hands of a capable and imaginative teacher.

While the learning activity package, mastery learning, and contract learning have been discussed primarily as relatively discrete strategies, it is relatively apparent that there are striking similarities among them. It is also apparent that the best features of each can be synthesized into alternative strategies that can greatly extend the possibilities for learning flexibility.

INNOVATING THE SHORT-TERM ELECTIVE

In recent years the short-term elective course has been making steady inroads into the 180-day content blocks of the traditional curriculum. This has been particularly true in English and social studies, in which conversions of this type have been a matter of long-standing necessity. Actually, semester length courses have been part of the educational scene for a long time, but for the most part they managed to retain the prescriptive and stifling characteristics of their longer counterparts.

The evolving short-term elective has a duration that ranges from a week or less to a full semester, with an average of about nine weeks. These courses differ so widely in purpose and content that it is difficult to offer a generalized description of them. Some are offered for credit, some are not; some are taught by regular faculty, others are taught by teachers who are drawn from a diversity of professions and occupations within the community. In some cases, students themselves serve as instructors. What they do have in common is that they are a direct outgrowth of student interest and planning and that they frequently open hitherto inaccessible areas of knowledge and skills.

One aspect of this trend has been the "free choice English curriculum" that has all but done away with regular English courses in a growing number of schools. In the free choice curriculum, students are offered a wide variety of learning units that are usually either nine or eighteen weeks in length. The content of these units is developed through student–teacher cooperative planning.

Selection of units is often made through a catalog that contains perhaps dozens of offerings. As a rule, brief descriptions of the units are included along with a listing of major areas or works to be covered. Some schools group the units into lower and upper divisions to accommodate prerequisites, to reduce the risk of haphazard selection, and to make the problem of scheduling more manageable. While thematic and topical literature offerings are usually dominant, a substructure of essentials for communication skills is built into the well-designed program. Such essentials are either identified as a major part of the unit or else they are taught incidentally as the need for them occurs. Consequently, the basic skill areas of reading, writing, speaking, and listening are never neglected or left to chance.

The free elective system completely eliminates any need for ability or achievement grouping since the students group themselves by election. It also offers each student a wide variety of educational experiences through which he or she can round out a highly personalized sequence of as many as sixteen elective units over a four-year period.

Unit courses are appearing in increasing numbers in the social studies also. It has been reported that 28 percent of the secondary schools in Kansas are offering short-term electives such as "Doves and Hawks," "A Nation Is Torn," "Making Your First Million," and "Rise of the City" among others.

Every area of human knowledge or skill can provide content for the minicourse. They can deal with the arcane or the practical affairs of everyday life, and they can be taught by a diversity of people from all walks of life. They are by no means restricted to a formal school setting.

HIGHER EDUCATION AS PACESETTER

Over the years, higher education has been more responsive to the need for change than the public grammar and high schools. But in fairness it must be said that colleges and universities serve constituencies that differ greatly in their composition and demands. Higher education has enjoyed relative freedom from the public scrutiny and blame that is the constant concern of public school officials and teachers. Also, higher education has had to a much greater extent the advantage of human and material resources that are the necessary ingredients for adjustment and change. But even so, some of the more recent innovations in higher education have been mostly products of student unrest rather than administrative foresight.

New York State has been developing a partnership between high schools and colleges that has resulted in the "seven year sequence." Some centers are working with a four-year-of-high-school, three-years-of-college program, while others are developing three–four programs. A three–one–three program is also being tested, having a middle transitional year between high school and college. The college segments will operate through learning centers that have been established throughout the state.

The open university, a concept that began in England in 1969, is yet another form of higher education that operates without a campus. It reaches out to its students through radio, television, tapes, learning packages, and localized discussion groups. It is a technologically updated extension of the long-established practice of correspondence learning, and it has enormous potential for opening higher education opportunities to a widely scattered clientele.

Integrated learning semesters, with their interdisciplinary approach, are becoming a common feature in higher education. As opposed to juggling five different courses at once, this approach opens the opportunity for in-depth inquiry based on a single theme. The University of Delaware ILS is based on two seven-week blocks per semester.

Free universities, which usually operate on the fringe of conventional institutions, offer learning opportunities that embrace almost every imaginable aspect of human experience. All that is required is an instructor with the needed expertise and a few interested students, and a content is developed around that interest whether it is belly dancing or small-appliance repair. Instructional meetings can take place anywhere, at any time, and under whatever conditions seem most appropriate.

SUMMARY: TOWARD OPTIMAL ACCESS

Subject matter is not and cannot be the substance of education at any level. Questions such as: "What subject do you teach?"

319

or "What subject are you taking?" reveal the shallow concept of learning that often characterizes our thinking—or not thinking—about the truly worthwhile aims and outcomes of education.

There is, to be sure, nothing wrong with the term "subject matter" as an expression that generally describes an area of knowledge. But there is much more to the business of learning than subject matter per se regardless of how hard one tries to make it legitimate with courses of study, syllabi, and prescriptive guides of various kinds.

It is probably disconcerting for many instructional specialists to admit that it takes only small degrees of overenchantment with the structures of knowledge to reduce the survival potential of a school program for some students. Content, as a concept in program design, has connotations of permanence. It is, therefore, associated with the educational universals that the general public knows as the "basics"—that is, things that are so good that they must be good for everyone.

Programming that grows out of this conviction necessarily becomes prescriptive. Rigidity has never had positive meanings for educators but this has nevertheless become the most common residue of prescriptive teaching. In extreme cases, students frustrate everyone by forgetting the basics but remembering forever the abrasive features of an overstructured school.

One of the perennial alternatives to overstructuring is to place more emphasis on process than outcome. The process-centered school, thus created, is itself one step behind a more recent emphasis on student performance, the most widespread examples involving state-level prescribed minimum standards for high school graduation. This remedy is rigid in its uniformity but flexible in that the performance test can sometimes be separated from the teaching act, thereby becoming an alternative to structured schooling.

The most radical conversion models for traditional content-centered schooling focus on life-style options for both students and teachers. Theoretically, process, performance, and content can all be subordinated to the relatively stable value systems that undergird alternative life-styles. If resources and people can be regrouped (scheduled) to genuinely reflect various life-styles, then one might expect a new level of authenticity in schooling as well as the flexibility required for a high survival factor. Meanwhile, a powerful inertia continues to focus the attention of educators on the most traditional of all program components, academic content. From this vantage point, the invention of conversion options may fall far short of a dramatic remedy but still be a justifiable means for school improvement.

17

High-Power Supervisory Strategies

Supervisory strategy is very personal. What works well for one person can easily cause another's failure. However, the problem is not totally relative. Authenticity and predictability in human relations are universally successful approaches. They have always been important but are more so when the intent is to induce openness in individual thinking, hopefully followed by a group generation of open curriculum models.

Traditional supervisory strategies are hardly relevant at all to present needs. They were orginally derived from a different set of assumptions to meet equally different conditions, and those conditions are not likely to ever return again. The first of the classical assumptions was that supervision meant "supervision *of instruction*"—that is, influence on the teaching act within a given classroom. This *excluded* questions now identified with the word "curriculum." Instruction was a *methodological* proposition; curriculum, a matter of program design (and, incidentally, an administrative rather than a supervisory prerogative). Hence, classroom visitation and demonstration teaching became the operational model.

The target was typically the beginning, isolated, or troubled teacher. All others were virtually exempted—and, for a very good reason: the teacher–supervisor ratio was so high that there were not enough supervisors to oversee each teacher. If, for example, one supervisor was responsible for 360 teachers but the school year was only 180 days long, the supervisor had to choose between the total exclusion of some teachers or conduct extremely superficial, multiple visits within a given day. Group supervision, incorporating group teaching demonstrations, was to evolve out of this dilemma but it would never entirely replace the classroom visit.

One can only conclude that other largely hidden functions were being performed. It is rarely admitted, but nevertheless true, that supervisors have always been a part of management's "authoritative presence"—the school's counterpart of the ever present uniformed police who serve more as a symbol of community safety than as actual crime suppressants. One can, however, argue that the police do some good even if no arrests are made and that supervisors are likewise "helpful" even if they only provide social contact for the teacher. Consider the lonely role of the young, transient teacher and a strong case can be made for nonpurposive supervision in education.

Another now obsolete supervisory assumption about strategy has to do with the speed of change. Many supervisors, even now, build their careers around yearly "themes" for inservice education programs. One year it may be reading; the next, science; and the year after, the arts. Thus, a given discipline or skill area might come up for serious development as infrequently as once in a decade. Of course, the thematic model is sometimes used to cut across disciplines and grade levels, as in the case of topics like "behavioral objectives," "humanizing the curriculum," etc. Even so, the presumed obsolescence rate is far from the actual. The schools do not yet have a "throwaway" curriculum, but sometimes the curriculums seem to approach this concept. An accurate assumption would be that every major program component now requires a review and some updating each year. Consequently, the supervisor's in-service calendar can no longer suffice as the controlling model for reform. The reform movement proper will have to be more diffused but the supervisor is needed to set the concept in motion.

Having previously questioned the process known as in-service education, or staff development, it becomes necessary at this point to concede the obvious: the supervisor is in the best position for becoming the required change agent for major program conversion. Program conversion requires many of the traditional supervisory skills; however, the dimensions of the problem are larger than specific subjects, designated skills, selected age groups of learners, or specified disabilities. The target is overall educational reform, an awesome assignment requiring high-level authority and accountability. Special competencies in institutional design are required as well as experience in the proper uses of authority. Formal training in supervisory role conversion has to be personally fabricated or established by an interested superintendent. Much experimentation along this line is bound to happen in the future.

DESIGN ISSUES IN OPEN EDUCATION: A SAMPLE IN-SERVICE BEGINNING

What are the larger dimensions of knowledge, inside and outside the schools, that either give impetus to, or condition, the drive toward openness? Whatever *your* answers may be, there is a chance that many of your teachers have simply been too preoccupied to really notice. Everyone in the academic community has a better than average chance of gleaning significant new knowledge. What counts in job reorientation is that which is examined carefully and thoroughly for its reconstructive potential and significance.

This suggests that a beginning in-service program should be designed to critique the larger issues, especially those in which a direct transfer of content to the public school curriculum is possible. The "past" orientation of the schools sometimes makes it easy to forget that new content should be filtering into the social studies, or that the literature curriculum may focus on the daily paper. But, since curriculum design is more than history plus current events, the teacher's job is to search out the larger concepts and theories that the current scene reflects. The issues of open education are really the issues of the open culture; hence, a teacher's professional reading list can often be merged with the students' bibliographies and class agendas. Teachers and students can learn the same things at the same time, thereby dealing realistically with change rates that do not permit one generation to reduce its experience to "truth" before beginning to teach it to the next generation.

The Valley View School District, a consolidated rural area north of Scranton, was among the first to build a major in-service program around the concept of open education. The model used was simple in basic design but quite complex in the interrelationship of its component parts.

The first decision was to allocate time equally among four big types of topics, namely:

1. Contested concepts
2. Tools of independent education
3. Curriculum design components, and
4. Content conversions for direct student access

In the first category, the selected topics were (a) deschooling, (b) alternative education, (c) contingency management, and (d) reality therapy. The reasons are, perhaps, obvious. The Ivan Illich deschooling movement provides leads for open access curriculum models by challenging the very nature of the education establishment. Options come from the short-circuiting of unnecessary bureaucratic control mechanisms, particularly those that interfere with the randomization and personalization of learning.

Alternative education is not antithetical to these ideas but has a uniquely urban flavor. It is a liberation movement with a particular clientele and accepts programming of any type that alleviates deprivation and prejudice.

The consideration of a contingency management will, to some, appear like giving the fox an invitation to the hen house— an improbable means of initiating open education if not an outright contradiction. However, contrast does have value in sharpening choices, even if the above is true. An earlier chapter presented an even more appealing position, namely that by looking for the proper (and necessarily limited) applications for prescriptive teaching, the remainder of the curriculum can be freed from this particular threat to openness. But, it is also fair to acknowledge that certain basic skills, even if acquired prescriptively, can have a liberating effect in the long run.

Reality therapy challenges prevailing Freudian interpretations of learner motivations. It is particularly relevant to open programming by its equation of mental health with responsible behavior. The minimizing of clinical and therapeutic techniques (and the assumptions of illness and disability on which they are based) returns to the normal realm much of the affective domain that teachers had gradually lost to the expanding psychological specialities.

The second major emphasis on the tools of independent education was similarly subdivided, beginning with "direct access technologies." The idea was to create a clear distinction between the technological facilitation of personal learning and the more common use of technology to reinforce teaching.

Dealing with contested content presupposes a significant difference in teaching methods when the goal is debate and discussion as opposed to intellectual closure or some type of performance demonstration.

The topic of tools of prescriptive teaching, is self-evident. The assumption is that a thorough knowledge of tools—including those that appear to constrict access—is necessary before teachers can make appropriate selections for personal use. It is unfortunate but true that school administrators reject many useful tools simply because no one has bothered to learn how to use them. The critical decision should not be how but when to employ a given teaching–learning tool. At any given time, the "tool kit" should be full, the "master mechanic" determining the appropriate selection.

Finally, evaluation and accountability were viewed as tools capable of either stifling or enhancing open education. As is so often true in human enterprises, conceptual tools and pure technology merge indistinguishably. Technological gains in processing data via computers, for example, have boosted achievement testing to the point of distortion and have filled more than one data bank with meaningless trivia. There are few legitimate reasons for data collection beyond the researcher's ability to formulate decision models. Yet, conceptual model building is lagging so pathetically as to make data collection moratoriums easier to justify than the wasteful practice of letting machine capability determine how much is collected. Either way, educators must decide and their intentions regarding open education can draw the line quite decisively.

"Curriculum design components," as an agenda item, invites teacher input for the formulation of the school's master schedule. The factors are:

1. Space utilization
2. Technological requirements
3. Talent authorization
4. Time distribution
5. Authority delegation

The final agenda item simply invited teachers to start making specific individual lesson plans aimed at sharp increases in the

328

personalization of learning. The almost foolproof techniques of content randomization via "learning activity packets" (LAP's) and short term courses were recommended. However, no constraints were placed upon more complex or more inventive approaches.

The chart depicted in Figure 17.1 shows the relationship of the workshop components to each other. In summary, it should be noted that the approach assumes:

1. comprehensive curriculum change;
2. short time-tables;
3. teacher involvement in management throughout the curriculum planning process;
4. the necessity for diffused invention as an appropriate teacher response to openness;
5. the utility of open education as a tool for working through the current crisis in cultural values; and
6. the self-sustaining nature of the open access curriculum once a critical mass of change has been achieved.

IMPLEMENTATION

The chart in Figure 17.1 does not dictate what to do when school opens. Teachers can have specific lesson plans of a novel nature; guidance counselors can be keyed up to individualize programs; librarians can order new resource-center materials reflecting a wider range of student interests; principals can openly announce open curriculum intentions—and, still, nothing significant will happen. The establishment rejection mechanism is powerful, even when it does not overtly block the initiation of a new practice. Innovators are sometimes, even from the outset, made to feel that they are constantly swimming upstream. Eventually, they grow weary and quit, the programs return to their

EXAMINATION OF OPEN EDUCATION: VALLEY VIEW, PA

	Monday	Tuesday	Wednesday	Thursday	Friday
			CONTESTED CONCEPTS		
9:00 to 10:15	**Orientation:** The Administrative Charge Introductions Tentative Workshop Agenda (Craig Wilson)	Forum Chairman. Jim Crouse "Deschooling"	Forum Chairman: Bill de Coligny "Alternative Education"	Forum Chairman: John Gaynor "Contingency Managment"	Forum Chairman: John Gaynor "Reality Therapy"
			TOOLS OF INDEPENDENT EDUCATION		
10:45 to 12:00	Curriculum Design as an Issue of Access (Craig Wilson)	"Direct Access Technologies"	"Dealing with Contested Content"	"Tools of Prescriptive Teaching"	Forum Chairman: Jim Crouse "Evaluation and Accountability"

CURRICULUM DESIGN COMPONENTS
(Teacher Thoughts on Scheduling the New School)

1:00 to 2:00 — Schooling "Regularities" at Valley View (Ann Hatala adapting Sarason, "The Culture of the School and the Problem of Change")

Task Force 1: *Space* utilization — "people paths" in an open environment
Task Force 2: Learning *technology* needs — tools for independence
Task Force 3: *Talent* utilization — new dimensions of teacher roles
Task Force 4: *Time* utilization — arrangements beyond prescriptive teaching
Task Force 5: *Authority* delegation — planning authorizations clarified

SHORT TERM COURSES: SELF-STUDY PACKET

2:00 to 3:00 — A word from the Teachers (Moderator, Bill de Coligny)

Task Force A: "Post-Watergate Civics" — contested content in the Social Studies
Task Force B: High School Reading — remedial Language Arts
Task Force C: Career Education — applications to Humanities and Social Studies
Task Force D: The New Relevance in Literature — thematic approach updated
Task Force E: Self-study Grammar
Task Force F: Writing for Future Authors

Figure 17.1. *The Relationship of Workshop Components*

original forms as if they had been on an elastic lease all along.

Phase II strategy must, therefore, deactivate the rejection mechanism—clearly, openly, decisively. The administrator cannot escape a career-shaking, unilateral decision because an organizational rearrangement, including revised delegations of authority, is the only move to which the rejection process will yield.

The memo in Figure 17.2 illustrates rather clearly how everybody involved has to take risks beyond present authorizations. Note, for example, that the consulting team continued to brainstorm program design alternatives while it was still "between contracts." The introductory paragraph, additionally, makes it obvious to all that an open education experiment cannot possibly succeed under the leadership of a nervous administration. Everybody has a limit to his "comfort index"; if project directors go too far, their subsconscious "survival behaviors" may override their stated intellectual purposes, thus killing the innovation they wanted credit for but emotionally could not tolerate.

The operational model, no matter how tentative, has to be sufficiently specific to delineate specific development tasks. This necessitates not so cautious proposals concerning the school calendar, staff organization, and resource differentiation to this point—but not beyond. This is the step that separates, once and for all, the open curriculum designers from the open classroom existentialists. One approach leads to institutional change; the other to psychological gains only.

The memo is, hopefully, self-explanatory and will not be further critiqued. Suffice it to say, the example is of only one more step in a logical series that the reader is invited to brainstorm. Our plans do not always come to pass; however, it is likewise true that few things indeed become practice in the absence of plans. The trick is to plan so that practice is decisively slanted in an open direction—not necessarily toward the designer's personal choice but toward a new arrangement that will

UNIVERSITY OF DELAWARE
NEWARK, DELAWARE
19711

COLLEGE OF EDUCATION
DEPARTMENT OF PROFESSIONAL SERVICES
WILLARD HALL EDUCATION BUILDING
PHONE: 302-738-2323

October 22, 1973

MEMO TO: Former Valley View Consultants –
            Dr. Crouse
            Dr. Gaynor
            Dr. deColigny

FROM: Craig Wilson

RE: Brainstorming Next Steps – Just in Case

The next step in the Valley View project, whether it is done with our
help or not, will involve setting forth the preconditions for teacher
planning. These are design parameters that represent both the desired
direction and administrative tolerance for such programming.

Just to start the thinking, how do you react to this possibility?

Preconditions: A

First Look

1. Teaching year divided into six semiautonomous terms of six weeks each;
    students permitted to sign up for any five (Mr. Davis' version of the
    quarter-system junior college).

2. "English" hereafter referred to as "Communications" to reflect a
    suitably broader scope; "Social Studies" changed to "Social Sciences"
    to reflect needed specialization and inclusion of the new disciplines.

3. Specific terms to be designated to reflect different dimensions of
    content and the resultant differences in student access routes to
    knowledge and skill. The master schedule would make specific provision
    for:

            a) concepts and skills
            b) labs
            c) cross-discipline electives

Diagramatically, it could look as follows:

COMMUNICATIONS

Term I	Term II	Term III	Term IV	Term V	Term VI
Concepts and skills in communications →	Cross-discipline electives in the combined field of communications and social sciences →	Lab-contested and exploratory content in communications (emphasis on performance) →	Concepts and skills in communications	Cross-discipline electives in the combined field of communications and the social sciences	C. Lab-performance orientation as in Term III cont. →

SOCIAL SCIENCES

| Concepts and skills in the social sciences → | As above → | Lab-contested and exploratory content in the → socail sciences (emphasis on forums, invest-igations, individual and group projects) | Concepts and skills in the social sciences | As above → | SS Lab-issue orientation as in Term III cont. |

Figure 17.2. *Sample Memo*

332

4. In addition to the two department chairmen, the following special coordinators would be needed:

   a) communications concepts and skills
   b) social science concepts and skills
   c) cross discipline electives
   d) communications performance lab
   e) social science investigation lab

5. Different themes would be worked out to reflect the several grade levels thereby reducing the probability of accidental overlapping and simultaneously facilitating the development of differentiated resource collections.

6. Students would be assigned to the two centers on a cross-graded basis with planned heterogeneity in all respects; hence, specialized groupings reflecting interest, ability, or need would always be made by teachers not the master schedule.

7. Our assignment was limited to specific disciplines; however, wouldn't the suggested model, perhaps, work for a whole school, with only minor variation being encountered, moving to the arts, the natural sciences, and the humanities?

Development Tasks

Assuming the model above, would not the development work include the following? (I'll just illustrate here since the model itself is speculative)

1. Identification of the content in the communications field most suitable for performance lab development (patterned perhaps after the California Theatre Arts model). Same for social science investigations.

2. Generation of elective offerings in communications and in the social sciences. (Clues taken from "Deschooling" and "Free University" models).

3. Definition of possible cross-discipline topics (Model: University of Delaware Integrated Learning Semester).

4. Delineation of sequential stable content (skill and concept levels) to be systematically taught.

5. Sorting out of library resources and technological aids appropriate to the above distinctions.

6. Alteration of testing procedures for compatibility with the model (for example, no "achievement" testing in contested areas).

7. Alteration of pupil record systems for program compatibility; likewise, parent reports.

   There are others but I'll stop here.

   Now, what do you think?

CW/pk

cc: Miss Hatala
    Mr. Davis

333

be perceived as a reduction of constraints not considered relevant to the protection of open concept. What the schools need is a structure for personal liberty.

AFTER THE LESSON PLAN

The teacher's lesson plan has always been a supervisory target. It presumably declares the teacher's intent, noting its relationship with district curriculum guides, and identifies one or more acceptable strategies. The latter then becomes what the supervisor observes in practice.

Such plans have several clear limitations. They are short-term—a day within an academic unit. They do not have to be, but usually are, prescriptive in content, teacher-controlled in strategy. They thus tend to be more informational than performance oriented. Even when the so-called "behavioral objectives" approach is used, the behavior induced is teacher selected rather than student innovated.

The modern need is for something more open, perhaps having such characteristics as:

1. Mapping the total academic territory to be explored, regardless of time—one year, two years, a lifetime
2. Developing from the processes of mastery rather than quantities of content
3. Identifying general levels of performance without mandating either the highest level as a necessary student objective, nor comprehensive coverage as a more desirable achievement than excellence in a restricted area
4. Revealing all resources and making them available on demand for either students or teachers, for formal lessons or for self-teaching, at the discretion of the initiator of the learning process

5. Refraining from the presumptive treatment of "student needs" as a basic operational principle; accepting declared student "interests" on face value as the only legitimate programmable "needs" of the individual: and stubbornly resisting all forms of target group resource earmarking in advance of student declarations of purpose

With these specifications, one ends up, not with a lesson plan, but with a rationale that can be used to generate an unlimited number of "learning plans"—quite a significant shift from the assumption that learning and teaching are synonymous. Examples are scarce due to the newness of the concept; however, there is an experimental model in use in California that comes close. The field is theatre arts, the grade span is twelve years, and the controlling assumption is that this performing field is a component of "general education," not just a high school elective. Figure 17.3 identifies the model's major parts, noting their novel relationship to each other.

Since no chart is really self-explanatory, a few of its intended novel characteristics deserve special mention. First of all, the fourth category across the top of the chart, "Resources," lists five topics, two of which are traditional public school subject matter fields—literature and history. The lesson plan, as opposed to the performance plan approach, would have considered these as the content sources for teaching units. The rationale is, in contrast, active rather than historical. It specifies expectancies in three progressive levels of performance, each being approached with appropriate teaching strategies. The behaviors that result can then be analyzed in terms of the "concepts" to which they contribute, the "resources" required, and the ultimate "processes" served.

The whole operation is activity centered, the three basic processes being "originating and performing," "producing," and "responding." The teaching becomes quite specific, for example, when "producing" is broken down into directing, managing, and

PROCESSES	ACTIVITIES	CONCEPTS	RESOURCES	PURPOSES
I. Originating and Performing	A. Sensory and Emotional Awareness	Intent Purpose	Literature	Self-development
	B. Rhythm and Movement C. Pantomime D. Oral Communication E. Improvisation	Idea Theme Message	History	To communicate effectively To solve problems intuitively
	F. Playmaking/Playwriting G. Formal acting H. Designing	Structure Coherence Unity Emphasis Rhythm Climax Conflict Balance	Aesthetics Techniques Models	To learn from and contribute to society To use critical and creative skills
II. Producing	A. Directing B. Managing C. Executing Technical Elements	Effectiveness Entertainment Information Illumination Inspiration		To be aware of theatre as an art form To approach other art forms with insight
III. Responding	A. Viewing B. Reviewing	Worth Profundity Validity Depth		

BEHAVIORAL EXPECTANCIES

Performance level	I	II	III
Teaching Strategies	I	II	III

Figure 17.3. *Performance Orientation Chart (Theatre Arts)*

executing technical elements. The performance chart supplies numerous other examples.

The familiar lesson plan still has an important place, but it is within the more confined area of prescriptive teaching. Rationales of the type just illustrated are the working tools of open-access programs, especially where personal performance is stressed.

STRATEGY AS POWER

There are only four ways to increase the effective power of the supervisory effort as the role was brought into existence as, and remains, a totally dependent satellite to administration. These are:

1. Personality and persuasion
2. Political alliance and subtle power usurpation
3. Role conversion to include "line authority" (a curriculum directorship, for example)
4. Strategy conversion from personal service to group leadership in environmental and institutional design

In this chapter option 4 has obviously been advocated. At first glance, it might appear that this new order of strategy takes some control away from the administration. The truth is that neither teachers nor administrators have been very active, or successful, in the design field; consequently, collaboration is in the interests of both. There is no need, or excuse, for adversary assumptions as the new types of supervisory strategies begin to emerge as the results of cooperative planning, not only between supervisors and administrators but including teachers as well. Equal partners make the best collaborators when invention is needed. The only authority required is the quality of a new idea.

Index

INDEX